The Obsession

To Fionnuala, Eva, Clara and Seán, *my parents and brothers for their unwavering support, encouragement and acceptance of this obsession of mine over the past 20 years.*

The Obsession

Seán Cavanagh

MY AUTOBIOGRAPHY

with
Damian Lawlor

BLACK & WHITE PUBLISHING

First published in 2018
by Black & White Publishing Ltd
Nautical House, 104 Commercial Street
Edinburgh EH6 6NF

1 3 5 7 9 10 8 6 4 2   18 19 20 21

ISBN: 978 1 78530 182 7

A CIP catalogue record for this book is available from the British Library.

Typeset by Iolaire, Newtonmore
Printed and bound by CPI Group (UK) Ltd, Croydon, CR0 4YY.

CONTENTS

PROLOGUE

Sunday, 27 August 2017
All-Ireland semi-final, Croke Park
Dublin 2-17, Tyrone 0-11

The sound of a final whistle can do funny things to you. It can make you laugh, cry, despair or jump for joy. Today, I get the entire range of emotions delivered to me in the one package. We're out of the Championship and I'm done. There's massive sadness. But there's relief too.

'It's over, Seán,' I say to myself. 'You don't have to beat yourself up any more.'

I see Fionnuala and our two daughters, Eva and Clara, sitting alongside the Tyrone dug-out. They had been quite a distance away earlier but had made their way across the Hogan Stand when I was taken off, so they could be with me at the final whistle.

I had no idea they would be so close, but I'm delighted to see them. At the end of every club and county game I played, the girls would always come over to have a chat, though I had asked Fionnuala not to let them over if I lost a match. It wouldn't be

1

fair to them. On this occasion, however, she knew it was the end of the line and she wanted the girls close to the Tyrone bench.

Seeing them, it hits home. There is huge sorrow but there is clarity too. Some sort of release. With the three girls waiting for me, it strikes me that I can relax a bit now, step away from the relentless treadmill of responsibility that's needed for this level. Maybe this obsession of mine can finally end, and I can stop worrying about tactics and fretting over defeats. Become normal again, more of a family man. Enjoy things other than football.

The wins, the trophies, the glory days: they've been great. I've had the best of times and have loved every second of it. Now, though, I can get on with life.

Fionnuala has tears in her eyes. She is a GP. She has to deal with matters of life and death every week and can take the rough with the smooth and so, when I see her upset, it really throws me. We share a private moment, or so we think, on the steps of the Hogan Stand, the four of us bound tightly together again, totally unaware of the TV cameras trained on us. Fionnuala just hands me wee Eva and, God bless her, she gives it to me straight: 'Daddy, I'm so happy that you don't have to go to Garvaghey any more!'

I start laughing and it brings on the tears.

'Daddy, you'll be able to spend a lot more time with us now.'

Jesus, this is surreal.

'Don't worry, Daddy, it's okay. Dublin just practised a bit harder than you.'

Trust a six-year-old to put it all into perspective!

Fionnuala hands Clara over too. At age four, Clara knows her daddy plays football for Tyrone, but she doesn't really get the bigger picture. When she sees me her expression is priceless.

Something like, *Ach, Daddy, it's yourself. What brings you to these parts?*

As I hold the two girls in my arms it's like they sense something is changing. I hug them close. I'm sad and proud. A tumble dryer of emotions.

Brian Dooher passes, gives me a slap on the back. An old warrior, our captain back in 2008. He walks out of the stadium and merges unnoticed into the droves of people making their way down Jones' Road. I watch him leave, shaking my head that even a diehard like Brian who pushed his body to the limit eventually had to move on too. We all do.

Fionnuala takes the girls back and I make for the pitch. The victorious Dublin players are hugging and enjoying their moment. They have bookended my career. I made my Tyrone senior debut in March 2002 against them in Dungannon, and now here they are again as the curtain falls. Some symmetry there, I suppose.

I bump into Stephen Cluxton. We've been playing against each other for sixteen years. We also played together for Ireland at international rules. He's a quiet lad but good craic at the back of it. We had many a lively night out.

He throws an arm around me. 'It's been amazing playing with and against you, Seán. We've shared a field together and you're an incredible man.'

I rest my head on his shoulder and return the compliment: 'You're the best, Stephen.'

I look for Paul Flynn and Bernard Brogan, others I went to battle against, fellas I have huge respect for, but before I find them, a gaggle of the younger Dubs greet me.

I'll be honest, I don't know the half of them by name. That's the scary thing with these fellas – they have a conveyor belt of new leaders coming through. With other teams you can target one or two players and hope to soften them, but with Dublin, where do you start? Here are these young lads queueing up to shake hands, gents off the field but deadly and clinical on it.

I don't linger out there. Back in the changing room, teammates come over one by one, say nice words and embrace me. We're all in shock that the game-plan we had refined, that seamless season we'd been having, has been shattered into pieces. We felt we would beat Dublin and go on to win the All-Ireland. Instead, we're going home after a thrashing.

Mickey speaks, and he too says some nice things. And then I get a chance to address the boys. There's not much to say.

'Lads, I've been here a long time. I have always tried to make Tyrone better, to leave the dressing room in a better place, make us more successful and pass it on. Now it's your turn.'

All my life I've been chasing something.

In school, I targeted straight As in exams but they didn't come without hours and hours of late-night studies.

A Tyrone jersey wasn't handed to me. I had to wait and fight hard for it.

When I started winning All-Irelands, I lapped life up for a couple of days. Maybe a week. And then I went on the trail of more success.

After years of studying I qualified as an accountant and took on a great job. But I still wasn't content. I wanted my own business; I hankered for the control and creativity to do things my way.

Sometimes I wish I could rest up a bit, but I can't see it

happening. No matter what age I live to be, I think I'll be searching for something; it's just the way I'm wired.

This afternoon, though, is a massive reality check. The only thing I'm chasing is shadows.

I'm thirty-four years old. My lungs are burning, my legs aching and for the first time in my football career I'm a spare part. Playing piggy in the middle with Dublin during my final act with Tyrone. For nearly two decades I played on centre stage and enjoyed everything that came with that privilege. This afternoon I'm running around like an understudy, not really sure what to be at. I call on whatever reserves I have left, tap into the bank of muscle memories long since stored away and grit my teeth. I dig my heels in one last time and resolve to muster some shred of pride.

Go back to the checklist: little things I can control.

I can always run faster and work harder.

So I do.

I try to prise the ball from the Dublin lads and I chase and harry.

But the harder I go the bigger the fool they make of me. They make eejits of all of us. For every blade of grass that I cover, there's a pass whizzing over my head in the opposite direction. My arms flail wildly in the wind, but it's hopeless. I have no impact on the game at all.

Here's the madness, though. As bad as things are, I still want to play to the bitter end. I could plead to be taken out of the front line and protected from the shrapnel, but I see this as the ultimate test of character. Dublin are battering us, but I have never hidden in my life and I won't start now.

Mickey Harte thinks otherwise. He has seen enough. The

number 14 lights up on the sideline and my heart sinks as he beckons me ashore. I wanted to walk off that field with my boots dirty, shield pierced, my honour intact. Those were the dreams I brought with me to Croke Park that afternoon. Reaching another All-Ireland final, going on to captain the team and lifting the Sam Maguire – that was the aim.

Those dreams are gone now, swept away by a blue storm.

Apart from my brother, Colm, the whole team was off-colour. Listless, completely dissected and shut down. Dublin had us sussed. They studied how we had played with two flankers all year and so they put four men out wide to counter that. They tied Petey Harte and Mattie Donnelly up completely, swarmed those two lads like bees around hives. They blocked our runs and effectively took the key from our ignition. Cut us off at source. We toiled hard but there was nothing to show for the hard labour.

Dublin, meanwhile, throbbed with life and played keep-ball like carefree youngsters in a park.

As a designated first line of defence, I was placed in the middle, delegated to track and hunt when not in possession and to drive forward when I had the ball. But every time I got near Ciarán Kilkenny he seemed to have two or more outriders waiting for the offload. It felt like I was back in the schoolyard chasing ball while it sprayed around me.

Trouble came early. Four minutes in, Dublin cut through our centre, Con O'Callaghan broke forward and with all the swagger of youth smashed home a goal in front of Hill 16. We were down before we even started. I couldn't but catch the irony – that had been me sixteen years earlier, cutting through the Armagh defence in Clones, scoring a goal in the closing minutes of my debut. I could relate to the exuberance of O'Callaghan and envy

6

it, too. The road ahead of him is open and long. My journey is at an end.

Our game-plan? Hold Dublin for as long as we could, confine them, and break away near the end with our strike runners. That method had worked a treat all year long and we could see no flaws in it. It was like Mickey had us convinced, we were uber-confident, believing that our 'system' was watertight. Looking back now I honestly can't understand why we were so confident but I just couldn't see any way we would be beaten. Mickey talked our style up, talked our players up, and had us utterly convinced that we would be in an All-Ireland final.

He had me fully on board even though I'm quite old-school in my thinking. I feel that systems are only necessary for teams with lesser talent, whereas we have always had great playmakers and finishers in Tyrone. We have long since been labelled a dour, negative team, but that was never actually the case. This time as the semi-final plays out it enters my mind that this 'system' of ours is curtailing the talents of the players we have in our team. The game-plan almost binds us.

Dublin sensed as much and forced us out into the open to see what we were made of. They exposed us, dragged us around and we had no answers. Mickey had told me, as captain, that if we won the toss I was to force the Dubs to play into the Hill 16 end in the first half so that they wouldn't have the advantage in the second half when the game would be in the melting pot. I could see the reasoning behind that, but that ploy badly backfired. In the first half it was like the energy from the Hill sucked the Dublin players in towards them every time they gathered possession. The game was gone before we even switched ends.

You hit autopilot in such a scenario. Keep on trucking. Aim to win the next ball, maybe burgle a goal out of nothing. One peg up the hill at a time until you eventually near the summit. But we never came close, and at half-time our changing room was in panic mode. You could sense the inevitable. We were already a beaten docket.

I put my head down and listened to the nervous hum around me.

'Who the fuck is marking him?'

'We have to push up, lads!'

'Why is he getting his kickouts away so handy?'

When we return to the field I get another twenty minutes before I'm taken out of the line of fire.

That's it then. Sixteen years and eighty-nine Championship games for Tyrone. My head is swirling. I'm brutally disappointed. Throughout the year Fionnuala would often say to me after games: 'I'm sure you weren't happy being subbed off.' And she was right; I wasn't happy. Like all sportspeople who compete at a high level, you always feel there is something more to give. I believed that I still deserved my starting and finishing place on the team. I worked hard to make sure that was the case.

But coming off against Dublin I was angry. Mickey knew it was my last game for Tyrone and, while I wasn't setting the world alight, I felt there were a few other lads who could have made way before me. Maybe I was looking through the lens with pure sentimentality. Or perhaps it was arrogance on my part, a misplaced belief in my ability at the twilight of my career.

Still, it was that same single-mindedness and arrogance, the lingering belief in my ability, that had made me who I was.

When it comes to sport, however, Mickey's not mawkish. I see young Conor Meyler waiting on the sideline and they are trying to get him on the pitch. He deserves his shot, so I hurry over to make way for him. People would ask later if I heard the huge cheers that went up for me, but I didn't. All I heard were the jeers and jibes from the Dublin supporters in Hill 16.

I jog up into the Hogan Stand, join the subs, and look on in some distress as Dublin canter to a twelve-point win.

When it's all over, I shower and go outside. Some of the stewards and caretakers, fellas I've been meeting for the best part of two decades, are waiting to wish me well. That's a lovely touch. I stop and speak to the journalists. I spot a few that have been there throughout my career and I take time to chat to them too.

On the bus home I send out a tweet. I want to get it out there quickly, maybe just to underline my decision. A few words, but it does the job:

> My incredible journey ends. Blessed to have shared the highs and lows of our game with some amazing people.

We head up the road, and back at home in the Moy, Fionnuala and the girls seem chuffed. The narrative is clear.

'Mummy says you'll be about the house a lot more, Daddy.'

'You should be so happy, Daddy, because we can do all these things together. We can eat chips, chocolate and ice cream now.'

Maybe we can. All I have known these last sixteen years is getting up at 7 a.m., going to university or working until 6 p.m. Like a spare tyre, my gear bag was a constant in the car boot. And the car would nearly drive itself to Garvaghey, it had tread that path so often. Garvaghey Centre, by the way, is surely the coldest place in Ireland, a modern-day centre of excellence pitched on some of the iciest, most unforgiving terrain in Ulster. It would be 9.30 p.m. at the earliest before I would leave there on midweek nights, getting back home at 10 p.m. Straight away I'd take one set of gear out of the boot and put another set in for the next day.

That was my life five days a week. The other two days were centred around rest and recovery. In recent years, most mornings I left my kids around 7.30 and as I walked out the door I would say, 'I'll see you tomorrow.' It killed me leaving them.

On Wednesdays I managed to get home from work for fifteen minutes of playtime with them before leaving again for a gym session in Omagh. It meant that once a week I had to explain to two very disappointed girls why I was in and around the house but still couldn't put them to bed!

Now the girls are all over me with excitement. 'No more gym in Omagh, Daddy.'

Tonight, back in the Moy, I finally do get the chance to put them down for the night. They were exhausted, so it didn't take long. Then a ramble up the village to Tomneys, a wee old-school, traditional bar with Armagh owners. It has plenty of small, quiet rooms where you can be quite anonymous. It was in Tomneys that Philip Jordan was infamously accused of tearing down the Armagh flag during the height of the 2003 rivalry, causing such a stir around the village. I still can't confirm or deny whether or not Philly was involved! I head up there with my brother Colm and Harry Loughran, another Moy player on the Tyrone squad. We summon Philip McCann, a good pal, better known as 'Moy's Philly Mac' and spend an hour or two there. All our lives Colm and I have been close, but Philip has been there for most things too. Any time stuff goes wrong in my life he is around. Philip had to cope with the loss of his younger brother Mark in 2012. Mark was Colm's best friend, so we have been very tight down through the years.

The four of us are supping our pints when Colm throws on a WhatsApp video recorded in our hotel room at Carton House a few hours before the game.

As it happened, Colm and I had been lying down, watching the Tyrone under-17s play their All-Ireland final against Roscommon, chilling out before heading for Jones' Road ourselves. Then he let a roar: 'Hey, there's a mouse, Seán! It's after running behind the curtain!'

Given that Colm spent too much time being mollycoddled by Mummy when he was growing up I knew he wouldn't do much about it, so I phoned reception, said there was a mouse in our room and asked if they would send up the resident mouse-catcher. I took a shower, and when I came out a few minutes later, wrapped in a towel, Colm was grinning.

'The wee thing is after hopping into your gear bag!'

Jesus, all my clothes were in that bag, and we had to be dressed and downstairs in a few minutes for the pre-match meal.

I wouldn't be the bravest when it comes to mice. I ran into the corridor and saw Cahir McCullagh, a big culchie of a lad, a farmer. A fella like him wouldn't be afraid of a mouse. When he came in, a bunch of the lads followed with a phone set to record.

There I was, squealing, standing on the bed, clutching the towel for protection, while Cahir scattered the contents of my bag and trashed the room as he chased the little fecker from corner to corner. Watching the video of Big Cahir flailing around, chasing shadows, I was half-thinking, 'God, this could

11

have been a metaphor for what just happened in Croker. I should have known what was coming!'

The couple of pints among pals, the craic of the whole mouse episode, and the howls of laughter at my expense in the familiar comfort of Tomneys bar make for a soothing end to a raw day. Drawing the night to a close was almost symbolic of being back among my friends and community after such a long time on the road with Tyrone. It's when times are bad that I have always found comfort with the club friends. Mind you, they were also very quick to cut me down when I might have got above my station!

I wouldn't have wanted it any other way.

PART ONE

JOURNEY'S END

1

DESPERATION

5.10 p.m., Saturday, 6 August 2016
All-Ireland quarter-final, Croke Park
Mayo 0-13, Tyrone 0-12

When you are in the business of looking for magic doors to open and chasing fairy-tale endings to your career, the most unexpected things can happen.

As a player I have mostly ignored the dark arts, nearly always played the ball and not the man, and backed myself to make things happen for the team. I've been spat at, pinched, verbally abused and I've learned from all of that. I'm not a choirboy either and in latter years I have been unpleasant, more desperate to win at all costs. In the 2013 All-Ireland quarter-final, I took Conor McManus down as he tore in on goal and fouled him to make sure we would win the game. It was cynical, but I would do it again if I had to.

Now I'm standing in front of David Gough, the match referee. He won't even look me in the eye, so I know I'm fecked. If those lads can't look you in the eye it usually means you're gone. It's my own fault; I rose like a leaping salmon to the bait, took a

15

leading role in the Punch and Judy show along with Lee Keegan.

At the start of the game I was expecting Kevin Keane to pick me up, but instead it was Keegan who came over. His job was clearly to disrupt me. I wasn't going to shy back from him either, so the inevitable yellow cards came our way and it was tightrope time from then on. With fifteen minutes to go, and the game on a knife edge, I caught Aidan O'Shea both high and slightly late with a tackle and knew instantly I was in trouble.

I looked over at Gough and started to plead the case for the defence. But the one-man jury was already back with its verdict. The red card was brandished – my first and last sending off for Tyrone. I had only previously got the line after picking up a black card against Donegal in 2014.

The Mayo fans cheered as I made my way off.

Every block of progress we had cemented down during the year was now in danger of coming unstuck. Despair must have been written on every line of my face. I was Tyrone captain, but was no longer any use to them. The final few minutes filled me with anguish and I held my head in my hands as we hit four late wides and lost by a point.

My nightmare was only beginning.

The pain that I endured after that loss came as no surprise. The game of Gaelic football has stressed me out and dominated my every waking thought for the past twenty years.

In 1997 I captained St Pat's, Dungannon, to a Corn na nÓg title. The final went well, and I scored 2-3. But the night before the game was torture – I lay awake imagining and replaying worst-case scenarios. Such has been the pattern through my career. Even in victory I agonise.

In the 2008 All-Ireland final I scored five points from play and was named Man of the Match. I was king of the hill, top of the heap. It seemed like the entire county was partying like crazy in the Citywest Hotel and they all wanted to hug me, buy me a pint and talk to me. But by midnight Fionnuala and I had had enough of the madness and slipped away to our room.

The hero of the hour, I should have slept soundly, but at 4 a.m. I was still wide awake, listening to the sound of the N7 awakening, and replaying episodes from the game. Or rewinding back over missed chances, to be honest. That time when I got through on the Kerry goal – why did I fist it over the bar? Why didn't I go for the jugular? Jesus Christ, I could have scored a goal in an All Ireland final!

To this day, I regret not going for that goal chance. Is that balanced thinking? It's not. It's crazy. And that lunacy, anxiety, whatever you want to label it, gripped me even more intensely as my career entered its latter stages. The closer I got to the end, the higher the stakes rose and the more my personality changed.

Deep in the winter of 2015 it was high time to release the pressure valves. I decided that 2016 would be my last season in a Tyrone shirt. Within the camp there was a feeling that we were again on the verge of something special. In some ways it was like we were about to commence a new project; there was a young team coming through. I felt I could be a meaningful part of that new-look side and could then walk off into the sunset with nothing left to prove.

In the 2015 All-Ireland semi-final we had pushed Kerry all the way, and though we lost by four points (0-18 to 1-11), we showed signs that we were ready to threaten for a championship again.

We had eight different scorers on that day, a healthy spread, and the likes of Connor McAliskey, Darren McCurry, Mark Bradley and Ronan McNabb had all stepped up.

We only lost after a couple of late points went against us, but on the road home that night we deemed it less a missed opportunity than evidence that we were a serious team again and going in the right direction. A new Tyrone team was in production and I wanted to help develop them, to lead them up the steps of the Hogan Stand.

It wasn't a difficult decision to commit to 2016. I would have found it hard to turn off the tap at that stage anyway, as I had become infatuated with my prehab, a proactive way of avoiding pain and injury. I was preparing fanatically for games and it was exhausting for everyone – me, Fionnuala, my family and friends.

All through 2015 I had carried injuries and never felt quite right. The left knee was a wreck and needed either six months' rest and rehab or a new-fangled infusion technique, where they drill through the middle of the knee and into the blood vessels in the hope of triggering the body's own healing response – basketball guys get it done to prolong their careers.

Ironically, my original issues were with the right ankle and right knee, and so to compensate I had been leaning more and more on the left. In time the left knee began to suffer from overwork and eventually gave me gyp every time I trained or played. Throughout my entire career my body has been far too reliant on anti-inflammatories. Since I turned eighteen I have had a constant supply to alleviate pain and even got to know which brand works best, and when they should be taken. All to help me cope with pain in the knees, never mind the screws in my ankles, shoulders and the constant concussions. It's like I had a pain-relief strategy, all legal and ratified of course, to get me through games.

When I researched this latest injury, I discovered how elite players in various sports were using ice machines throughout the day to reduce swelling and pain. Icing was the trend, so I started on that. Harmless enough at first, a few times a week. But when the knee responded I upped the dose to once a day and before long to several times a day. Everywhere I went, the ice packs and, in time, the machine, followed. Like the fairy story, where Hansel left white pebbles for him and Gretel to make their way home, I was never too hard to find – you just had to follow the drips and puddles!

The Tyrone guys nicknamed me Jackie Moon after the Will Ferrell character from the movie *Semi-Pro*, who walks into a nightclub with ice packs strapped around his trousers. The boys would give a running commentary whenever they saw me arriving with the bag strapped to my knee. I didn't care. I had one more year of my career left, and Jackie Moon was going to do whatever it took to get back fit and help Tyrone win another All-Ireland.

Fionnuala kept telling me that, whatever about temporary relief, ice was not going to cure such a chronic injury. Given her medical credentials I should have listened, but in my mind the ice was helping so I stuck with it.

Louis O'Connor, the Tyrone team's long-serving physio, treated me through most of my career, and he sourced the right machine for me. It was a game-ready device, a kind of compression system, and it came highly recommended – seemingly it was the same model the former Republic of Ireland midfielder

Steven Reid carried on his travels when he was plagued with knee trouble late in his career.

The combined compression and cryotherapy worked. I had to use it in forty-five-minute cycles, so once I showered and changed after a session, I would get some food and head back home to yoke up the machine, get the wrap on and then get into bed frozen solid with a core body temperature of around minus five. This drove Fionnuala, who loves a bit of warmth, absolutely mad.

My days went like this. Rise early to get on the ice for forty-five minutes before going to work. If that didn't happen I would do it at night instead. With the gym equipment out in the garage it usually meant I would start doing weights at 10 p.m. I trained some part of my body every night of the week, before going back on the machine until 11.30 p.m.

At one point, deep in the month of November, Fionnuala asked me what had happened to the off-season. It was a valid question; from October to December I was training as hard as ever and was absolutely unbearable to be around in the process. All of this to get myself primed for the last hurrah.

Almost unaware, during that winter of 2015 and beyond, I went deeper into obsession mode. Nothing else mattered bar trying to get the body to maximum efficiency. It was lunacy. It began to impinge on my work as an accountant at Cavanagh Kelly. But worse again, I sacrificed more and more time with Fionnuala and the kids because it was so easy to do. The girls would just smile: 'Good luck with the football, Daddy!'

It's funny how the most important people in your life, the ones you love most, are often the easiest to take for granted when the selfishness kicks in. The truth is I could have been away working overseas for five days and it would have made little difference at home. They were used to me not being around.

One December night Fionnuala and I headed to Dublin for the *Irish Daily Star* GAA awards, always a great event. A few of the Tyrone boys, including Tiernan McCann, Ronan O'Neill and Mark Bradley, went down too, young lads looking forward to a Saturday night's craic in the big city.

I was the odd man out. A text message had gone out from the Tyrone management earlier that day – training had been called for nine the following morning in Garvaghey. I should have let that one slide, but instead I said to Fionnuala that we'd go down to Dublin, stay with the festivities until about midnight, hit the hay and then head home early the following morning. We did all that and on Saturday morning we crammed some breakfast into us as soon as the kitchen opened at 6.30, then poor Fionnuala followed me out to the car and we were on the road by 6.40. Almost everyone else that night had made use of the complimentary bar and gone on to Coppers, but of course I had to be different. I look back now and cringe. But once you're in, you're in. And this thing sucks you right in.

The other boys at the awards, naturally enough, were marked absent at training, which Mickey remarked on as we warmed down. I was left thinking: 'Hang on! I'm thirty-two, I've actually won a bit and I'm still willing to do all this. Maybe those boys should be here trying to win as well.'

In fairness the lads were only doing what young lads do. And it was December, for God's sake. But I couldn't put myself in their shoes. That's how obsession takes over.

*

Coppersgate or not, we cruised through Division Two of the National League, winning games without having to get out of third gear.

We beat Derry in the first round of the Ulster Championship but hit a speed bump when we leaked three goals to Cavan and got only a draw.

I wasn't worried. In fact, the more I think about it, the more I marvel at Mickey Harte's skills. His greatest strength is his ability to convince you things will work out. When we sat down to prepare for that Cavan replay by reviewing the drawn game he showed us only clips of the good things we had done, or cameos where we were unlucky not to score. A masterstroke. We went home believing we were miles better than Cavan – and proved as much in the replay.

But Mickey isn't just about building belief in a team. After a handy win, such as that replay – and just so we didn't fall in love with ourselves – he would show us ten passages of poor play, including butchered chances. It always got us grounded again.

We were utterly convinced we were going places – especially after running Kerry so close the previous season. People outside the camp – pundits included – argued that we lacked the fire-power to win a championship, but we dismissed all that as begrudgery: 'Ye're just out to get us,' was the mantra.

That 'us versus them' attitude was often our default mentality. In many ways it can be a sad and narrow stance, one that I grew weary of, to be honest, and yet it was never more needed than when we played Donegal in the Ulster final.

This was the big test. They had just beaten us four times on the trot and in fact had dominated us since Jim McGuinness took charge. We finally cracked their code and broke them down to win 0-13 to 0-11. I hit three points, a couple of them late in the game, to help us over the line, and my last point skyed straight up in the air when it left the boot, a perfect rugby Garryowen. I never thought it would get over the bar but somehow it did. To this day I believe that was fate.

Shortly before that final, Fionnuala's dad had passed away. In the match programme notes I wrote a wee ode to Charles Vernon, a beautiful gentleman, and I'm convinced that Charles coaxed that ball over the bar for me. By all the laws of physics there was no way it would have got there.

It was all written in the stars. I was kicking the crucial points as captain. To have Colm and the girls there, standing with me on the podium as we hoisted the Anglo-Celt Cup. A historic day for the family and the county. A landmark day too, but one I felt was just another step on the journey back to the top.

At the end of the match Peter Canavan jumped into my arms and hugged me fiercely. That showed me just how much the win meant to Tyrone people. A lot of folk said it was better than winning an All-Ireland. Donegal's grip on us had been broken.

We were drawn to play Mayo in the All-Ireland quarter-final and my mind wandered with the glorious possibilities of what lay ahead. We always knew Mayo were a threat but having seen Galway take them out of Connacht and then Galway beaten by Tipperary, we had no fear at all. We could take Mayo and if we did we would face Tipp in a semi-final. No disrespect intended to Tipp, but we would most likely beat them too and reach an All-Ireland final.

I couldn't help thinking: *This is it. This is where it ends.* Even if Dublin beat us in a final we would have shown serious progression and I could at least walk away on the biggest day of them all, knowing I had done a decent job in captaining my county.

With Mayo, Mickey refined the battle plan. He told us at training that Kevin Keane would play full-back on me and that I would have the measure of Kevin all day long. The message was simple: kick the ball to Seán early and often and we'd go to town on them.

We perceived Mayo as being soft. They had seriously skilful players, but we would not be mastered by them. We would be the more aggressive side.

How disastrously wrong we were! Not for a second did we think they would come with such a defence-laden style – a 'negative' system not unlike the one for which we ourselves had long since been ridiculed. But they did. And they caught us on the hop, disrupting us by deploying a cagey game-plan we could only envy. We thought it would be a shootout but instead it was a dogfight.

Maybe we hadn't been strung together tightly enough for that. From the start they were brash and ballsy, while we were nervous and vulnerable. We struggled all over the field. We didn't know how to react to the curve ball we were thrown. It was tight and tense. We managed only five points from play while they got nine.

Did we, in eager expectation of an All-Ireland final, take our eye off that semi-final? You wouldn't want to think so. But looking back I do feel there was a strangeness about the squad in the build-up. I can't quite put my finger on it.

At the start of the second half I could see Lee Keegan lining me up for a shoulder and I didn't back away – we hit each other a right wallop. We then got into pulling and dragging and picked up two silly yellow cards.

Soon after, I was floating down the Cusack Stand side of the pitch when Lee came on a collision course again. I tried to be cute, to cut right in front of him to win a free – he might even get booked and that would be him gone.

Instead I was done for carrying, and worse still, David Gough, the referee, copped what I had tried to do. I knew from then on that I wasn't in his good books and had to protect myself for the rest of the match.

With no ball going in to me at full-forward I started to drop back. I retreated and made a few tackles, just to get myself back into the game. I was captain, I needed to contribute something!

That was when Aidan O'Shea came into my path. I genuinely tried to flick the ball away from him but in following through ended up striking him in the jaw. I sensed my day was done, yet when the second yellow was brandished I felt harshly done by. The incident looked bad enough on screen, but it was really no worse than clumsy.

As Gough put the card back in his pocket something happened I had never experienced before on a football field. I went into shock.

The fairy-tale ending had become a nightmare. The enormity of what was happening hit home and it was all too much for me. Everything I had thrown into my preparation, all the effort I had made trying to captain Tyrone to an All-Ireland title, trying to make our people proud; it had all gone up in flames.

My body went numb and my mind went blank. It was all I could do to get myself off the field.

Somehow, I managed to reach the far sideline, but I couldn't face going up to the stand to join the rest of the subs. I didn't want to look them in the eye. I felt I had let them all down. Let the county down. If we lost it would all be on me.

I collapsed onto the ground and stayed there for a while on my own until Richard Donnelly, one of our subs, came down pitch-side.

'Seán, head up here to the rest of us, come on,' he said, grabbing me and bringing me up to the boys. Still I didn't sit with them or watch the rest of the game. I just went in beside D.D. Mulgrew and fell to my knees. I started to pray as the match entered its final phase.

Darren McCurry had a chance near the end and Niall Morgan had one from a long-range free. Each time I looked to the skies and prayed to Charles that the ball would go over. I'd say D.D. was thinking, *This lad here beside me is completely nuts*. I look back now and imagine I made a complete fool of myself, but I wasn't in the right state of mind either.

I begged Petey Harte or Mattie Donnelly to go on one of those surging, lung-bursting runs, to try and win a free, maybe even get a soft one that refs sometimes give near the end of tight games just to make a draw of it.

'It can't end like this,' I groaned as the game entered injury time and the Mayo supporters screamed for the final whistle.

But it did. And a cloud of despair gathered around me. To this day I remain grateful to Joe McMahon for getting me out of there, because physically and mentally I couldn't bring myself to cross the pitch under my own steam. Because Dublin and Donegal were on after us and were stationed in the changing rooms on the Hogan Stand side, we had togged out on the Cusack Stand side.

'Joe, I cannot walk back onto that field,' I said.

'Come on, Seán, you're coming with me!' Joe replied as he took my arm, and with him beside me I managed to trudge across the pitch. On the way, Andy Moran, great lad that he is, came to shake my hand and I congratulated him.

That was nearly the last piece of conversation I would have that day. It was by far the worst I have ever been after a match.

2

THE WALK

As the years go by the pain of losing games becomes more acute.

Not just because of the results, or seeing the flames being extinguished for another year, but just as much because you know your time on the big stage is ebbing away. There is a nagging burn that you carry with you in your latter days as an inter-county GAA player. You feel you have to go to extra lengths, prepare better than everyone else, recover better than the others. It makes losing hurt all the more.

In his book, Cathal McCarron described a feeling of desolation, painting a picture of men slumped on the floor of the shower room after that Mayo game, and it was every bit as haunting as Cathal portrayed. Now as I sat in the changing room, head bowed in my hands, all I could see was the scattered debris of our journey's abrupt end.

A deathly silence prevailed, worse than any I have ever encountered in a dressing room. We had poured ourselves heart and soul into getting back to a final. I had become a fanatical, even selfish, man in the pursuit of the dream. Now I was the man who had cost the team.

I was also the last man to take off his boots, the last to get out of the showers, the last to get dressed, and the last to leave the changing room. All because I was devastated. I couldn't look anyone in the eye.

There were the usual end-of-the-road soundbites.

'We'll come again, lads.'

'We'll learn from this.'

'Nothing went our way.'

I tried to say a few words through salty tears, but I was in shock mode. I should have kept schtum.

We got on the bus and the hell out of Dublin. Colm and I stepped off at the Carrickdale Hotel in Dundalk and were picked up there by our clubmate Harry Loughran, who would himself be called into the Tyrone squad a year later.

I sat in silence in the back seat and when we reached the Moy around six I still hadn't said a word to either Colm or Harry. All the way there I had only one thought: *I can't go home.*

I was wearing only shorts and a tracksuit top but when we reached Moy Square I asked Harry to stop the car and I jumped out, leaving my house keys, wallet and phone behind. Neither Harry nor Colm tried to stop me; they just drove on. I had no idea where I wanted to go but I needed to clear the head and I knew I didn't want to meet anyone or talk to anyone.

There's an old road just off Moy Square that leads down toward the banks of the Blackwater and turns down to the Moy GAA grounds. Huge trees stand guard on each side, sheltering the river bank. At the end of the stretch there's a nine-foot steel fence, topped with spikes, which you have to negotiate to get into the GAA field.

As I scaled that fence I remember wondering what would

happen when I landed. Would I finally bust that knee I had been mollycoddling the previous twelve months? I remember thinking it would be the first serious impact in a while on the same knee. But what the hell? We were out. I was no use to anyone.

I jumped down, survived the landing, wandered onto the field and stayed there for about fifteen minutes, just looking around and trying to make sense of everything that had happened in Dublin a couple of hours earlier.

Then I climbed back out of there and headed out onto the main road from the Moy to Eglish. I had a choice there and then: turn right – up toward home and back toward everyone who loved me – or trail off left into the darkening countryside.

The brain was addled, and so I took the left turn and headed down country lanes. Before long I found myself in unfamiliar territory. I've never retraced the route I took that night and I don't want to. All I know is I was far from right in the head. I wasn't in control. It was a scary place to be.

Initially I walked about a mile toward Benburb. The village lights looked welcoming, but the one thing I knew was that I didn't want to go in there, meet people and have to make conversation. So I took a little byroad on the outskirts.

I wandered along, losing my bearings and losing track of time. It wasn't easy walking; it got hilly and the light was fading. I had no watch, no phone and no wallet. As darkness fell on that lonely road I felt confused and empty.

Out of nowhere a car hurtled around the bend in front of me, the driver in full rally mode. A boy racer with his foot to the floor on a country lane barely wider than the car itself. I threw myself onto the ditch and I doubt he even saw me, but I saw him and in a split second of clarity I even saw the number plate. I still spot that red Merc around the Moy from time to time. The lad behind the wheel doesn't know it, but he almost wiped me out that night.

It was a narrow escape, and yet in my numbed state it hardly even shook me. I just continued meandering aimlessly. Here and there an isolated dwelling would throw out enough light to lead me on another few hundred metres.

I got back onto a main road that looked like the Benburb-to-Eglish stretch leading to Dungannon, and I was loitering there, without serious intent, in shorts and tracksuit top, when a VW Golf drove past, stopped and reversed.

Inside was Matthew McGleenan, son of Mattie, another man who gave his life to Tyrone football. It was now about 11 p.m, and Matthew was with a few pals heading out for the night. I also recognised Francie Kelly, one of the Moy lads, in the back, but I didn't want to talk to them. I was curt.

'You alright there, Seán?'

'Well, lads, what's wrong? I'm only out for a walk here. Have a good night, lads.'

I cut them short and walked on.

'Do you want a lift, Seán?' Francie persisted.

'Nah, lads, I'm only out clearing the head here.'

And I walked on. It was only in the following few days, when recalling the incident, that I realised how bizarre it must have seemed and how worried the boys had been.

I remember walking toward lights and after maybe another two hours reaching a crossing of the main Dungannon–Belfast motorway. It's a busy stretch and tricky enough at the best of times.

When I crossed that motorway I saw something that I still

remember vividly – a few feet away, a small cat calmly dragging a huge rat by the scruff of the neck across the carriageway. I blinked and looked again, but the cat, intent on its prey, never even threw a glance as it passed in front of me. Was this really happening? Or had I entered the twilight zone?

Much of that night remains a blur but I do remember the cat and the rat. And that I couldn't stop walking.

Eventually I made it to Dungannon. And as I did a taxi drove by and the driver slammed on the brakes. I don't know who he is, I never got his name and I haven't met him since, but I have no doubt I'll meet this guy along the line again somewhere.

'Are you alright there?' he asked.

'Aye,' I replied. 'Only out for a dander.'

I looked at the clock in his taxi: 1.20 a.m. I was still in shorts and a top.

'You want a lift anywhere?'

'No, thanks, I'm dead on.'

He dropped the formalities then.

'Seán, just get in the car, will you, please?'

'Ach no, I'm alright. Honestly.'

'Seán, please get in the car. I'll take you home.'

I looked at him and he seemed a lovely man. I was weary now, numb with shock and shivering with cold.

'Look, Seán, I will never say word about this to anyone, I promise you. I'll drop you home and that will be that.'

I climbed in. I was frozen alive. I don't know what I said or what I didn't say but that taxi-man from Dungannon dropped me home and I finally walked in the door at 1.40 a.m.

Colm's wife, Levina, was inside babysitting while Fionnuala was out searching for me. As soon as she saw me Levina picked up the phone and rang Fionnuala. 'He's back. It's okay. He's here now.'

Levina looked at me. 'Seán, Fionnuala will be home in five minutes.'

I didn't make a big deal of it and Levina didn't either. Fionnuala arrived in and she was brilliant. She didn't lose the plot or tear into me, as would have been her right – she knew that something inside of me, a wire or something, had tripped. She asked when I'd last eaten.

'I don't know. I don't think I ate after the match, maybe.'

In fact, it had been fifteen hours since I had eaten anything. In the interim I had played an All-Ireland quarter-final and walked fourteen miles of Tyrone countryside in the pitch dark. Fionnuala went into the kitchen and rustled up something from a frozen batch of food kept in my famous ice freezer out in the garage.

But I couldn't eat it. My hands were shaking.

'I can't control my knife and fork,' I said.

Fionnuala looked down at me. 'Seán, you're not retiring. Not like this.'

'Ach, Fionnuala. I can't keep doing this. I don't know what I'm doing. I don't even know what's happening now.'

She got me something to drink, said we would call it a night and talk tomorrow. I still marvel at how she didn't make a big deal, but she was smart enough to sense I was in a dark place.

The next day she opened up. She wondered why I hadn't come home to the people who loved and cared for me most.

'Are we that bad, Seán?'

That broke my heart. The people I love more than anyone, the closest to me. It was true that I would have been safer at home than any other place in the world, but then at home I'd be looking at the people I had most let down. I couldn't handle that. And that's the truth. Eva and Clara were only babies – sure they wouldn't even have known there was a match on, never mind if we had won or lost, and yet I felt I had let them all down.

My family.

I have to be honest here: it wasn't my first time going AWOL. I'd done it in the past but in a less dramatic way. In 2003, six days on from the high of winning my first All-Ireland senior medal, I was at midfield for the Tyrone under-21s in an All-Ireland final that we lost to Dublin by five points. For a few days after that game I refused to go home. I stayed away, licking the wounds in isolation.

The more I think back, the more extreme it all seems. Sleepless nights before games, the obsessive need to make my dad, my family proud, to do it for others, at times to sacrifice mental and physical balance just to make the people up here happy.

I had great times but that was the price I paid to be a Tyrone footballer.

When I started off in 2002 I entered into a competitive bubble. Fourteen years later I was still inside, still trying to prove myself, still lacking that overall perspective you need.

Winning three All-Irelands was no small achievement, and yes, for a while after those wins I knew we had done something important – but there was always that cycle of feeling that I had to prove myself all over again. Be better than last year. Make everyone proud again.

You know what? There is not one medal or trophy in our house. Before Fionnuala moved in, there was only one sports photo – and that was one of the proudest – a picture of myself and Colm with the 2008 Sam Maguire Cup. Even then, because he had always been my closest friend, I was probably prouder for Colm that day than for myself.

I threw that picture up inside the front door. Then, when we got married, Fionnuala replaced it, naturally enough, with a wedding photograph – so even that little snapshot of my career didn't last. If you're looking for GAA memorabilia, the Cavanagh household is not the place; it's barren of anything related to Gaelic football. I would be constantly reminded that football was my hobby and not my life – not that I paid much heed to this.

I would say there are twenty boxes of crystal, Beleek china and bronze statuettes up in the attic, most still unopened, awards from various games. Mummy and Daddy, on the other hand, have loads of our medals and cups. Their house is like a shrine to me and Colm – but that was never my idea. They have trophies on show because they are proud, but my house has nothing, and that, I would have to admit, is a touch perverse.

The point I am making is that I was never content or fulfilled with what I achieved in the game. I never once felt I had done enough. I got to many brilliant places, did well and was happy for brief periods, but there was always a higher bar to be cleared. Maybe it comes from when I was a kid. I would score seven or eight points in a game, but Daddy would ask how I managed to miss the free from out on the left. Whatever the reason, the gauge never went near full for me when it came to measuring success. It's a bit sad, isn't it?

As the Mayo disappointment diminished over the next few months I got back to some kind of normality. Started to engage with people again.

'There's more success to be had, Seán,' they would say. 'You can't go in these circumstances.'

Mickey called to see me at work and asked what way I was thinking.

'Mickey, this was meant to be my last year, but I can't leave it like this.'

'Yeah, I thought that was what you'd say,' he replied.

And that was it. Back for 2017. Hit the reset button and scope the targets again.

Slay the ghosts of 2016 and win another All-Ireland. Sport is a fickle mistress – from the desolation and meltdown of losing to Mayo I was back within a few weeks not only positive but in obsessive mode all over again. Another year for Fionnuala and the girls to endure.

But she was right. I couldn't leave it go like this.

3

THE FINAL CURTAIN

I had two aims going into 2017. To try to get that fourth All-Ireland was an obvious one. Keeping my place on the team was the first target, though.

Hungry young cubs were emerging at a rapid rate and they were laying down serious markers in training. I didn't want to finish my career on the bench, fading into the background. I didn't want to hear people say, 'Look, he's done. The legs are gone. Not much to offer now.'

I was actually in dread of that scenario and so I decided I would up the ante and make sure it didn't happen. I had seen Dooher push his body right to the end, to the very limit, until his body said 'no'. He drove through serious pain thresholds to pull on the Tyrone shirt, and I told myself I could do the same thing. Did I want to keep a young lad off the team? Only if I was good enough to do so.

With all the prehab work of the year before, I felt strong and confident enough to have one more twist. I trained six days a week. Monday was gym work. Tuesday was with Tyrone on the pitch. Wednesday we hit the gym in Omagh. On Thursday we went back to Garvaghey. And Friday nights we had club training. I would always go and warm up with the club lads, even if only to shoot a few balls and in recent years Mickey had us in on Saturday mornings for skills work and final tactical work. It was manic, intense and painful, but I hung in there.

Meanwhile I was starting to examine other areas of my life. In December 2016, Fionnuala and I celebrated our wedding anniversary with a trip to Iceland and headed from Reykjavik into complete barren wilderness to see the glaciers. For most of that six-hour drive, I melted Fionnuala's head about my half-formed plans to do my own thing and open my own business.

Her response, as always, was calm and measured: 'Look, see how you go.'

Fionnuala knew I probably didn't need added responsibility and hassle at the time, but I had an itch for change, which I needed to scratch. I had been working for years in a corporate environment at Cavanagh Kelly, a firm co-owned by my uncle Seán, and had really enjoyed it, but I had ideas too on how I might run my own business if the chance ever came.

Back home from Iceland, I decided to go for it. I would strike out on my own. It was the third week in December and I owed it to Uncle Seán to be up front about what was in my head. I'm really close with him; he inspired me to do accountancy and helped keep me sane through all my exams. Mummy and Daddy didn't have the opportunity to go far with their education, but Seán had gone down that road and I had admired him greatly for that. He has always texted me before and after games for both club and county. He's also a good man in times of crisis and I often turned to him for advice. I went straight to him and told him of my plans.

'Don't be daft! You're in a good position here.'

But I told Seán I had made up my mind and he accepted that. Cue mayhem. I guess I was reliving Seán's own career path. He had made a similar move from one of the North's 'Big Four' practices, as they were known. Now his nephew and namesake wanted to have a go at being as successful.

I had expected to have a cushion of sorts in serving three months' notice, but company rules dictated they had no choice but to put me on gardening leave from February onwards. That brought an unwanted urgency to everything, and I hardly slept for four weeks during January.

In fairness, there was a certain safety net in the fact that Fionnuala has a good job, but I still felt compelled to honour my obligations to the household budget and so, before the Christmas turkey was bought, the structure of Seán Cavanagh and Company was put in place. We officially opened in February 2017 and we were mad busy from the start. All through February, March and April – months I thought would be quiet – I was flat out. Thankfully, it still hasn't relented. A lot of people have placed their trust in me and my professional ability and my links with the GAA definitely played a role in convincing prospective new businesses to come on board.

Even amid the mayhem of becoming self-employed, opening an office and finding clients, I never shirked training. I longed for it and would leave home for the Garvaghey Centre around 6 p.m. Myself, Colm and Harry would travel in together from the Moy. All the other lads were the same – they would be there when we'd arrive at 6.15 p.m., getting physio, stretching, the usual preparatory stuff.

The actual session would start at 7.30 and run to 9.15. Most nights from early spring through summer, the likes of Petey, Mattie and Lee Brennan would stay on pitch doing extra runs, extra shooting and extra defensive work. I often pulled out of there at 10.15, and some guys would still be kicking around. Harry had a few injury niggles and some nights he stayed late for rehab. He told me Richie and Mattie would often be there at 11.15 p.m., still working hard.

Fionnuala warned me I was heading for a heart attack with all the coming and going, chain-drinking coffee, thinking constantly about the business, and then training like a lunatic in the evenings. It was all just another crazy time in my life. During the day I longed for the normality and familiarity of Tyrone training and those sessions were a huge de-stresser for me, whether on the pitch or in the gym. When I was with the lads, my teammates, the most pressing topic was normally who had posted what on social media.

I was disappointed not to start the 2017 McKenna Cup campaign, or the first few National League games, and fretted over the need to win my place back. But gradually I got some routine and sanity into the working day and got back in the team.

The game-plan had been formulated and partly refined from the previous season.

We had been playing very defensively since 2013. Contrary to outside opinion, that was the real start of the 'defence first' approach in Tyrone and it coincided with Gavin ('Horse') Devlin's first season as a selector with Mickey.

Now Mickey started talking about our wing-backs operating almost as flankers do in rugby. I suspect he was thinking of how, in the previous few years, certain teams inflicted damage on us by attacking up the wings.

We used a soccer-like formation for the 2017 season, with wingers or wing-backs hugging the sidelines, covering up and down the field, exploiting space in the opposition half and offering protection in defence. My role was to slot in and around centre half-back with a defensive remit, do a job there and also look for chances to initiate attacks from deep.

There was a small bit of trial and error during the National League and Mickey road-tested a couple of other things as well, such as putting me and Mattie Donnelly up front on our own. But that formation was binned after we played Donegal in the NFL on a horrible night in Ballybofey when the ball never came near us.

It was a night when you wouldn't put a dog out, and the mood on and off the field was just as dark and dirty. There was pure hatred in the air that evening. Venom poured down from the stands, personal battles raged all over the place and those duels overshadowed the football.

They got a lead and brought the game into a dogfight. As things went feral on the field, rows were breaking out between both backroom teams. It was all far worse than anything I had experienced with Armagh, supposedly our bitterest rivals.

Michael Murphy and I had played international rules together and got on well – he's a really good lad and I recall that when he was seventeen he said in an interview that I was his favourite player. But in Ballybofey, we put our mutual respect on hold.

Donegal got on top of us, Michael was pulling the strings, and as well as the physical stuff the verbals were flying between us. It was vicious and we were as bad as each other.

We changed tactics again after that match and Mattie, especially, moved back out the field. We tried to be progressive. Against Kerry in the League we agreed to leave three or four men up the field in the first half and attempt to take the game to them. But Kerry dominated midfield and we couldn't get the ball to stick inside in our attack. They hit us for eight points in a row and we were nine down at the break after having the wind at our backs. That was the end of that adventure – we reverted to a defensive style in the second half, just about stayed in the game and got a couple of scores. But we went back to basics.

That was our flight plan for the Championship. A couple of systems had been tried but, nah, we would go back to a defensive style with that touch of refinement from Mickey with the wingers. When the opposition got on the ball we would fall in behind the 65, soak up the pressure, hold them, and counter-attack at pace, using the centre as well as the wings to good effect.

There was no Plan B. We didn't think we needed another system; we felt this one was unbeatable. Mickey had drawn up and explained his blueprint at the start of the year and having listened intently we were all on message. We felt no team could pass their way through us – we had such tough tacklers all over the park.

We thought we had evidence of that from the Ulster Championship. That is never easy to win, but we got through it pretty much on our own terms. Playing Derry at Celtic Park can be tricky because they are tough to play on a tight pitch, but it was straightforward enough.

Once again, the big test was Donegal. They were looking for revenge after we had scraped past them in the 2016 Ulster final.

At their peak under Jim McGuinness, Donegal had been similar to Dublin in their on-field discipline. By that I mean they had a real toughness but also a genius for finding the edge and staying on the right side of it. They perfected the three-quarter foul, for example, and would push that one to the limits. They tackled in packs and dished out the verbals but showed unreal discipline, dropping back in unison when they lost the ball. They had been known for producing brilliant individuals – classy forwards like Christy Toye and Brendan Devenney – but under McGuinness they were a unit.

I remember the first time we played them during Jim's tenure in Clones in 2011 and they completely dropped off us. It struck me they had lost the plot – what sort of eejits were they? They were about to give us a shed-load of chances and we would surely go to town.

They beat us with a last-minute goal and won a lot more after that.

Their players were transformed there for a few years. The McGees, Neil and Eamon, and Neil Gallagher were always tough but suddenly they had bought into a collective system with added value. I had been used to those lads getting in my face – the bit of bad blood between us – but under Jim, instead of niggling me they set me puzzles by sitting back and dropping off.

This can't work, I thought. This is not how Gaelic football is played.

It did work for them. To such an extent that in 2012 and 2013 we tried different systems, but we couldn't beat them. Eventually we decided that, if you can't beat them, join them. So, after all the trials and tests of game-plan, Mickey decided to base our

Championship model on theirs. It was some shift in strategy and tactics. We went from being the so-called aristocrats of the counter-attack game to emulating a team we had seen as vastly inferior.

But McGuinness had transformed everything about Donegal; he set strict parameters and got his team playing within them. They did it expertly.

Anyway, with all the sledging from Ballybofey still in mind, we expected there'd be jibes and jabs flying from throw-in when we met them a few months later in the Ulster Championship. But there wasn't. We had huge motivation too and something just clicked. We schooled them for fun. We got so far ahead so quickly there didn't seem any point.

It was amazing. I was on Neil McGee for a while early in the second half. A few years earlier, Neil would have been standing on my toes and giving lip, but now we actually got to chatting. At one point he said, 'God, it's a warm day, Seán – I can't wait till this is over!'

We won by nine points, but it could have been twenty. In fairness we did wonder if we were really that good or if they were that bad. We Tyrone boys got the sense from that game that all was not right in Donegal, that they were less invested in the set-up than they had been. They were leaving behind the McGuinness structures, they had lost a lot of experienced men, and they were just not the same force. When they played Galway and leaked four goals they were all over place; you could see the McGuinness legacy was dwindling.

It was nice to captain the team to beat Down in the Ulster final but, to be honest, it was really only a stepping stone to the ultimate goal. That was my sixth provincial medal and it was good to get another photo of the Anglo-Celt Cup with Colm and the two girls beside me. But the main thing was, we were back in the All-Ireland series as winners with back-to-back Ulster titles.

Playing Armagh in the All-Ireland quarter-final meant a certain division of loyalties in the family. Fionnuala is from Armagh and Charlie Vernon, her brother, has been one of their best players over the past decade. When Tyrone play Armagh, radio silence rules.

I marked Charlie for the first time in a McKenna Cup game in Omagh in 2009 when he was with Queen's University and we've played against each other a good few times since. There would be times when we would sit in either Charlie's house or our own place and chat about how Tyrone and Armagh were going, but it would all be vague and carefully coded. Very little was given away! And whoever got the upper hand on any given day would have the decency not to brag about it.

We played them in the NFL in Omagh a few years ago on a bad night for us. We got only nine scores in total and Charlie put the shackles on me. And to add insult to injury on the way home, Fionnuala kept asking about the game, with an innocent smile. How did I feel it went? Did we get our tactics wrong? Did Charlie himself play well? And so on. Fionnuala has been on my side for so long, but the old Armagh heritage and bias come out at the worst possible times.

Within the extended family, though, the lack of noise when the two tribes meet can be deafening. In the weeks beforehand, neither Charlie nor I wanted to talk about the All-Ireland quarter-final. Every Monday I pop down to Fionnuala's mum, Catherine, to collect the two girls after swimming lessons, but the week of the big match I made some excuse that I couldn't manage it.

It's funny how sporting rivalry plays out. They are the nicest family you could meet. Charlie is a lovely fella – always in and out of our house. As I mentioned, Fionnuala's late dad, Charles, was a gentleman, a proper sportsman. All he would say was, 'May the best team win.' Against Armagh in 2017, the best team did win.

And that's all I had better say!

Coming up to that semi-final against Dublin, I genuinely thought we had all bases covered and the system was infallible.

What we didn't factor in was that Dublin had spotted our strategy ahead of the All-Ireland semi-final and countered it by putting two men on each wing. That meant we were outnumbered where we had hoped to make hay, and our strength became a weakness. We found ourselves in little triangles around the middle of the field, only to discover when it was too late that the Dubs, their early goal aside, would rarely choose to come through the middle. Whenever they did, it was because we had left space there while chasing them around the fringes. They outsmarted us, playing with their heads up and spreading both the ball and us around.

I went into that All-Ireland semi-final thinking, 'I don't care what Dublin bring to the table or throw at us – they'll not beat us!' Then one bit of loose play around the middle and they cut through and rifled that goal.

When Armagh had challenged our defensive line, trying to break tackles, we mostly won turnovers and counter-attacked. But Dublin were cute. Instead of trying to break the line via the direct route they would hold the ball and move us up, down and across the field.

Ciarán Kilkenny conducted the orchestra. Each time he flourished the baton his teammates were there in sweet harmony. We desperately tried to match them note for note, but we couldn't get in sync at all.

Their game management is unmatched. They were able to drag us out of position, shut down our kickouts and keep us away from their restarts. That takes some doing. It was far from pleasant to be on the receiving end, but it was still possible, even in the throes of defeat, to be impressed by their organisation and skill.

Before the game I had refused to buy into the hype that they had too much pace and power to be stopped. Why should they be that much stronger than us? Petey Donnelly couldn't have done more to prepare us. Never mind the countless hours we had given training and practising since November or before. I said to Colm before the game, 'I don't care how good they are – they can't be doing as much as us. Even if they are, there's no way they can be fitter and stronger than us.'

But they were. They were incredible. You couldn't give away a free because Dean Rock was so accurate. We didn't know if Diarmuid Connolly would start, but if he did we would have to put a marker on him. Against other teams you could sacrifice one player to man-mark, but these lads needed more covering than that.

I was really struck by how unselfish their forwards were. They didn't have a Conor McManus type whom a defensive unit could target and so limit his team's scoring chances. Instead the ball was going to Paddy Andrews, he was flicking and passing it to teammates, moving on at speed, and maybe taking a return pass.

As far as I recall, until Dublin got that goal we hadn't once been behind in the 2017 Championship. Suddenly we were lagging off the pace, and our game-plan was being ripped apart. Our blueprint had been predicated on staying solid as a team, keeping abreast of them and then depending on our strike runners, Petey, Mattie and Niall Sludden, to pierce holes and open them up. But they sealed off all the space in front of those lads.

The game was as good as dead after eighteen minutes. I was at the front of attack, chasing ball in the middle of four and five Dubs, while at the other end we were sitting back defending an eight-point deficit.

I remember when Armagh lost to Wexford in 2008 saying to Charlie, 'Ye were losing by two points and still ye had two sweepers lying back. Why not go for it at that stage?' Now we were the ones with thirteen men behind the ball, chasing shadows while we trailed our opponents. Madness.

There was mayhem at the break. We needed to settle. The message was to try a few long balls in, maybe plunder a goal or two. The game could change very quickly. Petey played one ball in and that was cut out. Eventually Colm decided himself that he would go inside and ordered a few long balls to be played in. He won two or three and earned a penalty. He should have been in there much earlier.

All that said, our Achilles heel was an inability to change or adapt on the pitch. We hadn't worked on anything else during the year. There was no contingency plan. It was all or nothing with one style of play.

When I spoke at an annual review meeting in Kelly's Inn,

Ballygawley, a week after the heartbreak of being beaten out the gate, I looked the group in the eye and told them that we had brilliant footballers and what we needed most now were leaders.

'Lads, I'm a positive guy, but the more I think about it the more I realise why we won those All-Irelands. It came down to personalities. Gormley, Ricey, Dooher, Brian McGuigan – those guys who were ridiculously resilient and would go to any lengths to change the outcome of a match.'

And, while they didn't spend the same hours in gyms or on alternate training methods, they knew how to win when it mattered most.

I meant what I said. Mickey Harte is a great manager and has done more than anyone else for Tyrone, but quite often those lads made crucial decisions on the pitch without waiting for Mickey to tell them. I guess the difference is that some current players are afraid to make a mistake for fear of losing their place, whereas the likes of Gormley and McGuigan feared no one and played it as they saw it.

I've tried to work out why we haven't won an All-Ireland in nine years and I think the answer lies in the personalities of certain players. The group that set out with Mickey as winning minors in 1998 won the All-Ireland under-21s in 2001 and just followed right the way through – they were a special bunch. But 2008 and 2009 marked the end point for them and the years since have really underlined just how important those players were. They came up from minor, won everything in sight on the way up and the likes of myself, Dooher and Canavan joined in on the party for good measure along the way.

'Lads, this present group is equally committed and just as skilled,' I continued. 'But it's that character and personality – we don't have enough of that. Go back to tight games that we lost over the past couple of years, to the likes of Donegal when we couldn't get over the line. Mayo in 2016. We just needed someone to be cute, someone to take the right option, to win a free when we were in trouble.'

I told them how the Mayo game, the 2016 All-Ireland quarter-final, was never far from my mind. We should have done whatever it took to get a draw that day. I think we would have beaten them in the replay and beaten Tipperary in the semi-final. I suspect the guys of ten, twelve years ago would have found the answers in those crunch moments.

And so, signing off as a Tyrone player once and for all at that review meeting, I wished the group well and insisted we weren't far from the promised land, but we needed on-field leaders and decision-makers like those of old – and they needed to emerge from within the squad. They don't grow on trees.

PART TWO

GLORY ROAD

4

THE TROUBLES

At the end of my last day at Primate Dixon Primary School, Coalisland, my dad, Teddy, arrived to pick me up and walked me out of the building for the final time. The principal, Mr Herron, walked with us to the car and chatted before bidding us farewell and shaking hands. As he turned to go back into the school he paused, looked at Daddy and said, 'You're taking away the best footballer Coalisland has ever seen.'

I was only seven and the significance of the words hardly registered with me, but to this day Daddy recalls them. It was some statement.

My mum, Dolores, came from Coalisland, and that's where we had lived since I was born. She and Daddy had set up home in Newtownkelly in the town and were happy there, helped by the fact that Mummy's family, the Fanthorpes, were well known. The Fanthorpe boys were handy footballers, but they were also keen snooker players, which probably didn't help their football careers. They gave as much time on the green baize as on the green fields.

Daddy came from Moy, or the Moy as we all call it, and was steeped in Moy GAA; he played full-back for the club for twenty-five years and was there when they won the Tyrone Intermediate title in 1982. But Coalisland was only seven miles up the road and it was no big deal for him to settle there and commute for training and games.

Our first house was a semi-detached with few frills, but it did the job. It was a good community. Not surprisingly, many of my earliest memories are of kicking a football. I think I was only three when Mummy got me a wee pair of football boots and I tore outside to break them in.

There was no park or playing field alongside, so I used the gable end of the house as a makeshift goal. The timing wasn't great. On the day I road-tested my lovely new Golas, Daddy had just painted that gable wall a lovely creamy white, but he was happy for me to dirty it again as long as it was Gaelic I was playing.

And so, given the freedom of the end wall, I was putting the new boot leather through its paces, only for the session to end in tears when I chased after the ball too eagerly and slid head first into the freshly painted limestone, splitting my head wide open and spattering blood on Daddy's handiwork.

That's my earliest memory.

When I was five, we moved to a small bungalow up on Annagher Hill, at the other end of town. It was near the GAA pitch, and we rented the house there for the next two years before finding what would become the permanent family home back in the Moy.

We may not have stayed too long up on the Hill, but while there I met Peter Donnelly, a great friend to this day. Petey lived just fifty metres from us and we clicked from the start. We passed our days kicking footballs up and down the twenty-degree slope. We went on together to win an All-Ireland minor title for Tyrone in 2001, and he is still heavily involved with Tyrone, working as strength-and-conditioning coach to the seniors.

I started my Gaelic football career with the Coalisland Fianna under-8s and also played for the under-10s and under-12s before we moved to the Moy. Everywhere I went, Petey was close by. When I was full-back with the under-8s, he was just behind me in the nets, and so on up the age grades.

Daddy was content to see me playing away. A Gaelic football diehard, he worked as a fitter at a builders' yard called Stephensons. He is and always was a hard worker. After leaving Stephensons he started with another builder, Malachy O'Neill, and would head off on his motorbike each morning, seven miles down the road to the Moy. It's funny how it goes – that housing development Daddy worked on is where Fionnuala, our kids and I live today. Colm and his family also live there.

Back then, though, we were Coalisland people. The town serviced three GAA clubs – Clonoe O'Rahillys and Brackaville were the other two – and that goes to show the local appetite for Gaelic games.

I have one very vivid memory from that time in Coalisland and it concerns my younger brother. It was a hot summer's evening. Petey and I were kicking football on Annagher Hill, and Petey's younger brother, Paddy, and Colm were playing nearby with our wee dog, Lady, just beside the house and alongside the main road. All of a sudden, Colm and Paddy went running across that main road, a thirty-miles-per-hour zone, and little

Lady chased after them. A car narrowly missed Colm but killed our wee dog. That's the standout memory I have of Colm in Coalisland.

It was a good place to grow up. It wasn't all that affluent, but sure where was in the late 1980s? It had a good community and lovely people. But it also had its own experiences during the Troubles, and I'm told those ultimately were the reasons we left there as a family and moved to the Moy, a village that also saw its fair share of problems.

None of us had political connections, but in Coalisland we were in the midst of the Troubles. From the back garden of Mummy's family home in Mourne Crescent, only metres from the RUC station, we'd hear petrol bombs go off. We were acutely aware of the dangers and, though we were never actually caught up in the conflict, we would hear stories of weapons being stashed around the place.

Bringing up three boys – Adrian was now turning eleven, I was eight and Colm was four – our parents obviously worried there would eventually be pressure on growing lads to be dragged into it all. Daddy, in particular, was very aware of the likely pressures and was more content to move to the Moy, where he grew up and still played football. He felt more comfortable in a more rural village at that stage. He had grown up on a farm outside the town, nestled peacefully in the countryside, and I think that was the life he wanted for us.

It was a difficult time for everyone in Northern Ireland, and few towns or parishes could guarantee peace and security, but Mummy and Daddy made their move.

As recently as the 1960s, the Moy was predominantly Protestant, as were the businesses along the main road which linked the village to towns like Dungannon, Portadown and Armagh to the south.

That dynamic has changed since and, in many ways, I think that the Moy has reflected Northern Ireland's wider battle for stability. There are about 2,200 residents in Moy, with some eighty per cent from a Catholic background. A survey was carried out there six years ago and twenty-six per cent of the locals said their nationality was *Northern Irish*, another sixty-one per cent felt their nationality was *Irish*, and six per cent described their nationality as being *British*. So that's the make-up of our village; quite a complex one. I would say that wounds are still open and sore after the years of violence, but no one really talks much about those times. We all just get on with things and thankfully there are no steel barricades, or walls daubed with tribal slogans that make divisions between Catholic and Protestant more obvious.

It's an affluent enough village to live in now, forty miles southwest of Belfast and surrounded by blackberry hedges and rolling hills. There is no tribalism and the only flag to be seen is the skyblue and white of Moy GAA, flying proudly outside homes and businesses to mark our journey to the 2018 All-Ireland intermediate club final. The colours were hung by all sections of the community in support of us. But that's the only colour you see around the place these days. You can drive around and not be subjected to kerbs painted the red, white and blue of the Union Jack, nor the green, white and orange of the Irish tricolour.

That's not to say the Troubles bypassed us over the last four decades.

For a while after we moved down from Coalisland, with

tensions still growing, Mummy and Daddy considered the prospect of emigrating and mentioned it to us a few times. Some of my uncles had moved away from Ireland to London and the US to get away from what was going on in the North, and Mummy and Daddy wondered if they should do likewise.

I think they came closest to moving early in 1992, just eight months after we moved to the Moy, after Kevin McKearney and his elderly uncle, Jack, were shot at their butcher shop. Kevin died at the scene; Jack in April. The shop is still in business and we go there to buy our meat, but what brought it home was that Mummy was working only two doors down at the Moy Inn, now known as the Ryandale, just twenty metres from the murders.

As a kid, I have to say that none of what was happening actually bogged me down; I was aware that the threat of trouble was always there, but I grew up in the middle of it almost obliviously.

Here's an example. Once or twice a week I played in a friend's back garden with a group of lads. At the back of his garden a deep-rooted ditch ran adjacent to a nearby chapel and car park. Countless times one of us would fire the ball wide of the posts and out through a jumble of briars. I would often be dispatched to retrieve the ball from the five-foot drop into the ditch.

One day, as I ran to fetch it, I had to step over a British soldier lying there with a sniper's rifle; I had to shift my feet to avoid walking on his camouflaged helmet. I looked down at him and he peered back up at me, his rifle held closely in his hands. I know this sounds crazy, but I wasn't terrified or anything; I just got the ball and got on with it. This happened more than once to me and my pals, but none of us knew anything different.

There is a huge supermarket beside our parents' house which

had served as an egg factory called Dobsons when I was a kid. The factory had shut down after an incident and, as curious nine- or ten-year-olds, we would wander about and explore the place with our friends. An entrance ran into the grounds from our own back garden and it was like a mysterious playground for us. In reality there was nothing more interesting than old docket books, staplers and abandoned fax machines lying about but still we opened drawers and cabinets, letting our imaginations run wild at what might have been inside. It was harmless fun. The reality, though, was that two men had been murdered there not long beforehand. Everywhere we went there were reminders of the unstable political environment we lived in.

With every hint of trouble Mummy would say, 'If this gets any worse we are moving abroad. We are taking the family out.'

She was right to be concerned because danger was never too far off until, gradually, the politicians from both sides of the divide started sitting down and talking to each other and tensions slowly eased a little.

We always had Granda Tommy's farmhouse to escape to. That was the meeting point for the extended family, and he was the man who seemed to link us all together when I was a child. Daddy had enjoyed a carefree and safe upbringing there and I think he wanted us out in his family home as much as possible for the same reason. My abiding memories are of Daddy's family being very close and we would pop down to Tommy's house every Sunday evening. That's how I think of Granny Jenny, or Jinny as everyone called her, and Granda Tommy – being at their house every weekend.

Daddy had seven brothers and four sisters, a large family, all invested in the GAA. Daddy proudly recounted how Granda went to every All-Ireland football final for sixty years. He worked on the rail lines and would use his connections to take the train to Dublin every September for the big event. But his biggest presence was felt at grassroots level. He was a stalwart of the Moy and had served in a number of roles, including club president.

Before Granda died in 2004, I got to bring the Sam Maguire down to him when we won it in 2003, and that was a special thing to be able to do. In the autumn of 2017 I saw a picture of Micheál Donoghue, the Galway hurling manager, bringing the Liam MacCarthy Cup back to his dad, Miko, and that photograph stirred a range of emotions inside me. Micheál's dad was in tears, and I remember that's how Granda was too. Two rural men, diehards for their own clubs. Granda had these huge hands and he shook the paw off me and clung onto the Sam Maguire at the same time when I visited. To see such a big, strong man struggling to keep himself together was very humbling. Such was his strength that I struggled to loosen his grip on the cup, and, in the end, I had to say, 'Here, Granda, this cup has to go on its way now. I only have it for a few hours.' Granda wouldn't usually have been one to show the emotions, but that evening, though he didn't say much, I knew he was proud.

Jinny suffered a stroke in the late 1990s and lost the power down one side of her body. On the day I played the 2000 MacRory Cup final she was lying in bed, but she and the rest of the family were able to watch on TV, and they told me she was in tears at the end. It's amazing the power of the GAA – the happiness it can bring to friends and family. We underestimate that clout half the time.

Anyway, that was the background to Mummy and Daddy.

Two lovely, typically Irish families, the Cavanaghs and the Fanthorpes. Both immersed in the community, one mad for GAA and the other slightly addicted to snooker!

I didn't feel any massive wrench to move to the Moy from Coalisland because it was only down the road and I wasn't in my new school a wet week before I had established my sporting credentials.

It was late August 1991 when we finally relocated, and I enrolled in St John's Primary School in the Moy. I have a good memory of my first day there because I met three guys who are still friends – Stephen Harvey, Stephen Millar and Gary Millar. After school they called to the house asking would I come out to kick football, and I have a real vivid memory of going down to the Millars and thinking: *I'm the new kid – I have to be really competitive here to fit in.*

The Millar house had a wee set of soccer goals outside, and I thought that was just amazing – back in Coalisland we had only jumpers or jackets for goalposts. Anyway, I must have made my mark because after a while kicking around, one of the guys said to me: 'God, you're handy at the football!'

Later, as we settled into our new house in the Moy, we got Mummy and Daddy to throw up a basketball net out front. And just so we didn't forget our roots, Daddy put up a set of goal-posts on some waste ground out the back. I spent much of my childhood on that unclaimed patch that backed onto the local credit union building, kicking balls into that net until darkness fell.

It was important for me to put down a marker as an outsider coming into the Moy. I felt I had to prove myself and everything else would roll into place. At the same time, I was still a shy child and was in many ways unsure of myself, especially in non-sporting matters, and so moving schools was always going to present challenges. One episode stands out.

A few months after moving to St John's I was told I had been rostered for Irish dancing, recorder and tin-whistle lessons, and the classes would start the following day. I wasn't a bit happy; the prospect of having to do any of that in front of an unknown and critical audience filled me with dread. I arrived home from school bound up with nerves and anxiety, broke the news to my mother and burst into tears. Fortunately, she realised I wasn't faking it, and so she wrote a letter to the school and they gave me a dispensation. It cost twenty pence for an exemption from the dancing, a fine that I was more than happy to pay!

I had sport to fall back on. I used the fact that I was good at football and, to a lesser extent, in the classroom, to help me get along with my peers. Even when I moved on to secondary school at St Patrick's Academy and, later, St Pat's in Armagh, I wouldn't have had a huge number of friends, but that didn't worry me. I never was the type of guy who fretted about being admired. I think by the end of my time in school I had gained respect, mainly through what I did in sport and study rather than by being Mr Popular.

The change of primary schools proved fairly seamless for both myself and Colm, who started first class in the Moy and had known nothing else. It was a bit tougher on Adrian, who was eleven at the time and struggled with the change; all his long-time pals were back in Coalisland and he missed them.

Adrian was an excellent footballer. He won a Division One under-14 county title with Coalisland and went on to break onto the club's minor team when he was just fourteen before playing a bit of senior too. Out of the three brothers he was the most skilful – and still is. He played a lot of basketball and that broadened his range of skills. He is also the most athletic and still runs seven miles a day. But as a footballer, at six foot one and much slimmer than Colm and me, he hadn't the Cavanagh 'ignorance', or the bulk and bullishness that we had. Colm would put his head in where others wouldn't put a boot and it wouldn't cost him a thought. Adrian didn't have that thickness. As the years went on and he played more and more basketball he just fell out of love with football and drifted away from it. But he was well recognised as a strong talent.

In fact, to rank the three of us in matters of skill, I would put Adrian first, myself second and Colm third. In the ignorance stakes young Colm was undoubtedly top, I was second again and Adrian was third. We all had different qualities!

Not only is Colm my brother; he's also my best friend. When we moved to the Moy we shared a bedroom and did so for years. Adrian always had a room of his own because he was older. Anything I did, Colm did. He always tagged along and nowadays many of my childhood pals are good friends with Colm too. That all started with me bringing him along for kicking practice – I drilled balls at him and he had to kick them back to me. You could say I used wee Colm for my own ends, but we became so close and still are. He was stuck in goals so much for my practising that he became a really good keeper and actually played there until under-14 level for the club.

In 1993, I did the eleven-plus in St John's, an entrance exam used in the North, a precursor to second-level education; it dictated what type of school you went to and what class you would be placed in.

My results were decent – I got an A – and that allowed me into St Patrick's Academy, Dungannon, a grammar school. Otherwise, in Northern Ireland, there are options to take a different pathway and go to a high school or comprehensive school.

Along with Gaelic and basketball, I was mad for soccer. In early 1995, when I was in St Patrick's, a friend, Donal Sage, asked me to come along with him and train with Dungannon Swifts FC. I went and joined their training session on an all-weather surface, and I recall that on that first evening we were being coached to do the Cruyff turn by a man called Joe McAree.

Joe's son, Rodney, is current head coach at the club – he was with Liverpool, Bristol City and Fulham during his own time playing across the water and made it into the Liverpool reserves, which is no mean achievement. But the dad, Joe, is a club legend. He was awarded an MBE in the 2013 New Year Honours List after giving forty years' service to the Swifts and leading them into Europe in 2007, and he still runs youth teams with Dungannon United.

Anyway, I joined the Swifts in training, and once again I felt I had to make my mark. I had never played soccer, but I didn't want to be anything but the best. I got stuck in, and after twenty minutes Joe called me aside.

'What's your name, son?'

'Seán.'

'Seán, I want you to come with us on Saturday. We have a game. Would that interest you?'

I told him it would. I knew that from the group of forty at training, only sixteen were picked for the game on Saturday. So I had achieved my first objective.

From there my brief soccer career went into orbit. It all

happened so quickly. A few weeks later I found myself playing against Manchester United under-14s.

The Swifts seniors were down to play Man United in a fundraiser for a new set of floodlights, so it was decided to give the under-14s of both clubs a run-out in Stangmore Park, Dungannon.

I'd been with the Swifts for only a month and had played just four games when Man United came to town, yet I was picked at right-back for the big occasion. It was a baptism of fire, but I loved the challenge. I knew a few of the Swifts guys, a couple of lads I played Gaelic with: Seán Webb from Coalisland, who went over to play in the Scottish League with Raith Rovers; another Gaelic footballer, Mark Hughes, who signed for Tottenham and ended up captaining the Spurs reserves.

Joe spoke to me before kick-off: 'Seán, if this goes well tonight you could go places in soccer.'

I didn't say much but I looked around and saw senior players like Phil Neville and Phil Mulryne (now the Catholic priest Fr Mulryne), who were playing for United in the senior game afterwards, and wondered if I could reach their level too. I reckoned I played well – but with time running out and the game scoreless, I was called ashore. I had barely reached the dugout when United went flying down my wing, the winger rifled a cross, and they scored from it. As I sat on the line I just knew I would have stopped that cross.

I loved soccer but only played it for the rest of that season before Gaelic took over again. I would like to think, had I stayed with it, I could have earned a move cross-channel, but sure who knows? All I know for certain is that guys I was on a level with were getting try-outs back then.

Anyway, despite that defeat, I remained a Manchester United fan, and I still head to Old Trafford several times a season.

The head of PE at St Patrick's Academy, Fintan Colgan, kept asking me to play rugby for the Dungannon under-14s and under-15s. He talked to me several times and mostly I dodged the issue because it clashed with Gaelic. One Saturday, though, there was a gap in the diary and I found myself free to go.

On the Thursday night beforehand I had gone training with them just to learn the 'laws' of the game, and when Saturday arrived they put me on the wing. Just before kick-off I reached for my gumshield – and realised I had left it at home. It was too late to worry, the game started, and I was in the thick of it.

If my soccer debut was good, my first and only rugby start was even more eye-catching. I got two early tries and set up another. And then one of those wee rucks formed, and when one of our lads, a small fella, was tackled and got sent flying backward, his head hit me full force in the mouth and knocked out two of my teeth.

Fintan was distraught. He had begged me for ages to enlist, and now here he was rushing me up the road to McArthurs, the dentist in Dungannon, with my mouth split. I remember landing home and having to tell Mummy I'd just had two teeth knocked out and had false ones put back in again. Poor Fintan couldn't stop apologising!

Back at school, however, once my new teeth had settled, he came to me again: 'Seán, you played seriously well. Would you come again with us?'

'Thanks, Fintan, but I'm sticking to basketball and Gaelic from here!'

I enjoyed the experience of playing rugby and soccer but would have always picked the GAA before either of them. With Daddy being such a GAA stalwart, I could really only fit in soccer or rugby if they didn't clash with a Gaelic football game. And as I got older there were clashes every week.

But dipping the toes in those other sports was a good learning experience. Not only a sporting experience but a cultural one too. Coming from a nationalist background, I remember a few wee flashpoints when playing against mainly Protestant soccer teams. Names like 'Fenian' and 'Taig' were flung at you.

There was one lad on the team who didn't talk to me at all. Whenever the two of us went to take a throw-in, or pick up an opponent, he wouldn't even acknowledge me. At first, I wondered what I had done to him, but sure I had done nothing. In his mind it was probably down to where he came from and where I came from, and that was just how things were. I guess I found that through sport you could work things out with non-verbal communication. Because that's what we had to do when playing on the same team and not talking.

The most bizarre episode for me was when, before that Man United game, I had to stand with the Union Jack raised in front of me and 'God Save the Queen' being roared out. I remember looking around and wondering, *Jesus, am I okay here? Will I get in any trouble for standing for this anthem?*

I grew up always facing the tricolour and that night I had to stand in front of the Union Jack. I just put the head down and did what was expected of me on that occasion. This was just the political side of things – there wasn't much for me to worry about as a kid. I was about to play Man Utd and that was enough for anyone at that age.

That sort of stuff broadened your horizons, though, and gave you a fair dose of perspective. The wisest course was just to stick with sport and work hard in school.

We had left Coalisland for a more peaceful life, but there were just no guarantees.

5

NEW DAWN

The IRA ceasefire of 1994 meant that, for the first time in many decades, the people of Northern Ireland could be optimistic about peace.

It was only a cautious optimism, but people rejoiced all the same. I remember watching the news and seeing crowds gathered on the streets of Belfast, flags being waved, and car horns tooted. For us as a family the ceasefire meant that we could stay put in this island and focus on all the normal things – each other, our hobbies and education.

In St Patrick's Academy I followed up on my love of basketball. Much and all as Gaelic football has been my life, and leaving aside the staunch GAA background I come from, basketball was probably my first real love. My admiration for the game came from Adrian, who adored the 1990s Chicago Bulls team that won six NBA championships between 1991 and 1998, with Hall of Famers like Michael Jordan and Scottie Pippen playing starring roles. They were all-time heroes to Adrian and to this day he still has hundreds of basketball video tapes, DVDs and posters. I grew up watching those tapes and shared the love of that sport with him too.

Each summer Adrian took me to the Dungannon Basketball Annual Camp where Jerome Westbrooks, a former American basketball professional who was involved with Killester in Dublin for twenty-seven years, held coaching clinics. Jerome's son, Isaac, is a professional in the Icelandic leagues and also plays for Ireland. Jerome lived in Dublin but came up north to run the camp in Dungannon each year. I was in P7, my last year of primary school, when Adrian took me along for the first time.

Unlike my later and short-lived stint in rugby, I had some sense of how basketball should be played from messing around with the brothers at home, playing on the hoof, although I had no technical or court experience whatsoever.

What I loved most about the sport was the walk-through, the inch-by-inch dissection of the game-plan. I thought it made sense, too, that there was a countdown clock, a shot clock, and definite rules that were clearly demarcated in black and white, not like in the GAA, where there are so many grey areas and the rules change depending on who is refereeing a game. In basketball, everything is so structured and disciplined.

Around three hundred kids from all over Ulster gathered for the first camp I attended and there were between thirty and forty coaches to help us develop. I had just turned eleven, but was summoned to play with the under-14s, which was a steep learning curve.

I was happy. I had started out in a group of twenty and just took it from there. All week we had to learn skills in that group. Leona Fay from Eglish was one of the best basketball players around and she was also my team leader and taught me a lot.

As the days passed a few of us were selected to play the best players in other groups. I was young and fearless and, as I was not far off six foot even then, I didn't pay much heed to who I was up against. As the duels were fought out and the numbers whittled down I found myself up against a lad from Belfast who at the time was known as one of the best players in the camp and very well regarded on the basketball circuit.

We were pitted together to see who was the best one-on-one player in the camp. With the stakes rising, the coaches moved us from the Dungannon Intermediate Grounds to the Dungannon Leisure Centre and even that change of venue heightened the tension. I took your man on and beat him. He was fourteen and I was three years younger.

Leona came over and said: 'Jesus, do you know what you have just done?'

Adrian just kept looking over at me with that perplexed frown. 'You wee bastard.'

On the last day I was selected as the 'most valuable player'. Our Adrian had played the game for years but come the end of the camp he was scratching his head, baffled.

'You wee bastard – you're only playing basketball for five days and you get MVP in front of the whole feckin' group,' he said to me on the way home.

I never publicly credited him, but it was surely down to Adrian that I won that award. Because he was five years older than me, and contested every ball with me when we played at home, I was well able to compete with the big boys in camp. I was as tall as any of them as well. When the event ended, I was so happy with that accolade, I genuinely can't describe how much it meant to me. A lot of stuff I learned from that camp stayed with me for the rest of my sporting life.

For example, in my latter years with Tyrone I turned to basketball over and again each winter just to stay fit and sharp. It also helped me hone my football skills all the way through too.

There was a time when basketball was my clear number one. The secondary school routine went like this – every evening after classes ended I went home, did my homework before grabbing a basketball and going outside to shoot hoops. I might stay there as late as midnight or until our neighbour, Mrs McAnallen, would finally lose patience. She regularly had to ring the police and ask Mummy to get me in off the road.

I was addicted. Aside from running the local rugby team, Fintan Colgan also coached me all the way up on the St Patrick's Dungannon basketball teams and along the way we won Ulster Colleges titles, beating all the big teams from Belfast. A lot of the St Malachy's Belfast players, our rivals, lined out for Star of the Sea, a club that has produced giants of Irish basketball. To play against these teams was huge. To beat them ensured a level of success unheard of for a Tyrone school.

I played mostly as a forward but had a few spells at point guard where I could see the whole game unfold. I later lined out for Dungannon Basketball Club, now known as Tyrone Towers, and one of the coaches there, Frankie O'Loane, came to watch me playing for Ulster against Connacht and sought me out after the game. Frankie was involved in the Irish set-up and invited me to train with the national squad. That was a huge honour, but it was also a huge commitment to invest in and it would have involved travelling up and down to Dublin on Saturdays, which would inevitably have resulted in a direct clash with Gaelic football. So, it never quite worked out.

On any given weekend there was always a Moy under-14 or under-16 game to be played and, because of my family links, Gaelic football was back-burning away and slowly starting to become the dominant sport in my life.

My height helped me in football; I stood out from an early stage. At fourteen I played on a Moy minor team that won a grade three county final. A year later we won the grade two minor final, and from then on I could never really squeeze in the basketball commitments.

I do remember, however, the craziness of trying to make it all fit in. One particular day stands out. The Moy beat Derrylaughan in that grade two minor football final and I scored a couple of goals. Later that afternoon I had a big basketball game for Dungannon and that night I had to fit the schoolwork in too. It wasn't easy.

But I felt there was an onus on me to make it work on the football field. From under-12 level onwards, as I towered above everyone else, the temptation for the coaches was to say, 'Give the ball to Seán and he'll do the rest.' Playing basketball had given me skills that other players didn't yet have, and as I was taller than almost everyone at that level, in most Gaelic football games I tried to take it all on myself.

I was standing out – but not everyone liked that. When I was ten years old, we played Derrytresk in an under-12 game. The game was only a few minutes old when I managed to cut through the Derrytresk lads and bag a couple of goals. Next thing I noticed this big row on the sideline.

'Unless you take the number eight off, we are walking off,' the Derrytresk coach roared.

I knew a few of their guys from playing local schools games and so I went up to their coach and pointed to one of the lads. 'Sure, your man there knows me, he knows what age I am.'

You'd get more response from an automated phone service.

'Unless you get that number eight off the field we're pulling the team,' the coach repeated, totally ignoring me.

'He's bloody ten,' our club officials roared back again.

It was all the one – they took the team off the field. A bizarre moment. A few of my friends, at least two years older than me, were playing in that game yet there wasn't a word said about them.

I didn't win that many underage titles with the Moy; we lacked a bit of strength in depth. But playing each week, a few grades above my age, and having learned to carry the ball through basketball – all of that helped me to develop.

Another day that stands out. We played Trillick in Omagh in a minor grade two final. I managed to score 1-4 and chalked it down as my first big GAA success. That evening all the lads were heading out to celebrate and I wanted to be with them. I was sixteen, we had just won a county title and I wanted to go off with my pals. But down south it was a bank holiday weekend and Daddy told me I was down on the roster to work that night in the Four Seasons Hotel in Monaghan, where Daddy did shifts as a bouncer. I refused, saying that I was heading out with the boys and we were going to have the craic. It led to bit of a falling-out with himself. He went off to work without me. As he drove down the Armagh road in his Peugeot 306, his car was rammed by a black bull that ran blindly across the road. It kicked its back hoof through the passenger side of the windscreen. The impact knocked Daddy unconscious. If I had been in the car I would have been killed stone dead. With my height, my head would have been taken clean off by the windscreen.

Sometimes you wonder if things happen for a reason.

Around that time, we played Derrylaughan and I scored 8-16. At one stage late in the game I was moved to full-back; I think the opposition manager requested that I be moved out of the way, but I remember being furious, thinking, *This lad is not going to stop me from scoring – no matter where I am*. Next time I got my paws on the ball, on the edge of my own square, I took off like a sprinter in a rage, tore up the field and scored a point. I shot a look to the sideline as I ran back down the field.

'Youse won't stop me from scoring,' I shouted over to the lads on the line. 'Doesn't matter where youse put me.'

I don't tell these stories to sound like a hero. It's more to demonstrate how I always tried to rise to a challenge, to show too that I was never content to sit back and reflect on what I had achieved. Both of those characteristics still define me to this day. Something inside of me always wants more.

I did learn another trick in those early days; one that I have kept in my locker for almost twenty years: the jink or shimmy that I became known for throughout my Tyrone career. In basketball, I played on the right side as a forward and, to create or get into space, I learned to dummy to the left, take a step inside, and then press back onto my right side. Poor Adrian was on the receiving end of that dummy a thousand times in the street at home. It was as regular as the Angelus before the six o'clock news – me feigning to the left, taking a bounce as if to keep going on the left and then twisting back onto my right. Adrian fell for it every time. He wasn't the only one, mind you. I used it to fair effect against opponents for twenty years.

Even as recently as last winter, when the Moy went on our great run, which started by landing our first county intermediate title since 1982, it worked. That county final was my first adult title with them in nineteen years of heavy toil and in that match against Derrylaughan I tried the dummy once more – and the fella I was marking fell for it again. He jumped to my right to block my run and as I tore off to my right all I could hear was his teammates chastising him, 'Jesus, not his left, not his left, he'll turn to the right!'

It was only natural that, when playing Gaelic, I should use every tool and skill that basketball had given me.

All of these stories look great in black and white, but they meant little to me at the time. For no matter what I won, I always hankered for further glory. There was never any fear of getting carried away; I knew I had a bit of talent, but I still had some concern that one day I would be caught out, that there would be someone better around the corner.

I often wonder if that constant yearning for more can be traced back to our upbringing, our family background. Like, even on the day I brought the Sam Maguire home to Granda, he never actually said the words: 'Well done, you played well.' When he grabbed that cup and clearly didn't want to leave it go, when the tears formed in his eyes and he looked at me, I just knew he was the proudest man alive. Still, the words never came out. 'Well done, Seán.'

As a kid I probably needed to hear those few words from time to time, whether it was from Granda or Daddy. I don't know, maybe I still do. What I do know is that I kept looking for the next crown to be captured, the next challenge to be considered. I wanted to make my family even prouder of me.

Yet, that's all in reflection. Back then, life was simply too busy to notice anything much off the field. I was playing for the Moy under-14, under-16, and minor teams, and that was enough to be going along with. I had other stuff to contend with too. At the age of twelve, I was working as a shelf-stacker in Costcutters. The following year, I worked at the Moy Inn (now called the Ryandale Inn) every Friday and Saturday night.

When I hit fifteen I spent my summer days out on a construction site with Daddy, lifting blocks of wood and labouring. I also got a part-time job in the bar of the Four Seasons Hotel in Monaghan, where Daddy was working as a doorman. It was a ridiculously hectic lifestyle, coming home from sports, trying to fit in the school work and then going working. But it was the way it was. And I kind of liked it.

One thing Mummy drilled into me right from the start was to get my study done, always. Playing so much sport, I often didn't get to sit down to my books until 10 p.m. – but no matter the time, or what I had done earlier that day, I always knuckled down to study. Education was a huge thing for my parents and so it became for me too. Combining sport and the books has given me a work ethic that I have carried with me all my life.

Always give one hundred per cent.

Always challenge yourself.

Always fit as much into a day as you can.

But all of that is what made me. That drive and work ethic. It comes from my dad who still works forty hours week in a labour-intensive job and then works at the Four Seasons at the weekends. Daddy doesn't need to go out and do all that work any more but he still does. I think he got that work ethic from Granda and it has been passed down. Daddy's brothers and sisters have that ethos too, so it's definitely in the gene pool.

Mummy and Daddy are both grafters by nature and they would accept nothing else from me. Like Daddy, Mummy worked in tough jobs as a cook and she has always said that they didn't get the opportunity to educate themselves properly, but we would.

Often at night I hit the hay half-wrecked but still went to sleep thinking, *This is brilliant. I have achieved so much today.*

In 1999, I played with Moy in an under-16 final against Ardboe, which would have been seen as a much stronger team. As the teams walked off at half-time I crossed paths with a lad, Jarlath McGurk, with whom I had a few run-ins around the time I was in St Patrick's Academy.

I was six foot one and Jarlath was about five foot six so I brushed him aside with a shoulder, and without thinking about it, headed back towards the huddle. Next thing I knew I was on the ground. Someone from Ardboe had jumped the fence, hit me from behind and pulled me down. Craziness ensued, with Moy and Ardboe supporters on the pitch fighting, and tensions spilled off the field as well.

To make matters worse we ended up losing by a last-minute Tommy McGuigan penalty.

Not long after we lost to Ardboe I was called in for Tyrone minor trials. I was still only fifteen but I played in the trial and scored 2-5. I never got a second trial! Instead I was dropped after the first and told to come back next year. One of the Tyrone mentors, Martin Coyle, was the Ardboe manager so I wondered if I had paid for what had happened a year before. Anyway, I was told I was no longer needed.

I looked on and watched the Tyrone minors of 1999, with guys like Fergal Donnelly and Kevin McCaughey in the team. I was delighted for the squad, but I had marked those lads in that grade two minor final against Trillick. I scored 1-4 in that final, mostly off the two boys. Yet they had made the county team and I didn't even get a second trial. That was sickening.

But it was more diesel to fuel the ambition for 2000. I knew I was good enough to play for Tyrone.

At sixteen I took my GCSEs, which determined whether I would go on to do A-Levels. A lot of kids leave school after their GCSEs and go off to trades, but I wanted to do well in my GCSEs at St Patrick's. The results allowed me to go to St Patrick's Grammar in Armagh, another school that requires pretty high grades.

There was another reason for changing schools. Fr Gerard McAleer suspended me from St Pat's, Dungannon, in spring 1999, for a high jinks schoolyard incident, moving gym equipment around. I was the one picked out of a huge group because, with my height, I was seen running about in the wrong place at the wrong time. They suspended me for a week, but I was disgusted to be the one lad singled out, as I genuinely hadn't been involved in the messing. I went home angry and upset and Mummy enquired what was wrong. I told her what had happened and how I felt about it. She knew I was genuine and said I would be in a new school by the following week if I so wanted. I didn't feel like I could go back to Dungannon after how I had been dealt with, so I agreed that I would move, and within a day I had been enrolled in St Pat's Armagh.

I later ended up playing for Fr Gerard for Tyrone in 2003 when he was in the backroom with Mickey Harte, but we have never since mentioned the war!

Going into 2000, I felt I had something to prove. And, that year, opportunities started to come my way.

Sure enough, myself and my friend Ryan O'Neill got called for Tyrone minor trials again that year. I was now studying for my A-Levels and also working nights at the Four Seasons in Monaghan. The place wouldn't be cleared and cleaned until 4 a.m., which meant that Daddy and I wouldn't get back home to the Moy until around 5 a.m., where I'd grab a sandwich before crashing on my bed.

Every Sunday, Ryan's dad, Fintan, would call for me at 9 a.m. to drive us to exotic places like Strabane for the trials. The doorbell would wake me and I'd jump up, dress, and head out. Fintan would laugh when I would instantly lie down in the back seat of his Audi A6 and nod off to sleep again. The only food I'd have inside of me would be that early morning sandwich.

But before I could prove myself with the Tyrone minors, winning the 2000 MacRory Cup was my first opportunity to show them all.

For the two years I had at St Pat's Armagh I played with Ronan Clarke. I played at number 11 with Ronan at 14 and we switched during games. A few years later I watched Ronan inspire the Armagh senior footballers to an All-Ireland in 2002 and it led me to think, Hey, if Ronan can do that for Armagh, I know that I can do it for Tyrone.

Big Mattie McGleenan was over us and I really enjoyed playing for him. We had some huge games along the way to winning. I first encountered Fergal Doherty of Derry when we played St Patrick's, Maghera in the quarter-finals in Donaghmore. They were heavily fancied at the time and Doherty was very much their leader. I ended up marking him for a good proportion of the two games we had with them, which we ended up winning in extra time after a replay. I was holding my own, finding my feet.

We beat Omagh CBS in the semi-final and, with players Chris Rafferty, Finnian Moriarty and Liam O'Hare on our side, all of whom later played for Armagh with distinction, we felt we were going places. But we faced St Michael's, Enniskillen in the final and they were the team to beat at that time.

The game was televised, and I knew it was my chance to really kick on and show people that I was good enough for a bigger stage. But once more I had to kill the nerves the night before. Around nine o'clock that evening a friend called to the house to take me for a spin in his car, which he had just bought after passing his driving test. I was nervous that I wouldn't sleep so I went with him and a couple of others, despite knowing it probably wasn't a good idea. We ended up being stopped by police in a car park in Cookstown, about thirty minutes from home, and questioned about insurance. I didn't get back home until after midnight. Mummy wasn't impressed, but it was just another example of me trying to deal with my insomnia from the pressure of big games.

The following day I was up against the likes of Marty McGrath and Barry Owens. I marked Barry for a while but the first half sort of passed me by. In the second half we turned the screw. Ronan and I switched positions and I started to get on the ball a lot more.

I kicked a point at the start of the second half after looping around my marker and it got my dander up. With six minutes to go and the game deadlocked, Liam O'Hare, a very good reader of the game, got the ball at wing-forward and saw me darting in behind him from centre-forward. My man followed me, but I looped back around Liam, who flicked it over the top, suddenly leaving me one-on-one with their goalkeeper. I bore down on goal, carrying the ball with my right hand, and chose my left foot to shoot home. My left wasn't that strong, but I struck it, caught it sweetly enough and put it in the bottom corner. We got over the line.

After being ignored for the 1999 county minor squad I had finally made my mark. Tyrone would come calling the very next day.

6

COUNTY CALL

Winning the MacRory Cup in 2000 was satisfying and, despite the big scores and hauls from underage level, that was the season it really started to hit home that I could be good at Gaelic football.

For all the levels of obsession I demonstrated with county teams for the bones of two decades, the truth is I played my first game for Tyrone in the spring of 2000 still giddy and groggy from the night before and definitely seeing double.

During that MacRory campaign Ryan O'Neill and I had received a call to attend county minor training, but as we were in the thick of the colleges competition they said they would leave us alone until after that series ended.

Forty-odd players were in the frame for the panel, but Ryan and I were told not to report for county duty until after the MacRory ended. We were told that an Ulster minor League match with Down was scheduled for the day after the final but, not surprisingly, that invitation slipped our minds until about

5 a.m. of the morning after we had beaten Enniskillen. The whole team had gone to a nightclub, the Arena, a few miles outside the Moy, where hundreds, if not thousands, of clubbers gathered every Friday, Saturday and Sunday night. It was St Patrick's Day, so they opened their doors on the night we won the Cup and we shacked up inside until we were kicked out at about 3 a.m. Next it was over to a house party in Ronan Clarke's, where we continued celebrating as if we had won the World Cup. To us, we kind of had!

After a while, as the first shafts of light broke through the Clarke household's curtains, I cranked my neck in Ryan's direction and said, 'Hey, what are we going to do about this Tyrone match later?'

'Ah, sure we'll go in to it, but they'll never ask us to play.'

Grand, I agreed, and we partied on. Around 9 a.m. we found ourselves at a bus stop in Armagh, with Daddy on his way in to meet us. He collected the two of us, dropped me off at home to get my football bag ready, and off we went to Dungannon to play Down at 11 a.m.

Neither of us had slept for one minute and we had both enjoyed ourselves a little too much. But we headed into O'Neill Park for the game, full sure we'd be onlookers only, so there was no panic. As I waddled into the dressing room I saw Benny Coulter pass by and I prayed for the lad who had to mark him. Benny was already one of the country's top prospects and I'd get the chance to study him now from the sideline.

All went to plan initially; we were named in the subs as the first fifteen was read out. In fairness to Liam Donnelly (father of current Tyrone player, Mattie) and his backroom team, they acknowledged the MacRory win and congratulated us. They had just stepped into their roles after Mickey Harte had moved up from the minors to the under-21s. We kept our heads bowed, trying not to draw attention to ourselves, weary from the celebrations the night before. We took our places on the bench without fuss, blended in, and tried not so stand out.

As rotten luck would have it the lad who was playing centre-forward for Tyrone went down injured after ten minutes and I got the call from the management. My head banged with the effort of trying to concentrate and respond to the selector. I looked at Ryan and he looked at me, the fear dancing in his eyes. Then I looked out onto the pitch and saw about three balls. I decided that, any time play came near me, I would go for the one in the middle. Three minutes in, one of those balls landed in my hand, I cut in from the end line and rammed home a goal. To this day I swear I don't know how that happened. I managed to stay out of the way until half-time and after the break I even shot a few points. My inter-county career kicked on from there!

We reached the 2000 Ulster final, losing by a goal to Derry. We had gone into that match as favourites, but they shocked us. I had an off day; I had played really well in the first few games, but I was tightly marked in that final and left a big display behind me. So did the rest of the team; we just didn't turn up.

I was puzzled as to why I didn't perform that day but found few answers when I went digging. The step-up from schools' level wasn't difficult at all and, if anything, I found inter-county easier. Maybe that's because the summer football, allowing me to carry the ball basketball-style, to shimmy and shuffle, suited me way more than the winter dredge that the schools' players have to endure. Everything that I loved doing in Gaelic football required a good surface, nice hard ground. Going in to play Derry, everything was set up for me. I was full of confidence – and yet I went absent without leave.

The Derry management had devoted the entire pre-match build-up to talking me up as the 'coming player in Ulster', the one to be tightly marked, the lad who could do no wrong. Maybe some of that seeped in. I vowed it wouldn't happen again.

At every landmark there was never a great recap or anything; it was always about what was next. It was hard at times and I had to work things out myself quite a lot but that only made me go even harder at it. I knew I had to do it on my own. I carried that through my whole life, both in sports and school.

As my school years ticked by, I finally realised the value of tying in a good education with sport. I see young GAA players now giving every second they have to their sport, but you can't ignore the education side of things either, whether that be academic work or learning on the hoof in your chosen trade.

Between school, club and county I was ignoring my school work and my results reflected that come the end of the year. There were times when I wondered if I could cope. I took economics as an A-Level in my first year at St Pat's, Armagh, but that year was centred heavily around Gaelic football and I didn't devote the time I should have to studying. At the end of a two-year cycle you either passed or failed the A-Levels and at the end of my first year I got an E in economics.

I was humiliated.

When the hurt and disappointment faded I vowed that it would never happen again.

'I'm going to beat this,' I said to myself. 'I'm going to study ridiculously hard.'

I stripped away all the sideshows and hobbies, cut basketball out of my life and soccer too. Everything went except for Gaelic football, in my final year at school, I actually put my academic future as the number one priority in my life. I began an intensive study period until June 2001, which involved me enrolling in after-school study, which ran from 4 p.m. to 6.15 p.m. each day, then heading home and out again to training, before returning to study from 10 p.m. until at least midnight. We were knocked out of the 2001 MacRory Cup at the quarter-final stage, though on paper we had arguably a better side than the previous year, with players like Brian Mallon and Mal Mackin coming on board. But St Michael's, Enniskillen beat us, and it gave me the opportunity to put the head into the books for the remainder of the school year.

By the time I finished school I was one of the top scorers in economics in Northern Ireland.

I remember the day I got those eleven-plus results as a P7 student. I knew my mum was really, really proud of me. Same when I got my A-Levels. When I opened the card, showed her the envelope and said, 'Look, Mummy, I got three As!', she hugged me.

As outgoing and warm as she is, it's probably one out of only three or four times that my mum has hugged me in my life. To this day I have never hugged my father. It's mad because we're actually very close. We are all emotional too in our own way, but it is what it is. Maybe deep down it is what drives me to go so hard all the time. I always strive to make them proud of me.

I was so proud when I got those results. I had lived by military precision in getting them, but the hard work paid off and that's a lesson I took with me for the rest of my life. The fruit of your own hard work is always the sweetest.

On the night my exam results came out I was at a Tyrone minor training session. The weather was so warm that I had made the call to get my head shaved. I was wearing a sleeveless top at training and, to be honest, I looked like a football hooligan. One of the Tyrone mentors came over to me and asked how I had fared in the exams. I told him of my decent results, but I could see he didn't believe me. I wouldn't blame him. I wasn't exactly giving off an 'educated' sort of vibe with my new image.

That summer of 2001, with the pressure of studies released for a few months, a friend of mine, Stephen Harvey, helped get me a job in a concrete factory, Acheson and Glover, just two miles from home. Stephen's uncle, Jim Devlin, worked in recruitment and he set us up there. We started work at 8 a.m. and kept going until 6 p.m. We spent our days lifting blocks and I was shattered every evening I came home, collapsing on the couch before I went off training. Again, though, I look back and see that it helped me build my physique.

I just didn't go in for gym work. I maintained that it made you slow on the football field. But lifting heavy concrete blocks for four months helped me with my stamina and strength, so I was getting a better aerobic workout at work than in the gym. The intense study had helped me develop a mental toughness too. The cogs were turning together. My Gaelic football career benefited from the fusion of the two disciplines.

I carried a shot of bitterness with me too. Deep down I was still sore that I hadn't made the 1999 Tyrone minor panel. Daddy had taken that pretty badly too. We had an inkling that I was going to be a good player but that guarantees little because you don't realise how near or far off the top guys you are until you reach county level and see where you stand. Moy had always played grade two and three football and sometimes even lower, so we didn't often have the chance to play against top players. My only gauge was the two boys I had marked in that minor club final against Trillick, Kevin McCaughey and Fergal Donnelly, when they had rotated on me and I still managed to do a bit of damage.

Now, with a year's inter-county football behind me, I was mad keen to make my name. When both Ryan and I made the cut with the 2000 minor team it was a huge deal for the club. We were following the trail that Philly Jordan and Ryan Mellon had taken with the Tyrone minors of 1997 and 1998 under Mickey Harte, winning an All-Ireland in the latter season. We wanted to win things too.

Liam Donnelly and Martin Coyle had taken on the mantle from Mickey as co-managers. Liam was a real player's man and is still doing great work coaching. He led Ballinascreen to a county final only recently.

Liam was also the first man who made me love Tyrone. That probably sounds strange but it's the truth. Although Daddy had taken me to games since I was a kid, and although I had originally studied at St Pat's Academy in Dungannon, the truth was I had almost as many friends in Armagh as I had in my own county. I had won medals with an Armagh school, lived only a few miles up the road, and a shedload of guys who came from the Moy originated from Armagh families and supported them at inter-county level.

I won't lie, when I first made that Tyrone minor panel there was a slight disconnect between me and the others. I looked around at lads who had played with the other schools around, like Holy Trinity Cookstown and Omagh CBS, fellas from the west of the county. I didn't think I had much connection with them at all. There wasn't a huge split between east and west or anything, but I felt there was a bit of a gap all the same.

Even trying to catch the accents of the other players from Strabane, Aghyaran and these places was fairly hard for me. The whole process helped me prepare for the parochial brogues I would later come across, like Brian Dooher's. Brian may as well have been speaking Mandarin the first few times I met him. I didn't understand one word he was saying. While these lads were only an hour and a half up the road from me, it seemed as if they existed in a different realm altogether. Before mobile phones and social media, we didn't have that many chances to gel or interact.

I was a little shy as an individual and that's where Liam came in, helping me to mix with people from the west, lads who lived on the Fermanagh and Donegal borders, helping me to broaden my horizons. Liam was really good at integrating us; he looked out for us off the field and you could have the craic with him as he wasn't a bit stand-offish. He would be constantly phoning the house to see how I was doing, and he and Daddy would have right chats about how the season was going. He loved us for doing all we possibly could to help Tyrone. But he was doing more than anyone.

In fact, all the Donnellys – Liam, Mattie and Richie – just love Tyrone. Most of their family had played for the county over the years; they had a huge connection with Tyrone and Liam brought me into that space, showed me it was a big deal to wear the county colours. Although we lost that 2000 Ulster minor final to Derry, which was massively disappointing at the time, there was a sense that big things were coming down the tracks too. We only had to wait a year to reap the dividends of what Liam and Martin had sowed.

Along the way I reconnected with Peter Donnelly, no relation of Liam's, but my best friend from Coalisland, as I tried to make my mark with Tyrone. Peter remains a lifelong friend but back then I had scarcely seen him since we'd moved down to the Moy. He was studying at Coalisland Intermediate School during my time at St Pat's, Dungannon, so we didn't even play against each other. The few times we saw each other was when Paddy, his father, brought horses to the Moy on St Stephen's Day to take part in the annual hunt. But I would say that I hadn't talked to Peter for five years before we linked up with the Tyrone minors.

Now we shared a dressing room and when I looked over at him I didn't see a childhood friend; I saw a chief rival for the jersey I wanted, and it felt really strange. Peter was the main man in the set-up. He was midfield for both the Tyrone minors and under-21s in 2001, which was an amazing achievement. He was captain of our minor team and he was everything I wanted to be. I love Peter to bits, so much so that he was groomsman at my wedding; but back then I was envious of him and saw it as a challenge to reach the level he was at. In training, I was always rocked up at midfield or centre-forward while Peter operated at midfield or centre-back. We faced each other almost every evening and I probably gave it to him hard in training whilst trying to figure out how I could get to his standard. I was in his face, but Peter yielded nothing. Both of us were pushing to get to the top. That insatiable desire on both our parts would ultimately help the team – even if we had to wait twelve months to get to where we wanted.

We faced Armagh in the first round of the 2001 Ulster minor Championship and that was a tricky enough one for me, with a lot of my friends there – the likes of Mal Mackin and others from St Pat's. Mal absolutely dominated the first twenty minutes until Liam pulled me out the field and told me to quieten him. We eventually got over the first hurdle by a few points.

We played Derry in the semi-final: mostly the same Derry team that had beaten us in the 2000 Ulster final. Liam Donnelly put his finger on it. Before we played that semi-final, he looked directly at me when he spoke in the dressing room.

'Seán, these guys have the same management team as last year and remember that they are the fellas who talked you out of an Ulster medal last year. Don't let that happen again today.'

I think Liam was right. Near the end of that game, we were ahead by a point or two. I ran through the middle of the field and shot from twenty metres out. It nearly ripped the back of the net and the goal helped us win the game.

Earlier that week, my friend Niall Kelly had helped me continue my hairstyle experimentation. Niall is a plumber, not a barber, and I had a dodgy line separating my shaven scalp and a kind of a crew cut. I'm usually conservative enough when it comes to celebrating scores but this time let loose on the emotion after ripping that ball in. I remember standing in front of the 'hill' end in Clones, with my dodgy hairdo, thinking that I was in this game to score sensational goals. To do the business when it was most needed. In reality, I probably looked like Phil Mitchell from *EastEnders* having a meltdown. It was a big game for me, though, and I really wanted to kick on.

It turns out that game wasn't the biggest deal of the day because later that evening I met Fionnuala for the first time. Ryan O'Neill was going out with her sister, Roisin. We got on like a house on fire and chatted away, so maybe the oul' blade-one haircut wasn't too scary after all.

In the Ulster final we beat Monaghan 2-13 to 0-13, even though Paul Finlay was up to all his usual tricks, scoring sidelines, 50s, 60s – doing whatever he wanted, basically. Near the end of the game Gary McBride, a Scotstown man, made a big dart upfield and went for goal. I was tiring but tracked him as best I could and got my foot to the ball right on the goal-line to divert it away, David de Gea style. That demonstrated once more the value of hard work, how vital it is to help out at both ends of the pitch. It showed that maybe my time with Dungannon Swifts had helped me too.

We beat Mayo in the All-Ireland semi-final in one of our best games of the year and later that night we celebrated, let off a bit of steam, before we faced up to the prospect of playing Dublin in the final. After our night out we headed back to Peter Donnelly's house in Coalisland to keep the party going. Someone threw on a video of the match and as we listened to the post-match analysis we got our first introduction to Joe Brolly.

He was in full rant and his words were cutting. Basically, he suggested that, while Tyrone were in the All-Ireland final and might even win the Championship, he reckoned this was a poor team and no players from that particular Tyrone set-up would make it.

Jesus, that brought us back down to earth pretty quickly.

I was insulted, I won't tell you a lie. I knew that day that I had been one of the best players on the pitch and I felt I would go on to bigger and better with the county. I knew others were happy with how they performed and wanted more from their careers as well. Our parents and friends were proud and happy too.

But God, as young lads, when we heard Joe's words we were downbeat. We were coming down off a huge high and reduced to a low by a man we had never met. His critique made us question ourselves. Maybe he was right; maybe we would never make it. It wouldn't be the last sweeping statement of his that I'd be a victim of. Our parents were upset that we had been exposed to such a blunt analysis so young. We were only kids. Do kids need to hear such things at a delicate age like that? Not in my book.

But these things galvanise you too, and his words helped create a defiance. That's something we still have to this day in Tyrone, and we take it to a ridiculous level at times. But back then, while our families were a wee bit miffed, we became more resilient.

I couldn't sleep a wink the night before the final. We stayed in the Spa Hotel in Lucan and I paced up and down the room that night, looking out onto the M4 motorway. I was sharing with Peter Donnelly and next door were the goalkeepers, Chris Greene and John Devine.

At the first sign of sunrise I looked out the window, disappointed that, once again, I hadn't slept and worried that I wouldn't produce it on the pitch a few hours later, yet full of enthusiasm for what lay ahead. My family and friends were on their way to Dublin and we were going to Croke Park on All-Ireland final day, for God's sake. Peter was fast asleep, but I heard a commotion from next door, so I popped in to John and Chris for the chat. John was white as a ghost.

'Jesus, are you alright, lad?' I asked.

'That mad bastard,' he replied, still shaking, pointing over to Chris. Turns out that Chris couldn't sleep either – and he wasn't even starting. Instead he had hopped out of bed during the night and crawled in under John's bed. There he waited patiently, like a sniper settling in for the long run.

At about 7 a.m. John rose and went to pull the curtains. As he walked to the windows Chris leaped on him from behind like a WWE wrestler, giving a huge roar as he flattened him and frightening the absolute living shit out of his goalkeeping brother-in-arms. Poor John thought he was being attacked and was still not right when I went in.

Aside from lack of sleep I had other distractions. On the week of the game I had started college studying accountancy at the University of Ulster, Jordanstown (UUJ) and had been out and about having a gander in freshers' week, doing a wee bit of socialising. I had a little fall on the dance floor and hurt my back. I carried that injury into the final and got a painkilling injection an hour or so beforehand into the middle of my lower back, which allowed me to get through the game.

I was only average. We were all only average. We thought we had it won but at the end Dotsy O'Callaghan, better known subsequently as a hurler, broke through and got a last-minute goal to salvage a draw for the Dubs.

The replay was held at Breffni Park. Dublin brought a huge crowd with them and, as we were chasing an under-21 champ-ionship as well, our county was on a high too and we had a massive following. The place was rocking. This time we did ourselves justice and we put them to the sword; a fine Dublin team that contained Dotsy, Paul Griffin, Bryan Cullen and Declan O'Mahony.

We walked off the field as All-Ireland minor champions and the following Monday I was back in college. I won't lie, I walked a little taller. We all did. We were champions, had just started college, and we had the pick of the girls. Life was beautiful.

7

FREE AND EASY

A terraced house on Canterbury Street was party central while I was in university. We lived there during my time at UUJ and it was there we got the ball rolling for many a night out. And that's where I was the night Eugene McKenna phoned to invite me onto the Tyrone senior panel.

If I'm being honest I dined out on the All-Ireland minor title for a good spell longer than I should have, and lodging on Canterbury Street didn't help, as every night seemed to be a party night. My college housemates had little interest in football, and neither had I much interest in tagging along 24/7 with football buddies.

Throughout my life there have only ever been a handful of people I would classify as real friends; I don't tend to let many get close. Maybe it's shyness; maybe it's the fact I have always had different things going on in my life outside Gaelic.

Back in school, I never had time for the nonsense of wee cliques and factions. I was focused on schoolwork, basketball and Gaelic, and that left little time or energy for trying to look cool.

Across my years with Tyrone there were shades of the 'cool club' as well – getting onto the team bus you would see guys who nearly had to be seen sitting beside someone for fear of being left on their own. I like to think I was dead-on with everyone I met, but I never chased popularity; I didn't mind being different.

Still, it was unusual, I guess, that the pals I made when arriving into university as an All-Ireland minor winner were not immersed in Gaelic football. Like myself, the lads I lived with on Canterbury Street enjoyed the few drinks and were keen on the girls, but unlike myself they had little or no interest in football. Ultimately, we were all there to get a degree, and I wanted to qualify as an accountant, and that awareness helped me in the long run to achieve some sort of balance.

There were evenings I would meet other Tyrone footballers around the city and we might have the few pints and the craic. But I didn't need to be around drink all the time either.

I was friendly with Michaela Harte and her friend Edel McCarron and used to hang around with them a wee bit. One major advantage of that was that the girls loved to bake delicious cakes and scones and that was another good reason to pop around for the chat.

Despite best intentions, it's fair to say that in those early months at UUJ the academic imperative was frequently obscured. The party spirit took hold as the pints flowed and the late-night takeaways mounted – and from September to Christmas I put on a crazy amount of weight. Each evening as the sun went down and the street lights came on, it was as if a Bat-Signal appeared above the Belfast skyline inviting me out to party. All too often I answered the call.

I was heading out one evening when, fifty metres away, I spotted Fergus McAnallen – brother of Cormac and Donal – who was also in college in Belfast. Whenever Fergus and myself hooked up we had great fun and banter, and so on a crazy impulse I decided he might enjoy being rugby-tackled on the public pavement, just for old times' sake. I took off at a run, built up a nice head of steam, came in from the blind side and clattered into him.

Major problem. Fergus was nineteen-odd stone and built like a brick shithouse, and there was only going to be one loser. He barely moved as I bounced off him, and as I hit the concrete I knew straight away the right knee was gone the same knee that had never been quite perfect since the under-14s.

Fair play to Fergus, he saw the funny side. He helped me up and dusted me down, and after we exchanged our bits of news and went our separate ways I decided I might as well continue my night out and leave worrying about the knee until the next day. I knew I was in bother but off I went into the night to ease the pain. The next morning the knee was three times its normal size and when I went to the doctor he told me I would be out for three months minimum. I had to relay the news to Damian Barton, the former Derry All-Ireland winner who had been put in charge of UUJ's Sigerson Cup team, that I wouldn't be fit to play Freshers football or the early stages of the Sigerson Cup.

The good news about that prognosis was that I would have more time to socialise, or so I thought, but at about eleven o'clock one night when we were draining the few cans in Canterbury Street, before we went out on the town, the old Nokia 3310 started hopping off the table.

'Seán, it's Eugene McKenna. We'd like you to be involved with the Tyrone seniors for 2002. We're meeting up next week and we want you there.'

Eugene and Art McRory were co-managers of that team, and as Eugene spoke I realised I was caught between a rock and a hard place. The news, coming completely out of the blue, was the stuff of dreams – I will never forget the buzz in that moment – but I knew that if in my excitement I started thanking him and talked at any length he would know I was half-cut, and that wasn't the impression I wanted to make. But if I said little or nothing he would conclude I was an ignorant and ungrateful sod.

Luckily, I was genuinely taken aback and dumbstruck, and I think that's what came across because he told me to take time to digest the news. Myself and John Devine were the only ones being called up from that minor team. I just thanked Eugene, briefly mentioned the knee injury – not how I caused it, mind – and then, from that front room in Canterbury Street, I phoned home.

In those days Mummy and Daddy wouldn't have been expecting frequent phone calls from their student son enjoying his newfound freedom in the big city, and especially not at that late hour. So Mummy's first words were full of anxiety: 'Seán! Is everything alright?'

Well, the reaction and pride when I told them! It was a massive deal for all of us. I also called Colm and we chatted it through before I headed out for the evening, fuelled by the good news.

We had another good night on the tiles. But I look back on some of the photographs from back then, late 2001, and I was colossal, and not in the right way. I had put on two stone, gone from winning an All-Ireland minor final at six-foot-one and fourteen stone, lean as a greyhound, to being a pudgy and stodgy sixteen-stone shaper.

Once I got the call-up to the senior squad, the coaches got to working on my physique. They prescribed these great big glugs of whey protein, stuff I found desperately hard to stomach. To make the shake less disgusting I would throw a bottle of WKD into the sludgy gruel, mix it around, gulp it down and hit the town. No night out would be complete without an eventual pitstop at McDonald's, around three or four in the morning. The next day, whatever time I rose, would start with a fry or a few sausage rolls. Over two months I blew up like a sumo wrestler.

What saved me from exploding altogether was that I had my very own fat-camp supervisor, Damian Barton. From late 2001 to late 2002 Damian noted my loss of form and fitness and embarked on a crusade to arrest the slide. He would bring me to a running track outside Belfast where he had some of the UUJ team working with athletics coaches on biomechanics, making sure our movements were correct. Damian had a very sound way about him and at that stage was way ahead of the coaching posse in terms of outlook and methodology. Not that I appreciated or thanked him for all he had to offer when he had me trudging around those tracks in zero temperatures.

'Seán, whatever you're eating, halve it and double the exercise,' was his mantra.

During one 'survival' session it hit home how much my stock had plummeted within a few months. As I huffed and puffed and struggled for air and lads coasted past me, I realised that most of these were average-to-middling division three players back with their clubs, and here they were overtaking me without breaking sweat. I was gasping so loudly after that session that one considerate fella asked politely if I was suffering from asthma.

Damian saw that too, so he upped the tempo and there was little let-up. One morning, shortly after Christmas, he phoned: 'Seán, come on, we're going to Dungannon!'

There were no further details, except that Mark Jordan, another clubmate, would be joining us for a run. With the belly still aching from hot turkey and plum pudding, I groaned and wondered aloud when this man would get off my back, but I answered the summons and we went into a playing field behind the intermediate school where Damian taught. And there he got myself, Mark and another chap, Aidan McCrory, doing laps and sprints. It was agony.

It got so bad I would often duck and dive when Damian came calling. He always found me, and whenever I was cursing him or giving him dirty looks he would just say in that soft way of his, 'Seán, the people of Tyrone expect great things of you. Don't let them down.'

But the pay-off was that Damian got me into some sort of shape to compete at senior inter-county level. I never really showed sufficient gratitude for all he did – I was half-thick with him much of the time – but the man went way above and beyond the call of duty for me and I cannot thank him enough.

A year or so later, when I had started to carve a niche with the Tyrone team, Damian wrote a column in *The Irish News* asserting that I had phenomenal athletic ability that just needed to be unleashed. Well, I don't know how in the name of God he recognised that in me, but he was the one who, with great patience and persistence, weaned me off the cakes, the fries and the WKD-protein shakes!

Thanks to Damian, when I finally linked up with the Tyrone seniors, I was back in moderate working order. And on my first night there I met another major influence on my career, Peter Canavan.

When I think back on my first session that night I still see Canavan wearing a shiny, sky-blue top, and it seemed the sheen from the top was giving off an aura we all knew he had anyway. I was in awe of Canavan then and I still am. I looked at him and wondered what the hell I was doing on the same pitch.

Art spoke up and said we would be playing two against two, backs on forwards. A bunch of forwards broke away in pairs, but I stood out like a sore thumb because I knew no one. Philly Jordan was my only friend and comrade there, but sure he was up at the other end with the backs. As I surveyed the gaggle of unpaired players I saw Canavan weaving his way past them – heading my way!

'Come on, Seán! I'm doing two-on-two with you. We'll work together.'

To say that made my day and my week and my season would be only the half of it. This man, who had been my hero for so long, had singled me out for welcome and was about to become my friend and teammate. Mad!

I pleaded with the powers above that I wouldn't drop every ball, but Peter put me at ease. He and Art were brilliant with their coaching.

Being neither lean enough nor mobile enough at the time for midfield, I was earmarked as a forward. But my movement in that position wasn't good and to this day it still isn't. I don't like to burn energy making what can often seem unnecessary runs. But forwards like Andy Moran live and die by those runs.

I learned so much from working with Canavan on the training ground. Throughout that winter and spring Peter was calling all the shots, coaching others while also playing. As I regained fitness I studied him intensely, and the more I trained alongside Peter in the inside-forward line, the more I learned. He was constantly tutoring: 'The run needs to be here! You need to go now!'

Peter and Art would break down every move and put all the elements together again for your benefit. It may have been a bit stop/start, but I was a sponge soaking up all the information, and I cherish fond memories of training on pitches in the likes of Eglish, where McRory, Canavan and Gerard Cavlan, another intelligent player, would have the likes of Brian McGuigan and myself working on our runs and finding space.

Tyrone haven't since had that level of hands-on coaching. It was simply exceptional, and you just had the feeling that Canavan was out to get the best from you. I was only a lad, but as I look back I can say for certain it was the only time in my whole Tyrone career when I got such one-on-one, individual, expert coaching.

I had been named to start at corner-forward against Roscommon in the first round of the 2002 NFL, but that game was cancelled due to snow and it was only in round two that I got my first taste of senior action.

My debut was against Dublin at O'Neill Park, Dungannon. There was a brilliant atmosphere, with the smell of burgers drifting onto the field and the crowd stuck to the pitch. I was on a high warming up that day and was euphoric by the time I got on the pitch for the last ten minutes, to play against the likes of Ciarán Whelan. When I came into the action I was still limping from tackling Fergus McAnallen, but you can't pass up the chance to play the Dubs. I only touched the ball three times, but we won that game and that was fine.

I was so big and physical even at that stage that there was no question of some lad flattening me, so I motored along nicely and made further appearances from the bench against Offaly and came on for the last fifteen minutes of the League final against Cavan in Clones, which we won pretty easily – the first-ever win for Tyrone.

That was at the end of April and when Brian McGuigan cried off injured a few weeks later I got the nod to start the 2002 Ulster Championship against Armagh, again in Clones. I was marking Paul McCormack and had a clear height advantage on him. Armagh were obviously expecting Brian McGuigan to be in that corner, so once we spotted the mismatch in height, we worked that corner.

After a while Paul was taken off and replaced by this older-looking lad with red hair. The new lad didn't say a word, but he did hit me a dunt into the back and then proceeded to stand in front of me, which I thought was brilliant.

This oul' boy is trying to work me from the front but sure I'm way taller, I'll take him easily, I told myself.

But this lad wasn't really all that old, and he wasn't marking me from the front either – he was just stepping out, then back, and digging his studs into my feet. Fair enough, I thought, it was his way of trying to shackle me.

I found out later who he was – Francie Bellew. Had I known then what I know now I might have walked in front of him, taken off my boots and genuflected. But I did alright; he spilled the next ball that came between the two of us and I capitalised by kicking a point. That kept him honest for a bit.

In the last few minutes, with Armagh ahead, Ryan 'Ricey' McMenamin broke up the hill side of Clones and sent in a crossfield ball. I rose above Francie, caught, turned and drove the ball into the corner. My first senior championship goal! What a feeling! It remains one of the best moments of my career.

We got a draw, and I scored 1-2 on my debut. That was mostly down to Gerard Cavlan spraying lovely ball right to my chest.

Armagh got the better of us in the replay, 2-13 to 0-16, on a baking hot day when we were minus the injured Peter Canavan. Huge disappointment. We were off to the qualifiers.

The first round was away to Wexford in early June, a fortnight after the Armagh replay. Now, if Damian Barton had seen me before that match he would have blinked and shook his head. We were in the hotel lobby shortly before taking the bus to Wexford Park. The lads, all with their game faces on, were having their pre-match salad sandwiches. But I, never having been able to stomach lettuce, was carbo-loading with two bags of cheese-and-onion Tayto and a nice king-size Mars bar, all washed down with a can of Club Orange. I glanced at Cormac McAnallen and his eyes were popping.

As we walked out of the hotel, Big Art came after me and said, half in jest but also half in earnest, 'Seán, just so you know, that's not the way a county footballer should eat.'

With the crisps still digesting we scraped past Wexford by two points. Canavan, back from injury, hit four points from play, and Kevin 'Hub' Hughes got the crucial goal that sent us through.

As we navigated our way through the 2002 qualifiers and I pondered Art's gentle rebuke, I realised I had been doing neither myself nor the county any favours with what I was eating. I still wasn't fit enough for this game. Art saw potential in me but knew my diet needed a massive overhaul. No point in training up a storm while eating mostly junk.

It was well known that both Art and Eugene had been sorely stung by how Tyrone had lost the 1996 All-Ireland semi-final to Meath – by all accounts we were bullied that day – and they vowed in the aftermath we would never again blink in a physical battle. Now it seemed I was going to be a designated case study for them.

Art, especially, was huge into weights, and one-legged squats were among his preferred exercises. I thought he was nuts. How could a one-legged squat help with anything? I expressed my doubts to more than one teammate: 'The man is bananas.'

By now, however, Art had assembled quite a following in his pursuit of perfection and I was increasingly the one out of step. McAnallen, Collie Holmes, Philly Jordan and I had started travelling to Tyrone training together and McAnallen was always at me about my diet. He was disgusted especially at my colossal sugar intake. Along the way we knocked a fair bit of craic out of it, but he was serious too.

I remember him nearly losing it with me around that time. We were staying in the Citywest Hotel. Cormac was there with his organic brown bread and I was there beside him with my usual staples: the Mars bar and the can of orange.

'What in the name of God are you eating?' he asked.

'Hey, Cormac, you know I don't eat salad,' I replied, a little tetchy. 'So when all of youse are tucking in, I'm starving and there's feck-all else to eat.'

With that Cormac got up and went over to Jim Curran, our liaison officer. 'Jim, for the love of God would you see if you can get this lad a few plain sandwiches somewhere? Without lettuce!'

McAnallen operated to higher standards than anyone else. In training if you turned a corner before the bollard he would call you out; he did it to me a few times. If you didn't see a sprint out to the end he would spot it and pull you up on it. He was so intense.

And then behind it all he was just great craic, the first man on the dance floor, a great man to share a few beers with. But when it came to sport, or whatever he put his mind to, he was on a mission and it was full steam ahead.

In training, from the moment the warm-up started to the second we cooled down, Cormac was switched on. He just did everything to the max in his life, and if we didn't follow suit he called us out. Lads accepted it from him because they respected him. If it was another fella, you might have told him to shove it. But with Cormac we knew he was genuine in what he was looking for and would lead by example.

I had come across him years earlier when himself and Donal would arrive at the youth club in the Moy every Friday evening and often ended up playing basketball, two-on-two, against me and Adrian. You could see then he was a born competitor.

Back when I was on the county minors in 2001 we took on a Tyrone under-21 team that included McAnallen, and because I felt I should have been with him on that team I was pumped up for it and went eyeballs-out at him. Cormac matched everything I did that day in Omagh and bettered it too. He never gave me an inch. I wouldn't be the only lad he snuffed out of a game.

Anyway, while trying to improve my eating habits I lost my place on the team, dropped for the qualifier against Leitrim at the end of June. I took the news badly, went home, raced up to

108

the bedroom I shared with Colm, lay on the bottom bunk and wept.

It was the last time I was dropped for a championship game and turned out to be the only time I was ever dropped in my entire club, county, provincial or international career. I took it personally.

8

THE ROOKIE

We needed two chances to get past Leitrim in the 2002 qualifiers. In the first game they led by a goal and a point to zip when the referee abandoned the game in Carrick-on-Shannon after monsoon rain had made the surface unplayable. I was half-hoping Leitrim would give us a good rattle in that game so that I might be sent to the rescue – that's the stuff that goes through your head when you're dropped. I got only a wee bit of action for the rescheduled fixture, which we won easily.

I knuckled down, trained hard, and was sent on with twenty minutes left in our third-round qualifier against Derry. Soon after running on I cut in from the end line and came up against Anthony Tohill – my other hero, up there alongside Canavan. I nearly stopped to shake hands with him, such was his aura, especially in Ulster; few footballers in the 1990s were as respected and revered.

Anthony had a show on UTV, *Tohill's Tips*, and I never missed it; as a young midfielder I was his most dedicated viewer. He had something masterful about him. I loved the way he would grab the ball in midfield, slalom sixty odd metres and either burst the net or fire over a point. A brilliant athlete, he looked almost nonchalant when on the ball – and he scored goals for fun.

Canavan was a legend and my main man, but Tohill was the player I wanted to emulate. When I saw him in action I always felt, 'Jesus, that's who I want to be!' I tried to copy him in every way.

And now here he was, coming at me like a train. I had the ball in hand and so the odds were on him flattening me. But my luck was in – he was slightly off-balance as we collided, and as I protected the ball and hit him a dunt with the shoulder, down he went. Again, I nearly stopped to help him up and apologise! But I kept going and, to huge roars from the crowd, set up a score. Another of those surreal moments in my development.

We thought we were humming again but ended up going out of the Championship with a purr. Injury ruled me out of the fourth-round meeting with Sligo, who handed us our arses on a plate. Watching from the Hogan Stand I was like an angry bear, willing the boys to win but not wanting them to shoot the lights out either because I needed my place back the next day. My chances of featuring again looked slim when the lads cruised to a six-point lead and Pascal Canavan, recalled to the squad, was showing well. At half-time we were relaxed, maybe even a bit too relaxed. We were NFL champions, and apart from one game, that replay with Armagh where we didn't get the bounce, the season had been encouraging. We were fast rediscovering our mojo.

Next thing, Sligo got a run on us. Eamonn O'Hara, with his lightning pace, started picking up ball everywhere. He was sidestepping our lads like they weren't there and sparked a come-back by shooting two super long-range points. Dessie Sloyan and company got on-message, and as they gathered momentum we went backward. We clocked only three points in the final fifty minutes and they beat us by five. I'll never forget it. We thought we had the bloody thing wrapped up after twenty minutes! Instead it was another tame exit. Everyone was in shock.

Life just got busier with every passing day and it became a daily battle to keep everyone happy. In the thick of my first season with the Tyrone seniors I got a call-up from Mickey Harte, who had just led the county under-21s to back-to-back titles. I respected him for what he had done, even if I was a little peeved he hadn't included me in that 2001 campaign. Having been part of the winning minors, I felt I could have played a role on both teams that season, like Peter Donnelly had.

Mickey, and maybe others to be fair, must have felt that I wasn't ready for the step up. Ultimately though, an All-Ireland under-21 is the only medal that has eluded me, and it would have been nice to complete the collection.

Now that I was also in the under-21 set-up I found it wasn't always easy to balance the books. The various managers I had around that time – Art, Eugene, Mickey and Damian – had, like the rest of us, different ideas and beliefs, various strengths and weaknesses. What they did have in common was that they all wanted me to train with them – every evening.

There was the morning, for instance, that I arrived from training at St Pat's Academy in Dungannon after an hour of one-legged squats with Art and the rest of the seniors. Later that day I turned up to another venue for under-21 training and informed Mickey that the hamstrings were a wee bit tight. They were too, and my legs felt like bags of sand. But Mickey couldn't understand why we'd been doing such work in the first place. Another was that Art was big into gym work and Mickey wasn't.

There was little compromise when it came to which nights I trained. Mickey didn't negotiate, simple as, so you always had to attend sessions. On the same night I might have Damian looking for me to go with Jordanstown and Art looking for me to go with the seniors. Maybe half sore about not making the under-21 panel a year earlier, I gave most of my focus to the seniors and didn't give Mickey's team the respect it deserved.

That 2002 under-21 campaign kicked off for us in April with a win over Down. We beat Monaghan a month later, where I came face to face with Vinny Corey and just about survived to tell the tale. I knew it would be a physical game and it was. I took a knee to the head, hit the ground, concussed, and started to vomit as I was taken off the field in real bad shape. I was sent to Craigavon Hospital, dazed and confused. My teammate, Joe McMahon, who was feeling unwell and had a slow heartbeat, was dispatched for further treatment too and ended up in the Erne Hospital.

That belt to the head was just one of a good few hammer blows to that area I shipped down the years, and when I sit down to count the exact number of concussions it scares the life out of me.

Four months later, we beat Cavan to win a third successive Ulster under-21 title, and that set us up for Dublin in an All-Ireland semi-final in Breffni Park.

The week before we played Dublin, at the start of September, the Moy played Errigal Ciarán in the Tyrone senior club quarter-final at Omagh. Mickey was managing Errigal and they were in right good form – they would later beat Crossmaglen Rangers and Enniskillen Gaels en route to the Ulster club title. But we pushed them all the way and that quarter-final was tied with fifteen minutes to go. With everything up for grabs I remember getting the ball, laying it off to a teammate and continuing on a support run – but that's about all I remember. Smack! Coming from the side, Peter Loughran (who would go on to join the Tyrone seniors in 2003) smashed me, and I hit the ground, seeing stars and wondering what day of the week it was.

Peter's blindsiding left me with two broken teeth, which were knocked out, a split lip and the blood flowing free, even though I was wearing a custom-made mouthguard. That was how strong the impact was. One of the stewards saw the pain I was in and rushed me to a dentist friend of his in Omagh for emergency work on the teeth. From there it was straight on to Omagh Hospital for stitches.

I'm told that after the game the Moy lads spent up to half an hour on their knees searching for my two teeth. I'd say they were well ploughed into the turf by then.

I put in a rough week, unable to chew and struggling to swallow. I had started seeing Fionnuala at that stage and on the Monday and Tuesday she came to the house and mashed up a couple of scones, so I could eat something. I would put a crumb of it on my thumb and try to swallow the morsel without using teeth or gums. It was torture.

I wasn't a happy camper, and when I arrived back to under-21 training a few nights later I gave Mickey a look of disgust, as if to say, 'This is what your club has done to me!' Of course it wasn't Mickey hit me, but still I was furious. In fairness Mickey came to me and said that what happened was out of order. I fully agreed.

The stitches were due to be left in for eight days but as we were playing Dublin that weekend I asked for them to be taken out two days early. To this day I have a lump of loose flesh where the fifteen stitches were and scar tissue at the back of my mouth.

I played the game and got a goal, but I still wasn't right, physically or mentally. I had barely eaten all week so there was little energy in the bank. I was rattled and angry, if truth be told. Ever since that rugby game when I first had teeth knocked out, I had worn a mouthguard, but for the Dublin game I had the old mouthguard which didn't fit over the new teeth. I was in too much pain to wear one anyway. I played with the niggling fear that another hit to the jaw could leave me in real trouble.

The Dubs beat us and our under-21 campaign ended in disappointment, as had my maiden voyage with the seniors.

In general, that year of 2002 proved a reality check for me. The Tyrone seniors were out; the under-21s lost an All-Ireland semi-final to Dublin; UUJ's Sigerson Cup campaign ended with a one-point extra-time defeat to UCC; and the Moy lost the Tyrone quarter-final to Errigal Ciarán. Talk about coming back down to earth!

The year also marked the end of Art McRory's three-year tenure with the seniors. I really loved Art. A good man, he gave three decades and more with both shoulders to the wheel, trying to heave Tyrone in the right direction – and we bloody well let him down in that Sligo game. There was a potential All-Ireland title in Tyrone in 2002, but we let it slip and it cost himself and Eugene McKenna, his joint manager, their jobs.

In October the Tyrone board released a statement confirming the end of Art and Eugene's involvement. The statement gave the impression they had stepped aside but it wasn't as clear-cut as that and Big Art and Eugene were hurt, claiming they had been kept in the dark, but that was the end for them.

As a young lad I just kind of moved on with things but the treatment of Art and Eugene hurt senior players like Canavan and there was a sour aftertaste in the county for a long time afterwards.

We had to look on as Armagh went on to win the All-Ireland that year. I say this with tongue in cheek, sort of, but it wasn't the easiest thing to celebrate as they went all the way. I travelled to Dublin for their All-Ireland final with Kerry, but I ended up giving my tickets to Fionnuala's brothers, Charlie and John, massive Armagh supporters.

I still travelled to Dublin with the lads, went to Coppers on Saturday night, and on Sunday watched the final from Quinns in Drumcondra with a friend and next-door neighbour, Karol McQuade, better known as 'Mooner'. I recognised plenty of Armagh people about the place, so I stayed quiet and neutral.

We had been brought up to support the other Ulster teams once Tyrone were knocked out. I remember being in the Moy Square with a Derry flag in 1993, waving as their team passed through, and I was shouting for Down when they won the following year. But because I knew the Armagh guys so well, because I had played against them and played with them and knew I was right at their level, there was bound to be a bit of envy at them winning the All-Ireland.

As the game ended and the crowd poured out of the pub

Mooner and I headed up Drumcondra Road. The streets were a sea of orange and white. I didn't know whether to keep my head down or take it all in. I turned to Mooner and said, 'Here, lad, if they can do it, we can do it too. And do you know what? We'll do it next year!'

I meant every word of it.

9

COMING OF AGE

Given the height of expectation in the county, there was only going to be one man getting the Tyrone job. Mickey Harte had masterminded two All-Ireland under-21 titles and was motoring well with his club, so he was a shoo-in.

When Mickey took over, he changed our approach and brought in a new system. He was very positive. He was big into training with the ball and those skills would be what set us apart from the rest. Attacking play was very important and kicking the ball was paramount. He constantly told us that we would be the best kickers of the ball. We had great kickers anyway and the lads didn't feel restricted in doing that. Mickey was on a crest of a wave with that same minor and under-21 team and times were good.

Everything the man touched turned to gold, so we did exactly what he said, working relentlessly as a team on his strategy of keeping the shape and keeping the ball. It was different from the stuff Art had demanded, but more often than not Mickey's ways worked for us too. Maybe also, with everything going rosy, he saw no need to be getting down to particulars at a micro level, as the boys before him had done. He was as ambitious as we were. Like ourselves he had looked across the county border as Armagh celebrated their historic 2002 win. And like the rest of us he was probably driven mad by the sight and sound of their whooping and hollering.

Tomas McNicholl, Moy's full-back, is from a football-mad family. On an afternoon deep in the winter of 2002 the Armagh midfielder John Toal arrived with the Sam Maguire to visit the McNicholls, family friends of his, who lived alongside us. Mummy and Daddy went out to meet John and admire the mythical silverware – but I refused to join them; I felt I had no right to touch the Sam Maguire Cup until we had won it ourselves.

That dream looked a long way off after we lost League games to Roscommon and Dublin. After three rounds we were propping up the NFL Division One table. I played at corner-forward in both of those losses and that's where I started against Donegal in round four. When we went into the dressing room at half-time trailing by three points, it seemed like déjà vu.

That was the first time I saw Mickey get proper angry. He roared, hammering the table, and flinging water bottles. On a more practical level he also took off a few lads and moved me out to midfield, where we were struggling.

Beating Donegal that day was the turning point of the season – and maybe also of my career. Switching me to midfield in that game effectively changed the dial on my flight path and sent me in an entirely new direction.

The game was played in Coalisland, once my home pitch, a

field a hundred metres from my early childhood home. I felt I had to make some mark there. The work with Damian Barton had kicked in by now, the weight was starting to drop off, and I was finding my range. And when they let me out of that bloody corner-forward spot, I felt liberated. I enjoyed one of my best halves in a Tyrone shirt, fielded five kickouts and scored four points from play. And at full time our season was back on track.

As I walked to the dressing room I was buttonholed by journalists asking for my thoughts on the move further back the field. In the heat of the moment and with all the arrogance of youth I shot straight from the hip: 'I don't know who ever decided I was a corner-forward in the first place. I was always a midfielder.'

When that came out, my teammate Collie Holmes and clubmate Philly Jordan were aghast. Did I really tell reporters Mickey shouldn't be picking me at corner-forward? I suppose I did. But I knew midfield was where I belonged. It was there I could exploit whatever athleticism I had. Maybe rather than single out Mickey for shoving me in the corner I could have reflected on how heavy and unfit I had been – that I just hadn't been fit enough for midfield in previous seasons. But when you're young it's easier to deflect blame.

I walked out of Coalisland GAA and as I headed down Annagher Hill to get a lift back to the Moy, my phone beeped with a text from Michaela Harte:

Can't believe how well you played today! Amazing! Daddy owes you one.

That text left a big impression on me. Getting a message like that from Michaela, who knew the pressure her dad was under at that point, meant a lot. Scoring four points from my favoured position at midfield, just the kick of a ball from where I grew up – well, everything seemed to click that day.

From then on, I played every game at midfield.

In early March we played Armagh in the fifth round of the National League in Omagh. Mickey named me at midfield for that game, without asking me if I was fit or discussing it further. That was the way things were. Fionnuala would buy the *Irish News* on the way to university on a Friday morning and text me if I was playing or not. Medical students obviously had an earlier start than us budding accountants!

It was typical spring weather; the pitch was heavy, but the days were stretching out and there was a real sense of promise in the air. As we prepared to leave the dressing room, the All-Ireland champions ran onto our field to a huge roar. The place was packed to the girders, and the Armagh supporters were as thick on the terraces as our own. We had been due to give them a guard of honour as All-Ireland champions, but they were out on the pitch before us, obviously meaning business.

Before running out we gathered in a huddle and, as we did, all I could think of was how heavy my legs were. That same week, I had played two Sigerson Cup matches for Jordanstown within two days – against St Mary's in Ballincollig on Thursday in the quarter-finals, and then down to Cork to play UCC in the semi-final, a game we lost in extra time. The rest of the Jordanstown lads then went on the lash in Cork, but Mummy and Daddy, who had travelled to watch my Sigerson games, drove me home from Cork. We arrived in around 3 a.m. on Saturday, and there I was in a Tyrone huddle a day later, worn out and dead-legged, but knowing I had to raise a gallop for what was to come against Armagh. That's player burnout any way you dress it up, but when you're young all you want to do is play every game. Miss nothing.

I looked around the circle and the boys were revving each other up, bouncing off the floor, bouncing off each other, roaring their battle slogans.

'Not in our fucking backyard, lads! They're the champions but we're every bit a match for them! This is where we make our mark! Today we make our mark!'

I looked at Horse Devlin, there with the iconic number 6 shirt on him, the backbone of our side, and he was weeping openly: 'I love you boys! I love you!'

I'll never forget Horse in that moment – that unbridled passion, that pure, raw energy as we prepared for a defining contest. Those are the most vivid and lasting memories, the ones that play out long after most of the mood music has died away.

We went out and it didn't take long for me to get the feeling back in the legs. We beat Armagh by two points, and three months into the 2003 season we knew we were on the scent of their crown.

I played alongside Cormac in most of our League games and it was an ongoing education for both of us, especially down in Killarney for round six, when the two of us spent the day trying to cope with the force of nature that was Kerry's Darragh Ó Sé. Cormac sacrificed his own game to try and nullify Darragh. He did everything he could to block him and stop him, but Darragh cleanly fielded fifteen kickouts that day and ran riot on us as Kerry held sway. Still we won the game and I managed to score a few from running into the wide open spaces. It turned out to be the only win I had in Killarney during my career.

With my Da, my brother Adrian and the Tyrone Intermediate Championship trophy – the Paddy Cullen Cup.

Accepting the Ulster Colleges 'Corn Na nÓg' Cup as captain of St Patrick's Academy, Dungannon.

My Da rented and converted a piece of ground adjacent to our back garden, where he built a set of wooden soccer posts. When I wasn't out the front playing basketball, I'd be here playing soccer and Gaelic with Colm!

The Moy club built a relationship with Carrigaline in Cork, and so I went with the 1993 group to Cork.

Above: I was a big under-14!

With my mum before the Ulster final against Down in 2003. I wasn't delighted with all the fuss as you can see!

Here I'm receiving under-16 Player of the Year from Oisin McConville. A few years later we would be on opposite sides of a huge Tyrone v Armagh rivalry.

The Gary O'Callaghan shield was the opportunity to play with Plunkett Donaghy – a Moy and Tyrone GAA stalwart.

Cormac doing what he did best – leading. Leading us through a guard of honour from Longford on 15 February 2004. A couple of weeks later we formed another guard of honour for the passing of our leader.

Me and my friend Cormac in action as a midfield partnership in the 2003 League final victory.

Impossible to make sense of: the passing of our leader and friend, Cormac McAnallan.

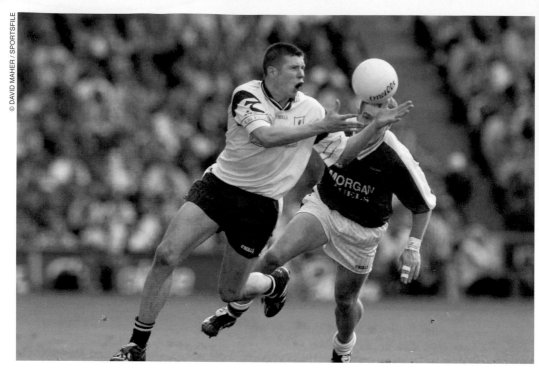

First of 89 Championship appearances. Scored 1-2 including a late equalising goal.

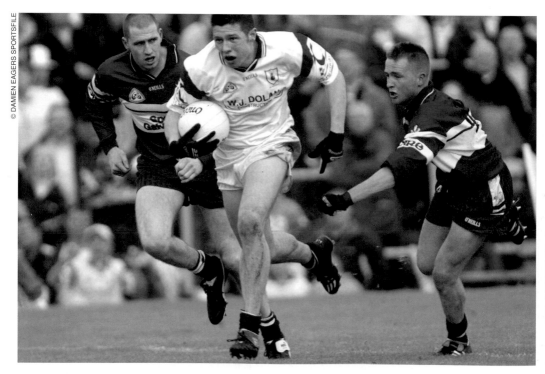

After a mediocre drawn game, I am determined to make my mark in this replay, playing against my childhood hero, Anthony Tohill.

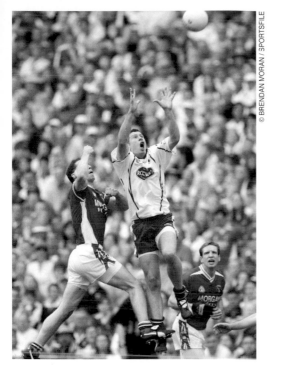

The most intense game of my career, winning a ball with Paul McGrane and Kieran McGeeney in close proximity.

Probably my toughest opponent. Ronan McGarrity was a fierce competitor.

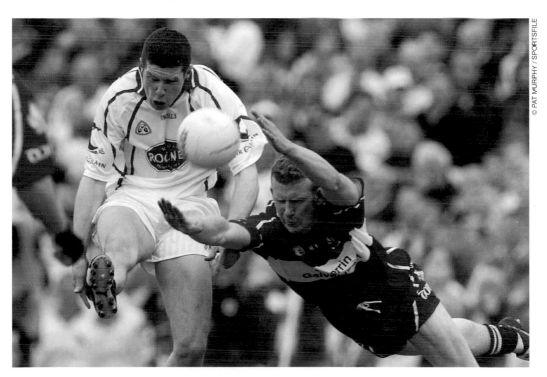

Fergal Doherty and I had plenty of battles, starting at school level.

Leading the troops out on my last appearance for Tyrone v Dublin 2017 at Croke Park.

Bursting past Tom O'Suillvan in the All-Ireland final of 2008.

Huge respect from a true great. Stephen Cluxton and I had so many battles beginning at under-21s level in 2002.

My proudest moment. Lifting 'Sam' with my brother Colm in 2008.

Overjoyed in 2016 at finally beating Donegal and getting my hands on the Anglo-Celt Cup.

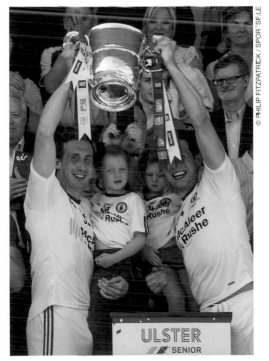

Lifting the Anglo-Celt Cup in 2017 with Colm and the girls in our arms.

We did it, Bro! Club All-Ireland victory at Croke Park with Colm.

The family, after an amazing All-Ireland semi-final victory v An Ghaeltacht at Semple Stadium, Tipperary.

Fionnuala and I enjoyed plenty of glamorous nights at the All Stars events.

A proud day for the family – the first Championship win for Moy in 35 years! Me and Colm with Da, Fionnuala, Colm's wife Levina, their daughter Chloe, plus Eva and Clara. Baby Seán completes the picture as Fionnuala was eight months pregnant that day!

I was working their other midfielder, Eoin Brosnan, and only scored those few points because Cormac was doing the heavier lifting across from me. Somehow the papers named me Man of the Match, but that was completely the wrong call; Ó Sé was the dominant figure in that game – something we wouldn't forget when we met them again later that summer.

Still, it was a fruitful partnership I formed alongside Cormac.

By the end of the League, we had won five games on the trot, trouncing Fermanagh in the semi-final and hammering Laois in the final. After an average start we just strolled through the League, but it didn't seem to count for much, since we had won the title in 2002 as well. This time our eyes were fixed on a bigger prize.

Paddy Tally, our conditioning coach, called me aside in early April: 'You're in ridiculous shape now, Seán. It's time you just went for it.'

That was another massive boost. I took him at his word and sprang like a greyhound from the traps in each game that followed. It was all youthful exuberance. I just loved the open spaces around midfield, and I loved kicking the few scores as well.

There were little landmarks along the way to indicate I was going well. Michaela's text was one. A memorable newspaper quote from the great Frank McGuigan: the way I played was 'how all midfielders should approach the game'.

My philosophy didn't involve rocket science. I could win a few balls in the air but mostly I tried to predict the trajectory of breaking ball. I would wait for the breaks and pounce. I had worked out that I could be really effective when judging the flow of the play and running into an open space fuelled by a twenty-metre burst of speed. From playing underage for the Moy, I also knew I could control the ball at high speed, and with footwork learned at basketball I could shimmy past opponents. When I combined those elements, open road often lay ahead. That's where I could do damage.

It helped that I arrived on the scene long before massed defences and sweepers were stationed in front of full-back lines, so my strategy was simple enough: just get ahead of your man and go for goal.

The Ulster Championship was both good and bad for us. We needed a replay to get past Derry in Clones. I managed three points in that rematch simply by deciding to stop fretting about marking big Anthony Tohill and just do my own thing. That's where those scores came from, and another Man of the Match award.

Imagine just playing your own game, being effective and actually enjoying what you are doing on the field. I don't know how many inter-county footballers get to do that these days; not too many, from what I can see.

Mind you, toward the end of 2003 we ourselves were held up as the Dark Lords of Gaelic Football. The ugly Northerners obsessed with defence and stifling opponents. And that too is garbage. There was no defensive system, no blanket, never any orders from Mickey to get thirteen men behind the ball. We clocked up big scores all the way through the League and Championship, managing on average almost twenty points per game in the Ulster campaign and sixteen points in the All-Ireland series when the stakes were even higher.

Those are the facts. You can draw your own conclusions.

Plenty of critics did that and lambasted us as the purveyors of all that was negative and unwatchable about the modern game. But here's how we lined up, and here's what we stood for.

Gavin Devlin always played and stayed at number 6; he was a holding man in defence and mostly held his ground. Brian Dooher just did what he always did through his career; he roamed around the field, hoovered up at the back and fed his midfielders. Brian McGuigan and Horse Devlin were best friends, from the same club, and had played together since the under-10s. We used to joke that Horse only ever gave the ball to McGuigan and we exaggerated only slightly. Horse favoured the hand-pass and whenever he got the ball he would look for McGuigan. I don't blame Horse because McGuigan was the best around. He would come deep and once he got the ball he was the best player on the park for controlling possession and spraying beautiful passes off the boot. He had radar vision, and as a free-running midfielder I just shot into space when he had the ball. Over the years he set up so many scores for me with cross-field balls.

McGuigan at centre-forward played on a string with Stephen O'Neill at full-forward. Essentially, wherever one went the other was drawn to follow. When McGuigan moved downfield, O'Neill stayed within thirty-odd metres. When McGuigan reverted to the half-back line, he drew O'Neill into midfield. There was always that link between them, so whenever Brian got the ball he just had to look around and there was Stevie riding shotgun. Most of our play went through Brian and he always had the option of laying it off to me or feeding Stevie, who was a sub for a lot of 2003, but was on the receiving end of passes from McGuigan for much of the next few years.

McGuigan just seemed to reach another level altogether

when our backs were to the wall. When we needed someone to take charge in a crisis, it was often McGuigan who came and demanded the ball from us midfielders, and you could tell by the look on his face – *I'm going to make something happen here!* – that he meant business.

Cormac held midfield for us while I was allowed to drive on. Kevin Hughes would do that holding role if Cormac was deployed elsewhere.

So there was always an anchor in that central position, with McGuigan and Dooher roaming up and down, in and around, and myself breaking forward. We worked it all out ourselves on the field – there were never any diagrams with X marking the spot on a chalkboard in the changing room. We simply reckoned that in Dooher we had the best number 10 in the land and in McGuigan the best number 11. And in our full-forward line we had Stephen O'Neill, Owen 'Mugsy' Mulligan and Peter Canavan. Blanket defence, my arse!

We played Down in mid-July in the Ulster final. On the morning of the final I was at home with all the flags outside and Mummy going around the place taking pictures of me. Even though she gave Colm and me everything as kids growing up, she generally didn't make a big fuss when it came to football. So when I saw her busy with the camera I knew the stakes were high.

That clash with Down was crazy – they grabbed three goals and early in the second half we were nine points in the red. We hit a temporary crisis after conceding those goals but with Collie Holmes and Chris, two of our specialist full-backs struggling with injury, we needed some solidity to avoid another goal rush.

It was helter-skelter but there was no panic because we had

leaders everywhere on that team. We had Conor Gormley, the best defender I have ever played alongside, settling and organising the boys around him. McAnallen was already established as our leader – along with Canavan – even at such a young age. So even as we lost those goals – they scored a fourth near the end – there was no shortage of inspiration.

Cormac stepped into the breach, switching to full-back to mark Dan Gordon, who had been wreaking havoc, and it didn't surprise anyone that Cormac revelled in that unfamiliar role. Everyone felt safer with him there. (In fact, in the four Championship games that followed his dramatic mid-season switch from centre-field to the edge of the square, we conceded just 1-25.)

At the far end Canavan and Mugsy, the teacher and pupil at Holy Trinity, Cookstown, began working closer in tandem and kept us in the hunt. They got on well off the pitch as well and there was always a bit of banter between them.

I look back now through a golden haze at that group. Born leaders all over the park. I just landed onto a team that was full of great men. And so I didn't panic when we went nine behind that day. I looked over and saw Hub shaping up for his next tackle, heard Ricey at the back telling the Down boys to enjoy the moment because it wouldn't last. I looked behind and saw Philly Jordan, calmness personified. Horse too was setting the tempo, taking ball out of defence, giving it to his best pal and organising boys in the process. Just doing the simple things.

And so we got those nine points back and were cruising to the win – only for Dan Gordon to flick another goal with seven minutes left on the clock. We fought back again to draw at the end and so we had to go to the well one more time.

Earning that draw was a real turning point for our Tyrone team. We had a flaky reputation after losing to the likes of Sligo and Derry in the previous couple of years, and emerging from the Down saga set us on our way towards changing the perception of us as being chokers.

We hammered Down a week later in the replay. Winning Ulster was a big thing in our development that year.

Just before the All-Ireland quarter-final against Fermanagh, Mickey decided we should all be able to sing 'Amhrán na bhFiann', and since few in the squad were fluent in the Irish language, Michaela wrote the words out phonetically and printed off a sheet for each of us.

In doing that, Michaela brought us closer together. Maybe she was well aware of what she was doing or maybe she did it without even knowing it. Over the years we would be called 'British bastards', 'Orangemen', 'The Queen's boys'. It wasn't a big issue until we got successful, but when we started winning things opponents would let fly. 'How's your queen?' 'Back to your crown, you English fucker!' That sort of stuff.

I think such abuse has strengthened the mentality of the Ulster footballer, those in the six counties anyway. We play on the perceived segregation and isolation card at times and maybe use it to our advantage. Growing up, I was always told to support whatever Ulster team were playing down the country, as the southerners didn't want us to win. It's very much a mindset and there is a belief, mistaken or otherwise, that referees, Croke Park officials and everyone involved would prefer that northern teams didn't win their competitions!

I remember standing in the Moy Square with a red and white

flag, after Derry won their All-Ireland in 1993, waiting to cheer on the likes of Tohill, Brolly and company. It was like seeing the Man United team bus pass through the village. We waited for hours and went mad when they arrived! All because we had to support the Ulster team. That was when I was a kid. It's mad how my mentality changed when I was playing against them in later years.

Nowadays there is a much stronger rivalry between the Ulster counties, though a certain type of clannishness still exists deep down. That was very much evident in the Railway Cup when virtually every Ulster team I played on fielded its best players as our respective managers realised it was a huge opportunity to compete against the southern provinces, who didn't seem to have much interest in the competition at all. The various Ulster managers and coaches never took the inter-provincial series lightly and always voiced their passion for the province in their team-talks.

Being called out for coming from Ulster is something that has followed me through my career. Right through to the 2018 All-Ireland intermediate club semi-final against An Ghaeltacht at Thurles, we got flak. One of their players started mouthing off about us being the Queen's followers and shite like that.

Some lads take offence and fight back. I never let it get to me on the pitch, but instead used the abuse to motivate me. I've played my entire career with that bullishness and it's only really and truly now that I know most of it is a myth, just the ramblings of some uneducated goon on a field, but the truth is that it suits us to believe that the opposition hates us.

Throughout my Tyrone career, whenever we played a 'southern' team, the perceived disrespect that 'northern' teams received from players, supporters and referees alike was mentioned. To be honest, I felt that all that started to wear thin but at the beginning I totally bought into it and believed that everyone in the south hated us. Now, maybe they did too.

Certainly, when we were put on hold and isolated during the whole foot-and-mouth outbreak in 2001 we felt we were out in the cold. After an outbreak of the disease was found in Ardboe, the GAA made the call – which was a really tough one for us – to take us out of the League and replaced us in the semi-finals with Roscommon. We felt we were sacrificed, and our under-21s were too when we were initially told we couldn't play in the Ulster final, although we were later reinstated. But there was no reprieve for the seniors, whom many felt would have had a good chance of winning the League title.

Peter Canavan's All-Ireland speech in 2003 would refer to how we felt we didn't get enough credit for our achievements and how northern teams didn't have any 'power down south'. That underdog mentality was kind of ingrained in us. Mickey had a way of making us despise most opposition teams – including the other Northern teams – but it wasn't exactly a hard sell either.

Ultimately, the lads from the south simply hadn't a clue what our parents had endured to help us preserve our heritage and keep us playing Gaelic Games. Eventually, as we clocked up titles, we laughed off the abuse. But I won't lie, it took a while.

With his emphasis on the anthem, Mickey reinforced our identity. Few people appreciated as he did the power of 'Amhrán na bhFiann'. Most of us had only a basic grasp of the language. We had three years at the start of secondary school where we could study Irish and one other language for one hour per week but it's a difficult enough language to learn and you wouldn't master much in that time. Nowadays there is much more of an emphasis on the native tongue and *gaelscoileanna* are popping up all over the place, but learning Irish wasn't a big deal when I was growing up. Sad to say, but the attitude at home from many people seemed to be: 'Why bother learning a language we may not need in the future?'

The Hartes had their work cut out to get us comfortable with the language but Michaela was determined we would get there. Rehearsing 'Amhrán na bhFiann' not only bonded us but also proved a valuable distraction, because as we focused on getting it right, not sounding silly in front of teammates, pre-game nerves were put on hold.

Just a week before we met Kerry in the semi-final, with Michaela's version learned off by heart, we stood in a room in the Citywest, clutched each other tightly and blasted out the anthem. We sang it with a ferocity calculated to drive back any opposition or army. It warmed our hearts with pride. We were as Irish as anyone! Just one week on, we would link arms again, this time in Croke Park, and sing our anthem without missing a beat.

Actually, as the big game rolled around, we sang it twice. On the bus to Croke Park, with tensions running high, just as we approached the bus entrance at the back of the Cusack Stand, a lone voice suddenly broke the silence: '*Sinne Fianna Fáil ...*' Soon the whole bus, including our backroom team, was belting it out at full volume. It was an emotional moment.

Since befriending Michaela in university I had often asked her about the language and its importance to her. There were times when I might even have joked about it. It was only later I realised its power and what it did for us. She would be very proud of that legacy, and it's fair to say she is having the last laugh.

She would have laughed even more had she heard me on the phone to my mum earlier that morning. All through the 2003 season I had worn these white Y-fronts for every Championship game but on the morning of the match, when getting up for breakfast, I noticed that I hadn't brought them with me. Mad panic ensued and, as the data roaming wasn't working on my phone, I had to beat down to reception in the Citywest to phone home. Surrounded by hordes of Tyrone supporters beside the pay phones, I asked Mummy to go find my lucky underpants and to then drive to the Citywest and meet me that morning. As I hung up, content that my lucky pants would soon be with me, I copped a couple of Tyrone supporters with plenty of drink on board beside me. They had some craic at my expense, joking about my 'Pringle' underpants and my phone call to Mummy on the morning of one of the biggest games in history. True to her word, Mummy successfully delivered the lucky pants.

Still, wearing lucky jocks or singing the anthem wouldn't get us to a final. Before the Kerry game there was no discussion, or anything like it, of shutting up shop or clogging our defence to keep their superstars at bay, but I do remember, during the week before the game, Mickey dragged Hub, Enda McGinley and myself into a summit meeting.

By now Cormac was playing at full-back. Chris Lawn made way and Cormac went back there, analysed what he had to do as a number 3 and, typically, never looked back.

But Darragh Ó Sé had hurt us so much in the League that now Hub's main job was to disrupt him any way he could. Enda was to get in his way, too, by pulling out from corner-forward and stepping in front of Darragh whenever he got the ball. We agreed it was manageable if he won a fair bit of ball when lying deep – as long as we stopped him in his tracks right there. Everyone else was told to just go out and play.

We had a real fear that day – a fear of losing heavily – and it manifested itself in raw energy that drove our efforts. It was a hot day and we were damp with sweat even before we left the dressing room. The excitement was huge. In fact I had never before felt and would never again experience a greater buzz of anticipation in any changing room. We knew that if the Kerry forwards got a run on us we were in trouble. We had to be tuned in and full on if we were to avoid being embarrassed.

As we warmed up I noticed immediately the lads were already at fever pitch. Dooher and McAnallen, doing their wind sprints, looked fit to overrun the pitch and end up among the spectators. This isn't natural, I thought. I'll need to find another level today if I'm going to survive.

It was ferocious in the warm-up and we just ramped up that manic intensity once the game started, swarming over and tackling anything in green and gold that moved. It's true that we dropped back a little that day too, fearing the potency of the Kerry forward line, but we stuck to our attacking brief and went six points up before they got on the scoreboard. We were like a well-tuned motor, humming sweetly in the high revs and the road ahead was smooth and inviting.

We blitzed them in that opening half. Ger Cavlan was plucking balls from the clouds, and even when Peter Canavan left the field injured we held our nerve and went in at half-time in good fettle.

If there was any danger of complacency it was nipped in the

bud when Canavan spoke to us just before we headed out for the second half. He stood there at the changing-room door in the bowels of the Hogan Stand, leaning on crutches, an ankle packed in ice, and looked at each of us in turn.

'I've never asked anyone to do anything for me on a football field, boys, because I've always done it myself. But now I'm asking. Go out there and get me to an All-Ireland final!'

We paused as the words sank in. I felt the neck hairs stiffen. Then someone roared, 'No more fucking words needed, lads!'

We drove back out, beat Kerry and got Canavan to that final. Mind you, for all the emotion, we didn't go headless. We protected our lead when we had to.

Maybe it was that second-half effort that inspired Pat Spillane's 'puke football' outburst on RTÉ television. It didn't sit well with our squad. Nor with our followers. I had grown up hearing about the great Spillane, Daddy telling me how he beat Tyrone virtually on his own in 1986, the huge respect he had earned. But with those two ill-chosen words, he lost much of that respect among Tyrone people.

I look back on that Championship and see the tallies we put up. We hit crazy scores in every game and steamrolled quite a few teams – only to be labelled puke footballers. We wondered could Spillane be serious, but it turned out he was. To my mind he was way off the mark. And from then on I found it nigh on impossible to take any of his comments seriously.

Not that we had much time to dwell on the pundits. We were back in an All-Ireland final for the first time in eight years. And this time we were back with a fresher-faced group. Young Turks used to winning. Confident lads who came through the minor campaigns of 1998, 2000 and 2001. The under-21s of the same vintage era. All of us looking to step up. We had no fear, we just went out and played each game.

Contrary to the negative press, despite all the flak we got for allegedly shutting up shop and shutting teams down and murdering the great game, the truth is we didn't unduly worry about what outsiders thought or said. We knew we were good and that was enough.

10

BREAKING BARRIERS

Ten days before the All-Ireland final, a scatter of us were invited to attend the *Irish News* Ulster All Star awards at the Armagh City Hotel. The event is a big deal around these parts, a prestigious, black-tie evening – supported by large corporate sponsors and with over five hundred attending – honouring the best player in each position as voted by the newspaper's journalists. I was one of the seven Tyrone players nominated, and it was a huge and welcome distraction for me ahead of the final.

I wanted to go for two reasons: it was my first individual honour of note with Tyrone; and it was my first opportunity to woo Fionnuala properly by taking her on a glitzy night out as my girlfriend. To mark the occasion, I bought a fine bunch of lilies, her favourite flowers. It was great that she knew very little about football at that time because we could chat away about anything and everything else. Her brother, Charlie, was only fourteen at that stage, and Irish dancing was the big thing in her life, so I could switch off easily when I was with her.

There was a real buzz to the All-Ireland build-up. I was in university with Armagh players, the likes of John Toal, Philip

Loughran and Aidan O'Rourke, and some of them were also down for awards. Living so close to Armagh and going to college with those lads, you would always hear stories on the grapevine – tall tales about fellas running out of weights to lift in the gym or word of Kieran McGeeney heading to New Zealand to train with the All Blacks. Everyone enjoys a good yarn, some get stretched no end, but it's all part of the hype. None of us lost much sleep over such tales.

But as the awards night loomed it was rumoured the Armagh lads would be marked absent – seemingly they didn't want to meet us up close and personal in the countdown to the final. We had no such problem, and so we showed up on the night, happy to be socialising and using the occasion as a distraction from the bigger challenge to come.

We didn't drink but we mixed and mingled freely, and, sure enough, as the formalities unfolded there was still no sign of the Armagh players. Then, as the desserts were being served, and just moments before the awards were to be handed out, they slipped in discreetly, like CIA operatives on the job, a small tight group, heads down, game faces on, no wives or girlfriends to be seen. They hopped on stage for their awards and then fled as quickly and quietly as they had arrived.

It was intended as a demonstration of their single-minded approach, and I suppose they left thinking they had made a point about their superior mental toughness and focus. To us, it all seemed a little too robotic. They looked far too uptight, and the result was we actually felt we had the edge on them. We were driven for sure, but also happy-go-lucky and well up for a laugh. I thought it was a great balance.

My biggest concern on the night was trying to impress

Fionnuala and make sure she enjoyed the glitz and glamour of the occasion. I was thinking less of football matters than of the possibility that another date might be on the cards!

But when Fionnuala wasn't by my side there really was no escaping the big game fever. Living in the Moy, the build-up to the final was a bit too intense at times. Philly Jordan's elder brother, Gary, acquired a black taxi from somewhere and had it professionally repainted in Tyrone colours – a brilliant job. I went with Gary and Philly to collect it, and as we drove through the Shambles, the main street in Armagh, which is peppered with GAA pubs and hotspots, we were showered with dog's abuse. This was only a week or so before the big day. We knocked a nice bit of craic out of it.

Deep down I dreaded the possibility of losing to Armagh. I had watched them in the semi-final against Donegal on TV and got a sinking feeling when Armagh won. I had headed straight to a driving range to let off steam. But the feckin' golf range was in Armagh too. Everywhere I stirred, there were signs and reminders of the old foe.

One thing we had to contend with was this narrative that Armagh would blow us off the field with their physical power. You had all the hearsay about their gym sessions. And then you had us in Tyrone who, at that point, were doing no collective gym work. Journalists were painting scenarios whereby Armagh would rough us up and stifle our free-running, free-range play. One GAA writer delved into a catalogue of match-day programmes for average squad weights (he should have known that very few players tell the truth in those programmes) and ran the story that the Armagh lads were several pounds heavier per man.

That analysis grew legs and pounds, and maybe Mickey was worried it would seep into our heads, so on the Saturday before the final he conducted a couple of psychological or mental exercises that worked a treat. Mickey passed around a small beanbag that fitted nicely in our hands and weighed a couple of pounds. When we had all admired it and pondered its size and weight, he spoke.

'Lads, do you think that little beanbag would stop you from winning an All-Ireland? Because that little pouch is the average weight difference between the Armagh players and yourselves. That little hill of beans is what all the talk is about.'

It was a masterstroke and his plan worked – it even got a few of the boys pumped up. I think Mickey later admitted that the little bag in question didn't exactly match the gulf in bulk between the teams, but sure who had the calculators out at that stage? It was another great example of Mickey getting us properly motivated. That skill surely was and is one of his greatest strengths.

Another clever ploy by the management initially left us scratching our heads. We were each asked to write a line on every other player in the squad. I had no idea what it was going to be used for. Most of the comments were highly complementary, but some of the lads put the boot in. Of course, it was all good-humoured slagging.

Good-luck cards dropped through the letterbox every day. I visited local primary schools to say thanks to the schoolkids for taking the time to write and draw posters. There were sideshows and distractions aplenty and, while I enjoyed it all, I was relieved when the big weekend dawned.

Usually on the Saturday before a big match, our team bus would stop off at the Glencarn Hotel in Castleblayney, after running the gauntlet of enemy territory in Armagh. Castleblayney is only a thirty-minute drive from the Moy, so instead of picking up the bus in Ballygawley, Ryan Mellon, Philly Jordan, Collie Holmes (who lived in Armagh at the time) and myself would get a relative to drop us to the Glencarn. That was part of our routine for the All-Ireland quarter- and semi-finals, so not wanting to tempt fate by breaking with a winning formula, we did the same thing for the final. Superstition and sport go hand in hand. What we didn't know was that, back at Ballygawley Roundabout, a whole gaggle of supporters had assembled to cheer us and the team on its way.

Missing that send-off took the four of us out of the spotlight a little, which probably wasn't a bad thing – and the coach trip down to Dublin felt almost normal. We had spent a fair bit of time in Dublin that year at training weekends and the like. The Celtic Tiger was in full roar and money seemed no obstacle. The team budget wasn't much talked about. How that would change as the years ticked on!

Most of those weekends away, we stayed at the Citywest complex, either in the main hotel or the golf hotel. It was often bedlam – almost impossible to take a walk around the grounds without meeting people eager to chat football. But for the final we were taken away from all of that and put up in Killiney Castle. It was an amazing spot.

We arrived there late on Saturday afternoon and, after getting our bags to our rooms, looked for a pitch where we could loosen up with a light kickaround. That routine had been straightforward when we stayed at Citywest, but since Killiney is not noted for its GAA fields, we ended up heading to a county council park near the hotel. That was quite surreal. There we were on a lovely evening in early autumn, just hours away from contesting the biggest sporting event on the calendar, jostling for training space on the hard, bumpy ground of a public park with youngsters playing hopscotch, rounders, frisbee and soccer. Not to mention other activities. Running to fetch a stray pass I sidestepped a bunch of teenagers headed for their favourite hangout, carrying the obligatory bottles and cans of cider. They glanced at me unawares, and all I could think, as I prepared for the biggest challenge of my sporting life, was how carefree they looked.

Of course it never occurred to us that Armagh might have their spies in the undergrowth. Managers nowadays would have a fit in case there was a spy in the trees. Everything now is about injury prevention and keeping cards close to the chest. Not showing who is or isn't fit, and definitely not revealing a glimpse of potential tactics. In the modern game, paranoia rules. But back then Mickey let us ramble in that park and we soaked it all up. There was a freedom about us, even a childhood innocence, as we eased through our paces one last time.

That evening kind of typified our team spirit – very little fazed us. We were a young, confident and determined band of brothers and we backed ourselves every time we came together.

Back at Killiney Castle, things got even better. This was a much more luxurious place than any others we had experienced. I stretched out on my king-size bed and slept like a baby after guzzling a full bottle of milk – something rare for me on the eve of a massive game. I phoned Fionnuala on Sunday morning and, rather than fretting and fussing over the game itself, I was describing the fabulous bed and all the other home comforts.

But to top it all, each player found a fancy yellow envelope on his bed. All the one liners we had written about each other the week before – good, bad and outrageous – had been collated, and it made for motivational stuff. When I read what had been written about me I was ready to run through walls.

That little exercise was only ever used that once, but it worked a treat.

Turns out our wives and girlfriends were also pampered by the county board that weekend. They were brought to Dublin by coach, stayed in the Burlington, and were given gifts such as jewellery to mark the occasion. It all helps make a difference to morale; our partners felt glad to be appreciated and we were pleased about that too!

Fionnuala shared a room with Cormac McAnallen's fiancée, Ashlene. The two had quite a bit in common – Fionnuala doesn't drink and Ashlene wasn't a huge raver either – so when the other girls were drinking cocktails and dancing the night away, Fionnuala and Ashlene were chatting over pots of tea. I told her to enjoy her day. That would have been difficult enough, as both she and Shona Holmes (Collie's wife) were Armagh natives and supporters. Once Fionnuala left the hotel she met her family and friends and to this day I still haven't a clue who she supported. I didn't mind either because, as I headed off to get the team bus for Croke Park, I felt free as a bird, totally at ease.

In Croke Park our dressing room was calm and focused. We knew our preparation had been thoroughly professional and we had the tools to get the job done. It just remained for us to stay on message and do ourselves justice, and the great prize was within reach.

Funny, though, how even at a time of intense concentration, something unexpected can pop up to blur the focus. When I went out to watch part of the minor game and taste the atmosphere in the stadium, I met a girl I knew from work experience earlier that summer, a staunch Armagh supporter from Maghery, Lisa Cushnahan. Lisa had spent most of the summer winding me up about the whole Tyrone/Armagh rivalry, and now here she was proudly wearing her Armagh jersey and wishing me the best of luck! It was just a peculiar thing. It brought home to me what was at stake, but it also reminded me that this was only a game. Win, lose or draw, life would go on. We'd all be back at work again soon, no matter what happened.

I retreated to the dressing room, where all was still comparatively quiet and calm. As team captain, Peter Canavan seldom got animated; most of the work was done by then, so it was just down to maintaining focus. Peter's dad had died before the Ulster final that year and I'm sure he was even more motivated to win to pay tribute to his father. Both he and Chris Lawn were very much the driving forces anyway when it came to mental preparation and in the lead-up to the final, both lads made sure that we kept doing the basics right.

Peter had been recovering from his injury in the semi-final against Kerry but there was scarcely a word said about it and he was around for all the training sessions, though largely doing his own thing. We never feared for one minute that he would miss the game, and we knew nothing of the plan to start him, replace him, and bring him on again. While he had trained very little, we were always told he would be okay on the day.

Shortly before throw-in we made reference in the huddle to Armagh being 'robots'. We said they would struggle to cope with the dynamics of the game, with our flexibility. We reckoned our ability to play off the cuff gave us a decisive edge.

They ran out to the Hill end to warm up, despite – or maybe

because of – the fact we were already warming up there. Whether it was planned or not, I can honestly say it didn't worry me, nor did I see any of our lads being unnerved by it. We took it as just another of their robotic rituals, and I still think it unsettled them more than us.

For the anthem they stood on the sideline under the Hogan Stand, along with their subs and management, rather than in a line across the field or spread across their own positions. That again suggested to us that these guys were badly overthinking the whole thing.

The game itself was edgy. The referee, Brian White, was perceived to be very strict, something we felt would surely work to our advantage because Armagh's physical approach was often too borderline for match officials. That was what we told ourselves anyway. We felt we were always in control and it was only a matter of time before we made that tell on the scoreboard. But goal chances came and went.

I had a great chance in the first half when played in by the man who could see things that others couldn't, Brian McGuigan. Lying in bed in the nights and weeks before the final I would visualise what might happen. I still do this before every game and it's something I have done since I was a child. It's not something I got from a coach; it just came naturally. One of the things I rehearsed mentally was being through on goal in the final. I played that reel over and over and arrived each time at the same conclusion – just do what comes naturally. That had worked a treat in the 2000 MacRory Cup final, when with time almost up and the scores tied I went onto my left side and finished the job.

Now it was actually happening for me all over again in an All-Ireland final. As I bore down on goal their keeper, Paul

Hearty, set himself to make the save. He would have expected me to stay on my dominant right foot, but I went to confuse him by switching onto the left. It didn't work out as I planned. I went left but Hearty had closed the space and I was off-balance when I swung a dodgy left boot at the ball and saw it trickle wide.

My chance to score a goal in the final was gone! I lay there for a second in disbelief. Then I jumped up and told myself in that moment I would put it behind me – I wasn't going to be blamed for losing an All-Ireland to our fiercest rivals, our next-door neighbours. As I ran back out the field I recalled Oisín McConville's words about the 2002 final, when he missed a penalty but resolved there and then to work even harder for the team and eventually got his reward, scoring a goal in the second half.

I never got another chance, but I did work even harder from then on and was fouled quite a bit around the middle third, a few knocks that slowed me down. But it did annoy me that I didn't show my best, nor manage a score, on the biggest stage of all.

Mickey managed the whole Canavan thing to perfection. Peter had been taken off at half-time, but we hadn't been alerted and the second half was well underway before I spotted him standing on the sideline and twigged what was happening. Half the other lads didn't cop it for ages either. That sounds mad, but we were all too hyped and too much in the zone to spot anything that was just off our radar.

Near the end of the game the biggest boost we got was probably the crowd reaction when Peter started to warm up again. That was such an intense moment, coming as it did at that point when we knew we had fingertips on the Sam Maguire Cup.

Then Armagh had Diarmuid Marsden sent off. Philly ran at him, Marsden instinctively put an arm up, and Philly went down. Armagh would always maintain it was self-defence, and they also accused Philly of diving, but Brian White was close enough to the action and showed Marsden a straight red.

I didn't really see the incident, but I did get great mileage winding Philly up about it for years afterwards. He still gets fierce stick from the next-door neighbours and isn't exactly the flavour of every month with the good folk of Armagh.

That red card was later revoked by the GAA but on the day, even before Marsden walked, it just felt like the game was ours to lose. We had missed at least three gilt-edged goal chances, and even if Canavan wasn't fully right, he still tapped over five frees.

Near the end Stevie McDonnell was through on our goal and looked home and dry. I was in the area defending at that point – with Armagh chasing the game I thought another lump of tall timber back there would do no harm. A high ball was kicked in and I remember it took an eternity to fall out of the sky. I called for it, but Cormac never heard, and as he challenged for it with an Armagh player they both clattered me, and the ball broke to McDonnell. It was then that Conor Gormley appeared out of nowhere, blocked McDonnell and prevented what looked a certain goal.

That intervention was typical of Gormley and, coming the way it did and at that precise time and place, it was possibly the greatest moment, and the most telling play, in the history of Tyrone football. Of course, Gormley, modest as ever, just went on about his business, no fuss at all, tearing after the next play. A legend of a man.

It was a poor enough game for the neutral, but we hung on

to win by three points and the feeling that hit me at the final whistle was like an out-of-body experience. I compare it now to the night I went walkabout after losing to Mayo in 2016 and met the cat carrying that rat in its jaws. *Is this real? Have we actually done it?*

I remember how loud the roars of the supporters were, but for several moments it was as if everything was happening in slow motion, noiselessly and at a distance, and I was there on my own. As I tried to take in and comprehend what had just happened, the spell was suddenly snapped, and I was engulfed by a roaring, boisterous red army, hugging and shaking and slapping me furiously on the back.

While I love the idea of the pitch invasion, and it's something you associate with huge GAA games, it wasn't ideal at that moment, to be honest. I just wanted a bit of space and a chance to be with teammates. I could see Canavan being lifted shoulder-high and weaving above the crowd to the steps of the Hogan Stand, while I had to fight my own way through, and it was a real struggle.

Eventually I was reunited with the lads and could begin to take in all that had just happened. Standing on those steps with most of Croke Park heaving in red and white, I looked up as Canavan's words boomed out: 'I can't think of a better place to be standing anywhere in the world right now!'

Hardly anyone ever said a truer word.

11

THE CIRCUIT

Donegal was the last place I expected to be the night after we won the All-Ireland, but that's where we ended up.

I'll be brutally honest. After you win a title, the sweetest moments happen in the changing room and on the bus back to the hotel, because that is when, free of interference from outside, you get to embrace the occasion, get your head around it all, with teammates. Once you emerge from that bubble you become public property and are fair game for all sorts.

Take that homecoming in 2003. As soon as the bus left the Burlington the next day, the songs were struck up, the beer flowed, and the craic was as you'd expect. There were pitstops in the likes of Carrickmacross and Castleblayney before we crossed the border to a lively reception at Aughnacloy. There was another gathering in Ballygawley and another massive welcome on the main street of Omagh, supporters packed on the pavements, people on top of traffic lights, monuments, walls. It was a sight to behold.

At each of those stops we were herded dutifully off and back onto the team bus and no one bothered to ask where we would end up. Reports filtered through of parties in various places, including the Auction Rooms in the Moy, which was owned by Philly Jordan's father, Mickey, and we heard the crowds were spilling out onto the Square. Being from the Moy I would naturally have enjoyed a piece of that. But, to arrive in the Moy, the bus would have had to go through Armagh, which might not have been ideal.

With the Moy ruled out, Omagh seemed the obvious choice. And when I saw the throngs waiting for us there, that was where I wanted to sling my hat. Yet we ended up in Donegal town, and to this day I wonder how it came to that. W. J. Dolan was our sponsor, and it seems he wanted to get us to a gathering in Aghyaran, a wee hamlet right on the Donegal border. We reached there at 11 p.m. and were ushered into a modest reception in the parochial hall.

By now it was becoming clear that because it was so late and there was a shortage of drivers and taxis that we wouldn't be rejoining the fun in Omagh or in any of the other Tyrone hotspots where fans were going crazy – it had gone too late and some of the lads had had enough bus travel for one day. And so, after keeping our appointment in Aghyaran we just moved on down the road to Donegal town and sought in vain for a party. But not much happened in Donegal on a Monday night and when we finally accepted that we crashed for the night in the Abbey Court hotel.

It was a huge regret that we missed the party in Omagh. I remember standing in Donegal town at three o'clock on the Tuesday morning and reading a newspaper report on the final. It said I had been largely shackled by the Armagh lads and had had minimal influence on the result. Feckin' brilliant! Bad enough at such a historic time to be stranded across the border in Donegal, but having to read, after winning an All-Ireland medal, that I was rubbish!

Still, I couldn't entirely fault the verdict. No doubt I could have done more in the final, and for that reason I didn't quite enjoy the celebrations as much as I might have otherwise. But I put it aside – sure wouldn't I have the chance to make up for it on many a future occasion?

We had a few more stops and receptions to negotiate on the way home from Donegal that Tuesday, and then it was back by our separate ways to our local communities and bars.

On that final lap the beers were still circulating – lads taking the edge off the night before – when I heard a commotion at the back of the bus. I turned around and there was Horse Devlin, buck naked but with the legs crossed, shouting: 'We are All-Ireland champions!'

Horse hadn't held back in the celebrations and was by now showing the wear and tear – only two days after playing number 6 on an All-Ireland winning team, he looked physically wrecked. It was one of those images that is quite difficult to unsee. Fortunately, the few sponsors and their wives at the front of the bus were spared the close-up view!

The annual GOAL challenge was in Omagh on the Wednesday night, and from there the Sam Maguire was booked to visit various pockets of the county and beyond, virtually every night for a year. Each player would pick and choose what we attended, but if anyone wanted to get out several times a week and enjoy the celebrations there was a clear road ahead.

Success certainly changed my life, and I noticed the difference in various ways. Sometimes referees in Tyrone would be accused of favouring 'county' players. That may have been true of some refs, but there were others who would go the opposite way and punish us for being supposedly fitter and stronger than 'ordinary' club players.

When the Moy played a club game soon after the All-Ireland final, John Kerlin, who still referees in Tyrone, was in charge. He sent off a couple of our players, we lost, and quite a few of us, convinced he had whistled us out the gate, let him know what we thought of him as we walked off at the finish.

After a quick shower I headed for the car, still raging, and was amazed to meet John, standing there with his daughter, asking for my picture and autograph. I obliged. Moments after chewing the head off the lad. No problem! I'm not sure if that would happen anywhere but in the GAA.

When we won the All-Ireland again two years later, in 2005, we had a League play-off with Clann na nGael not long after the final. I recall Stevie O'Neill and myself being told to wait in the changing room while our clubmates tore onto the Moy pitch. We had no idea what was going on, but as we ran out both teams gave us a guard of honour. A lovely touch, but of course Stevie and I just wanted to get on with things – after all, it was a straight knockout promotion game.

Mind you, as the game started I shipped a few not-so-friendly rib ticklers from their full-back, which suggested the guard of honour wasn't his idea. Normal service was resumed.

But 2003 was the start of a fairly constant (and to this day continuing) stream of requests and invitations for presentations, gala nights, birthdays, coaching sessions and school prizegivings. Fulfilling such obligations from year to year has taken me the length of breadth of Ireland and beyond.

I'm quite poor at saying no, but there's at least one good reason: I love meeting the kids and having the craic with them. I still remember as a kid when Oisín McConville presented our club with awards; it was such a big deal for me at the time. But there were times in 2003 when I attended three or four events in one night, and it did begin to take a toll. On the way home from a late-night function in Cavan I fell asleep for a split second at the wheel. That made me slow down and pace myself more sensibly.

Change was everywhere. People suddenly saw me in a different light. Lecturers and tutors at Jordanstown became more accommodating as I tried to juggle time or had to miss classes. Fellow students were willing to share notes. The university honoured me at a function alongside guys who were playing soccer, rugby, cricket – athletes performing on an international stage. I also received bursaries from the college. It all helped.

As winter rolled in we had the glitz and glamour of All Stars trips to look forward to, GAA awards nights in Dublin, international rules trips, invites to the USA. I knocked tremendous enjoyment out of those events, and I didn't have to worry as much about impressing Fionnuala, because the invites never stopped. Since 2003 Fionnuala and I have been to exotic locations all over the world and stayed in five-star hotels we could only have dreamed of, and that's all down to the GAA. It was some departure for me; growing up I would have looked on a week of bed and breakfast in Blackpool as the ultimate adventure.

Other avenues opened up, job offers included. I enjoyed the

limelight and would hardly have wanted it any other way. I took people as I found them, and most were sound and genuine. Once people start making a fuss and you get a taste of that lifestyle it's difficult not to want more.

Nevertheless, by Christmas of that year we were glad to get the heads down and go back into 'training' mode, which meant some sort of normality, establishing a routine and staying disciplined. But still the 'celebrity circuit' remained in season.

I ended up at birthday parties for perfect strangers, lovely people, but I would walk in the door and think, *What the hell am I doing here?* I once even went to a party for a four-year-old I didn't know. I should have been studying for accountancy exams but was blowing out birthday candles for some kid who had no idea why this big strange man was in his house acting the clown and grinning down at him. Just a trophy for the parents.

If I found it impossible to say 'no', so did my own dad, and we both got drawn into the social whirl. That's the hard part – trying to get the balance right between being a footballer, being nice to people, and keeping my focus on work or studies.

There were even times I was conscious of being used, but I put on the brave face and accepted that I was part of a special community, the GAA, and that success had its obligations. The downside was that all of the days and nights I was away doing stuff like that I was stealing time from my girlfriend, my family, the text books, and I was putting yourself under heavy pressure to please others.

There was the time my Tyrone and Moy teammate Ryan Mellon asked me to attend a club gala evening in Fermanagh. We needed that night away like a hole in the head – for one thing the National League was just around the corner and Ryan and I were off the drink – but we put our game faces on and Fionnuala even took the trouble to go out and buy a new dress.

We were put sitting at the top table – Ryan and Barbara and Fionnuala and myself – with the club hierarchy and the life presidents, and while they were all lovely people, it was a long night. We got back home at 3 a.m., pretty well wrung-out from eight hours of talking. The gas thing was that we often ended up being out of pocket and out of time on those occasions. As twenty-year-old students, neither myself nor Fionnuala were rolling in cash and driving to the other end of Ulster for the night and buying suits and formal wear wasn't inexpensive either. I might get a few bob here and there but nothing major. But I guess it always came back to this: we were in a privileged position and knew that we had to give something back.

The funny thing is that, despite their reputation, Cavan people were ridiculously generous in their expenses over the years. God Bless Cavan – they helped see me through university! It was more welcome than all the Beleek china I got in the way of thanks. I've enough china gathered to open a gallery at this stage.

I'm only joking really. The truth is I was my own worst enemy. I said 'yes' to so many people and that led to me missing a lot of what others take for granted. But it was my own doing. I've never been to a rock concert; I missed far too many friends' weddings; I passed up on family events too. I soon discovered that, while sports stardom was wonderful and brought with it amazing opportunities and experiences, it also entailed many sacrifices. Much more than people who aren't in that position understand. I learned that back in 2003. It's frightening to think how much greater are the demands on today's players.

When I lived at home, some of the pressure was deflected; Mummy is as sharp as the proverbial tack, and any time anyone called to the house or phoned uninvited or unwelcome, she could vet and filter them out, saving me the hassle. But nights out involved too much attention, and of course in recent times it has been all about selfies. It may sound glamorous but it's not in the real world. Often all you want is to be anonymous, particularly after a losing game or if you're out with long-lost friends trying to catch up.

I would enjoy trips to Manchester to watch United before heading out for a meal, and while even there I seldom managed complete anonymity – you soon realise there are Irish everywhere on the planet – I could go relatively untroubled.

I once had a few drinks with Ciarán McDonald of Mayo after an international rules game in Dublin and all he wanted to do was avoid people. With his braided blond hair and film-star looks he was an iconic figure, and I remember thinking he must love the attention. It was the complete opposite: he went out of his way to escape recognition. I admired that in him and could well relate to it.

Most of the reaction and interaction you get is positive but some of it is negative – even nasty. People will say that all comes with the territory, but does it always have to? Many a Monday morning on the way to work I tiptoed into the local filling station to grab a paper and check out my 'rating' and if it wasn't great it would affect me for sure – that feeling that you had let people down. And then you have to carry those emotions and feelings into your workplace or classroom, where you are expected to concentrate and perform.

There are in fact a fair number of downsides to success in elite sport. Criticism in its various forms is among them, and the arrival of social media hasn't helped. People can be quick to tear strips off you, but they tend to forget that Gaelic footballers and hurlers, not to mention camogie players and women footballers, are amateurs and have plenty of other stresses going on in their lives without some disgruntled fan or footballer on the ditch having a go.

One evening, officials of a team we were playing against stood on the line shouting obscenities at me at the top of their voices. I was about two feet away. I went over to take a sideline and one lad, in particular, absolutely laid into me. The following night, the same person phoned me to ask if I would present youth medals a week later. He never mentioned the abuse he had dished out, and for some reason I ended up obliging.

As my career progressed I put less and less store in public opinion, especially the stuff coming from certain quarters of the media. I have seen careless and uninformed criticism hammer the confidence of some of Tyrone's brightest young talents. If you think I exaggerate, here's an example.

Six days after that historic win, our first-ever All-Ireland, we had to play Dublin in the All-Ireland under-21 final. Of course, the scheduling was pure madness. For four days after beating Armagh I was on the razzle with the rest of the senior team. On the Thursday night – well, it was 2 a.m. on the Friday – I was at a reception in Coalisland (obligatory because I had grown up there), exhausted and worrying that I had another All-Ireland final in thirty-six hours' time. I doubt the under-21s from the senior panel were anywhere near right for that game, and though Dublin dominated and deserved to win, the short and hectic lead-in left a sour taste. Cue some really harsh reviews, but hardly any mention that several of those youngsters never got to prepare properly.

I guess that, overall, 2003 was very much about a bunch of fresh-faced, confident lads still riding the crests of waves made by winning at minor and under-21, and mixing with and learning from wise heads and steady hands like Peter Canavan and Chris Lawn.

Looking back there was one notable turning point in the season. A few days after we beat Down in the Ulster final replay, we trained at Edendork and the place was humming with talk of post-match shenanigans and in particular a party that had taken place in Gerard Cavlan's bar, the Bailey. Canavan and Lawn pulled us aside after training and gave us a pretty inspirational chat about realising how good we were and how far we could go. As young lads we didn't tend to look far down the track, but that night the two boys made it crystal clear that if we worked harder we could go all the way.

They were great times. Card schools at the back of the bus with Hub Hughes, Canavan and McGuigan, the high rollers. Hub lost seventy quid on the way to the Ulster final and got unmerciful abuse for his troubles. It broke the pre-match tension.

The 2003 All-Ireland quarter-final against Fermanagh always sticks out. After beating them we stopped overnight in Dublin. Kerry were playing Roscommon the next day, and since we would be playing the winners in the quarters, it made sense to stay back and attend the game. Mickey duly imposed a curfew – he wasn't a fan of alcohol and we were to get an early night.

As it happened, a couple of weeks earlier at a team meeting in Galbally the whole issue of drinking after games was discussed. We negotiated to get a few pints in on the night of the Fermanagh match, and after much debate, just when we thought we were nearing a breakthrough with Mickey, up jumps one of the lads: 'A few beers is no good to me, lads! I can't go out for "a few beers" – we either go on the tear or not at all!'

That was our 'few beers' cut off at source. It turned into an all-night jamboree.

I was rooming with Mickey Coleman, a musician who actually recorded a song with us after we won Sam and used to keep me up until 2 a.m. watching music channels. Mickey made contact with his Ardboe clubmate McGuigan around 9 p.m. and mentioned that a few lads were going to sneak into Saggart village and find a bar. And since Canavan was part of the raiding party, I decided it was safe to join in.

Eight of us snuck out through the back door of the Citywest and scuttled in pitch dark across the golf course, followed by a few muffled curses as lads fell into bunkers. We stayed out until 1 a.m. before wandering back to the hotel, well hydrated and content with the success of our daring expedition.

We hung around the lobby for a bit – it was a bank holiday and the place was still hopping – when next thing several taxis rolled onto the forecourt and disgorged most of our teammates. Virtually the whole team had slipped away, in small groups, and rocked up under the bright lights of Temple Bar for the evening. And there we were thinking how bold and brave we had been and we making it to sleepy Saggart!

As usual, word got back to Mickey, but he didn't make an act of Stormont out of it. A good job we had wiped Fermanagh convincingly earlier that day.

Once the 2003 All-Ireland celebrations were out of the way, I became much more focused on my weight and my performance. I cut back on the battered cowboy suppers and eased off on the chocolates. When university pals headed out drinking I would leave them at it and instead head to my little 'weights room' in my bedroom on the third floor of the lodgings. There I would pump iron and follow with maybe a hundred press-ups and as many sit-ups and dips.

Beans and toast became my staples. I often had them for breakfast, lunch and dinner. It's not a diet I would recommend to anyone – and it's one that present-day experts advise against – but it was my way of controlling the weight. I had my own layer of puppy fat to shed, and once I had managed that I was obsessed with keeping it off.

At the time our trainer Paddy Tally was a firm believer in carb-loading and I stuck religiously to his advice. When Fionnuala's mum, Catherine, made delicious spaghetti bolognese I would separate out all the meat and sauce and eat just the pasta. These days GAA players do the opposite: they leave the carbs and eat the protein.

At home I was skipping dinners; I wanted none of the meat and veg. I would pop down of an evening to my friend Jeff, who owned the Chinese restaurant less than a hundred metres from our house, and get a small portion of boiled rice, a handful, and a dash of curry sauce, and that was my main meal all the way through 2004. Colm followed suit and before long that 'meal' became affectionately known around our house as a 'BRCS' – boiled rice and curry sauce! That's a sad reflection of how I could convince myself that something was going to help me perform! The odd evening, I would substitute it with another helping of beans and toast – just to freshen things up!

I lived on those two meals for a year. I don't know from a nutritional standpoint what if any damage I was doing to myself, but I do know I felt brilliant.

12

MCANALLEN

In January 2004 we gathered in Quinn's Bar for the Tyrone team meeting. It was a night for drawing up a battle plan for the year ahead and the first step, Mickey told us, was that Cormac would be our new captain. It made sense; we would have done anything for that lad.

Early in the meeting Cormac spoke and set the tone. He left us in no doubt as to what he expected and demanded of us and mentioned his fear of retiring with a sense of having under-achieved: 'I'm not happy with just the one All-Ireland medal,' he said. 'I won't be happy until we've won multiple All-Irelands.'

I have no hesitation in saying I loved Cormac. I remember an occasion in 2003 when he and I ended up sharing a waiting room in Craigavon Hospital. We had both played the previous day for the Tyrone seniors in the Ulster Championship against Derry and this particular afternoon had been in action for our clubs. I had rolled ankle ligaments playing for Moy against Cookstown on a soggy day, while Cormac had broken a cheekbone playing

161

for Eglish. There we were, the sitting wounded, Cormac in the magpie colours of Eglish and myself in the sky blue of Moy. Fierce rivals from neighbouring parishes, side by side awaiting treatment. Chatting about the madness of it all.

When I look back it was a special moment that spoke volumes about the GAA. Both of us were used to being roughed up, especially in the tribal battles that marked the domestic championship, but neither of us would have swapped it for the world.

We started the League in 2004 losing by a point to Dublin and then beat Longford and Fermanagh. After a break from competition we hammered Donegal, 1-22 to 0-7, in the 2004 McKenna Cup final. I sat beside Cormac on the bus home and as we chatted I enquired what he was up to for the rest of the weekend. He replied he was heading to his fiancée, Ashlene's place. We said our farewells and I thought little more of it.

Cormac, as I've mentioned, was in many ways my minder when it came to discipline. He kept me honest and was quick to tell me when I was taking shortcuts. He also tried to correct my lazy eating habits, often with a well-aimed verbal dart. Because I looked up to him, I took everything he said on board. I saw him as both friend and mentor.

Early in the 2004 season I noticed Cormac had lost a fair bit of weight. I remember thinking he must be training to the max – he was that thin. He had always had a wee bit of the puppy fat on him, and it actually seemed to suit him. But now he was captain you could see him getting much leaner. It was natural to conclude that, even though he was already known to be a ferocious trainer, he had just upped the ante even more, especially in terms of strength and conditioning.

I admired Cormac so much that his attitude to training rubbed off on me and I was heading in the same direction. I saw how Cormac lived his life and I wanted to be like him. The 2004 season found me fitter than I had ever been. And like Cormac, I wanted to win another All-Ireland – and soon.

I think a fair few of us were obsessed. At training the bleep test would usually end with Cormac and myself battling for supremacy. That was until Hub Hughes, who just ate and drank whatever came to hand, would arrive from nowhere and blow us out of it.

Cormac and I always managed 14/3 or 14/4 on the bleep test. Hub and Dooher were also in the top bracket. The competition drives you on to train ever harder and prepare ever more diligently, and however unscientific my diet might have been I was motoring sweetly. I got a great run in 2004, with no injuries, which helped me no end. Cormac, though looking underweight compared to the rest of us, was ferocious in trying to win possession and could run for Ireland. We all meant business.

But none of that matters a jot because nothing – and I mean nothing – could prepare us for the news that we got just days after Cormac lifted his first silverware as Tyrone senior captain, the McKenna Cup.

Daddy came into my room at ten to seven that Tuesday morning, which was strange in itself – the running joke in our house was that Daddy, like clockwork, would put his head in the door and just say: 'Seán, half seven.' That was my rise-and-shine call. But this morning he was forty minutes early. He's not an emotional man, but I knew straight away something was up.

'Seán, I'm only after getting a phone call there now. Cormac McAnallen died last night.'

'What?'

'I don't know any details.'

I struggled out of bed in a trance, staggered downstairs and sat in the front room. I didn't know what I was doing. I think I poured a bowl of cereal and just sat there staring at it. I was numb, unable to process what I had just heard. Then Collie Holmes and Philly Jordan phoned, and those calls drove home the unbelievable news.

The only thing in my head was that Cormac must have crashed the car on the way to Ashlene's house in Derry. That was the last thing he had told me, that he was heading there.

We know now that Cormac died from sudden adult death syndrome, but none of us had ever heard of that, and when the diagnosis came through we struggled to understand what had happened.

We were distraught.

Philly, Collie, Ryan Mellon and I had travelled with Cormac to Tyrone training, and Philly and Ryan had travelled with him to county minor training – and before that to school training in St Pat's, Armagh – so we knew him better than most fellas on the panel. We were certainly close to him, and so we went out to the house in Eglish to meet his remains at half three that afternoon. We were among the first to see him, the four us waiting in the room. The coffin was brought in and the lid was lifted. That was reality, there and then.

We wept openly, but the howl of pure anguish that broke from Paddy Tally is something that has stayed with me to this day. In that moment Paddy simply could not contain his grief. Imagine how Cormac's poor family felt.

'That's our teammate there,' I whispered to no one in

164

particular as we stood there, numb, the tears streaming, looking at this image of a fit, healthy and exceptionally strong young man. Our comrade. Taken from us at the height of his great powers. It was just shocking.

Crowds started to file in. The Kerry lads landed around 4.30 p.m., Darragh and Tomás Ó Sé and others. Cormac had died in the middle of the night and the Kerry boys must have started out as soon as the news broke, because it would have taken seven hours of travelling from West Kerry to Eglish.

I looked at them and one thought struck me. These were the guys on whom we had inflicted 'puke football' a few months earlier. Fellas we were supposed to 'hate', who were destined to hate us in return. And yet here they were in Cormac's house, having driven the length of the land at no notice, their only thought to support the family and in turn to support us.

I may have whinged at times about being dragged from pillar to post to open a supermarket or present awards or blow out birthday candles, but here in front of me, in the persons of our fierce Kerry rivals, was the power of the GAA.

We knew then that Cormac's funeral was going to be an extraordinary event. Far beyond sport. And so it proved. It was so poignant. There were several guards of honour, from what I could see. Priests, endless lines of black suits, all heads bowed and soft music floating. At the graveside Mícheál Ó Muircheartaigh read a poem by Brendan Kane called 'The Beautiful Game'. It was haunting. It was beautiful. I saw men from clubs all over Tyrone and players from every county in Ireland line up to form the guard of honour. Behind all the shaping and carping, GAA people have huge respect and affection for each other. Not only GAA folk but also many outsiders, it seemed, were in awe of

Cormac and what he stood for. He was a shining beacon of all that was good about Irish life and culture.

I was glad to have the lads there beside me. I was a twenty-year-old who didn't know how to deal with such things.

A funeral reception for our team was held in Quinn's Corner on the evening of Cormac's burial. Someone ordered a round of drinks, and over the few pints we ended up reminiscing about Cormac and sharing personal memories. It ended up as an all-out drinking night, as lads struggled with their emotions. It hadn't been planned as such, but as it turned out there was some consolation, and I would say a bit of much-needed healing, in that little gathering.

It was when I was on my own in the following weeks that the desolation and fear played out. The prospect loomed of having to play football again, and I struggled with that; there was a real reluctance to even go back training with the team. Why would you bother? And then I just kept wondering. I had been training every bit as hard as Cormac. Was there something we had both been doing badly wrong? I can't speak for the other lads, but on top of my devastation at the loss of a friend and anguish for the McAnallens and Ashlene, I wondered if I was in trouble too. Cormac and I had been doing exactly the same training, the only real difference being that he probably ate much better than I did. A real fear came over me and lingered for a long time.

A few days after the funeral the team met again to bring our heads together for a game with Mayo in Castlebar the following weekend. We were trying to get the show back on the road, but everyone was fairly shaken still, including myself. Apart from the shock and grief, the fear was also there that we all could have whatever Cormac had and, to be honest, there wasn't a huge appetite to go back training right away.

As we lined up for the anthem in Castlebar we formed ourselves into the shape of the number 3, Cormac's number. We went on to win comprehensively. For the remainder of the season no one else would wear the number 3 shirt and instead our full-back would have '31' on his back, which was a nice touch. From then on, all the emphasis that year was to go and win another All-Ireland for Cormac. As the months passed we talked openly about it less and less, but it was the unspoken vow taken as a team.

I missed him so much. Cormac had played 8, with me beside him at 9, for large parts of 2003. I always remembered the game against Kerry early in the NFL and the delight I felt when Cormac came up to me beforehand and said that he would take Ó Sé. Darragh threw Cormac and the rest of us about like children and must have caught fifteen kickouts on his own. But Cormac being Cormac, he never gave in and scrapped it out with him until the bitter end. We ended up winning by a couple of points.

McAnallen was very much like that. Against Derry in the 2003 Championship he wanted to mark Tohill. He loved the challenge of taking on the opposition's alpha male and that was fine by me as I was a free-running kid who wanted to get forward, exploit open space and score as much as I possibly could. His style therefore suited me down to the ground.

After Dan Gordon had caused us all that trouble in the first 2003 Ulster final, I have to say I found it a strange call to move him back to number 3, as he was such an influence around the middle, but Cormac loved the challenge of that too. Tell him he couldn't do it and he went in all the harder. He was a big success back there and, meanwhile, I was lucky that when Cormac vacated number 8, Collie Holmes and then Kevin Hughes were able to slot in beside me. They were also happy to do the spade work, contest more tackles and challenges, and leave me to pursue my addiction of breaking free at every opportunity and running in behind defences with the likes of McGuigan, Canavan and Cavlan spraying balls into my chest from anywhere around the field.

The games following Cormac's passing are just a blur to me. We were All-Ireland champions, pushing ourselves to the limit and run ragged from being brought to functions all over the country. But Cormac was gone.

We still didn't understand this heart condition. Not long after Cormac's death, and after John McCall, a young rugby player from Armagh, died the same way, the whole Tyrone team was dispatched to Dublin's Mater Hospital for cardiac screening. I half expected to be told I was in trouble, and when the scan arrived I thought my worst fears were confirmed.

'Seán,' the consultant said as he pointed to the image, 'whatever way you are put together, and whatever way you are training, your heart has grown to this size, and it's well above average.'

'Is that good, bad or indifferent?' I asked, trying not to sound terrified.

The reassuring answer was that I shouldn't panic. The heart muscles had responded to the load being placed on them. It happened with athletes. There was no call to ease off training or playing.

Despite the assurances, I remained unsure. And if I'm being

168

honest I'm still nervous today about the whole area of heart health and hard training.

As the years passed I often saw Cormac's mother, Brigid, doing her shopping in the Co-op next to our house in the Moy. Cormac's grandfather Charlie O'Neill lived only a hundred metres around the lane from our family home, so we would meet him too quite often, a great man who passed away some years ago. As our basketball 'court' was on the front street, Charlie would regularly pass up and down and would often stop to give us tips. It was there that the Cavanagh brothers had played two-on-two against the McAnallens on many an occasion.

Until about four years back, Brigid drove Cormac's car, a silver VW Golf, and it was easy to spot. You'd get a boost when you saw it pass by. She is a lovely, lovely woman and it's great that we can always talk about Cormac when we meet.

For my part I always tried to mention Cormac in media interviews after big games. And whenever I played international rules, up to my last involvement in 2014, I was delivering the same message to my Ireland teammates: we have to win for Cormac. It was another motivation that the international rules trophy was named after him.

I like to feel that he was always there beside me down the years. People might assume that club or county teammates are automatically the best of pals, but it isn't necessarily so. In any team or workplace there are guys you gravitate towards and guys you wouldn't be close to. And that's the way it was with Tyrone. Cormac was one of those guys with whom I found a lot in common. Collie Holmes, Enda McGinley and Conor Gormley were three others.

It might seem strange – because when outsiders think 'Tyrone' they also think 'bunker mentality' – but I would have stayed in contact with only about half the lads I won All-Irelands with. The truth is, Mickey made us a tight-knit group and brought us together on match days, but that was about it for some of us. Even during games there were certain guys I wouldn't easily click with, nor they with me. And that's fine. That's just the way it is.

But I think Cormac had everyone on his side. He was exactly what I wanted to be: a highly educated man, captain of Tyrone, winner of All-Ireland senior, minor and under-21 titles, an excellent basketball player. The whole package.

When the shock of his passing began to subside – and it took a long time for that to happen – I decided I should live my life as he had lived his. I would aspire to be like him.

Considering what the Tyrone team and wider GAA community had gone through, we went on to put in a decent season. I was fit that summer, hitting three or four points a game, and in my crazy mind I related it all to the boiled rice and curry sauce. I had an edge and I wanted to keep it.

We won two games in Ulster before Donegal beat us and sent us back to the qualifiers. Four games on we played Galway in the last round of the qualifiers. The Sunday evening before that game we all convened as usual in the Vernon household, where Fionnuala's mum, Catherine, had made this really class chocolate cake, a speciality of hers that everyone knew I couldn't resist.

Catherine, knowing I was under starter's orders for Galway and so wouldn't be taking the usual supersized portion or two,

170

offered me this wafer-thin slice, saying, 'Surely that isn't going to slow you down in a week's time?' I thought of Cormac and what he might have done and then I thought of Joe Bergin and how he might be preparing in Galway to put shackles on me. I pushed the plate away.

'I'll not eat it, Catherine. Because there'll be no Galway lads eating cake today.'

Thanks to Cormac's influence and my own obsession I was in the zone. The small margins counted. As Páidí Ó Sé said when managing Westmeath – the same year, as it happens – 'A grain of rice can tip the scales.'

I was counting the beans on my plate, scraping sauce off the chicken leg, turning down the best chocolate cake in the country. All to win that second All-Ireland, and to do it in honour of Cormac's memory.

After we beat Galway, Adrian Logan of UTV interviewed me and asked if I felt I was the best player in Ireland. I replied that I wasn't even the best player in my house – Colm had been lighting the place up for the Tyrone minors. But deep down I knew I had found another level.

And yet, after Mayo beat us in the 2004 All-Ireland quarter-final, we were left to reflect on a year not only of loss and sadness but also of failure. And I considered myself largely to blame.

In the dressing room before the game the lads had warned me, as several times before, that the Mayo midfielder Ronan McGarrity was likely to get under my skin and distract me, and at all costs I was to keep my composure.

Fair play to Ronan, he was in my face that day right from the throw-in. He did his job and he got on top of me. Anxious from the start that I would let Cormac down, I took it personally as

McGarrity got the better of me and the game got away from us.

I was gutted at how I had allowed McGarrity to maul and drag out of me, to stifle my influence on that semi-final. Never having imagined Mayo would beat us, we were on such a good run, I ended up furious with myself and heartbroken for Cormac. He would have expected us to win another All-Ireland in 2004. Coming off the field that day I was convinced I had let him and his family down. That hurt me badly.

At the same time we were mightily close to beating Mayo and only for a few wonder scores from David Brady, and a few errors from ourselves, we probably could have made the final against Kerry. Maybe we would have beaten them too, as we had a knack of getting ourselves right for Kerry back then.

We didn't have the same edge that year following his passing. How could we? But there were also many other things that put us against a wall, including losing Canavan to injury for much of the year.

Cormac was impossible to get out of our heads, as you could imagine. I still think of him most days now and back then we were obsessed with trying to win for him. But a lot of energy was gobbled up by his loss. There certainly were nights in training where it didn't feel quite right without him and we were constantly having to motivate ourselves by saying that we were doing it for him; yet that was probably the thing that drained most of our energy and attention.

It didn't matter after what we had gone through but though I won an All Star that year I ended the season critiquing myself as harshly as Cormac would have done. Especially as the Tyrone minors went on to reach and win the All-Ireland. With Colm in his first year with them, I would have dearly loved to have played at Croke Park on the same day – with him playing the minor final and me in the senior decider.

Although Cormac wasn't with us, his influence remained. To this day I apply myself to challenges as I imagine Cormac would. It's as if he is there beside me as a kind of gauge or mentor. He still sets standards for me, and every couple of months I tip over to his grave to say a prayer.

13

NOISY NEIGHBOURS

Long before the recession cooled the reign of the foreign training camp, we looked on in envy as our next-door neighbours got ready to fly out to Spain and sun themselves.

By 2005 the Celtic Tiger had started to purr confidently and there were knock-on effects for those involved at elite levels of the GAA. If you had any sort of a profile you were in big demand. I was often asked to pop down to Croke Park for an endorsement gig and would get €1,000 or €1,500 handed to me as I made my way home that afternoon. The cult of the foreign training camp was rife and some of the bigger county boards in the country were fundraising for their senior teams to fly out to those warm weather pre-season training camps.

Early in 2002 Joe Kernan had brought Armagh over to La Manga in Spain and when they won the Championship nine months later the whole country started to follow suit. I think twelve counties hit La Manga in the immediate years afterwards and Armagh themselves went over four times in the next five years, each trip costing around €40,000 a pop.

At first Joe was ridiculed for thinking outside the box – and the island – but there were very few laughing at him in September 2002. We certainly weren't.

In fact we envied them. La Manga gave Armagh the first taste of a professional lifestyle. Rub downs. Pool sessions. Gym work. Training drills rather than a dreary old day job. All the dietary requirements looked after.

And when I say a lot of counties followed suit, I don't include ourselves. Mickey didn't like the notion of a foreign training camp and that was that. It was Mickey's regime and anything he didn't want didn't happen. We felt we should have been given pre-season trips over the years. There was often a slight bit of discontentment in the camp, but if we sent Dooher or one of the senior fellas to put our feelings to Mickey, the retort was always the same: 'Mickey doesn't go foreign.'

As time went on we did have a few weekends away at the likes of Carton House, but we were in the throes of one of the greatest rivalries in modern football history with our neighbours and we felt they were gaining an edge on us with all their perks. That grated with us because we reckoned we were the better footballers, though I'm sure they imagined they were superior. Most of the time there was absolutely nothing between Tyrone and Armagh, but as we faced into 2005, we definitely feared that their La Manga loyalty cards would give them a clear head-start.

While they were off sunning themselves in Spain we were stuck in Costa Del Greenmount Agricultural College, a primal enough institution for farmers of the future just outside Lisburn.

It was raw and felt more like a prison than anything else. On the weekend we visited there a lot of guys had taken the bus up, but I had accountancy exams and was cramming, so every minute was precious. I drove my car up instead and parked while the lads were handed keys to their rooms.

'We get rooms of our own,' one of the lads whooped at me excitedly as I made my way in to the reception.

'Great,' I said, thinking to myself that I'd get some study done now with no one to distract me. As the Celtic Tiger roared we became used to getting looked after in style – mostly once we reached Dublin and the knockout stages of the Championship. Then we usually stayed in Citywest Hotel, or Castleknock Country Club, where we enjoyed the lovely leisure facilities and the spacious rooms.

Mostly, though, we had to share with teammates, so getting our own rooms in Greenmount was a real perk. Maybe the place wouldn't be so bad after all. Armed with a giant key I made my way purposefully to the room, opened the lock and walked in to see a six-foot bed, a Bible and nothing else. It seemed pretty spartan to me. There was no desk for me to study for my exams either.

I put my bag on the bed, sucked it up, and got on with it. We all did. We trained like lunatics on the first day we were there, a Saturday. After training we converged on the canteen where our food was being prepared by what looked like a group of trainees. It was school canteen stuff and a few of the guys started looking at each other, maybe wondering what exotic food the Armagh boys would have been dished up in the searing heat of Spain.

After dinner myself and a few lads, including Mickey Coleman and Mugsy, hit the physio room for some treatment and we spoke about how bored we were. There was no pool, no lobby, nothing. 'Lads, I have the car there, will we take off and head down to a shop somewhere, get something to eat?'

It seemed like a fine idea. Out I went to the car and headed down a massive drive, arriving at the gate only to discover it was feckin' padlocked. We were literally stuck in school. There was only one entrance and it was closed up by the caretaker, who wouldn't be back until the following morning.

Crestfallen, we made our way back to the cells ... I mean rooms, and settled down for the night. The following morning, we woke up like weary inmates after doing hard time. We were grumpy and sore. We had worked so hard on the Saturday that we had stiffened up like boards and we were simply not up for anything at all on the Sunday. We treaded gingerly out onto the pitch, but it was soon obvious we wouldn't be able to train because we were knackered. Dooher had a chat with Mickey who just said to have a light jog, a small kickabout and turn back in.

Mark Harte got some infection while we were there as well and that was the end of the Greenmount camp experience. Thanks be to God.

All of that is only a bit of craic but on some level it did further fuel a serious jealousy and rivalry between ourselves and Armagh. Apart from the football games between us, which were always tense and fierce, we saw the likes of Kieran McGeeney, in full Roy Keane mode, demanding the highest standards from his players and county board officials. It felt like they were getting more resources and specialised preparation than us – without being any more successful.

But arguing was a waste of time. We were going to be stuck at home no matter how much we moaned.

Maybe we were getting a little carried away with ourselves too. We didn't enjoy the greatest start to 2005, for instance, when Canavan temporarily withdrew from the panel before returning at the tail-end of the League. Hub Hughes and McGuigan took off for Australia and missed most of that competition too. We fared only alright without them, reaching the semi-final against Wexford in O'Moore Park. That game was played in torrential rain with a lot of surface water on the pitch and one thing led to another. We were literally caught cold and Wexford beat us and deprived us of another meeting with Armagh in the NFL final.

Were we soft again? Or were we cocky going into that game? Maybe both. The night before we shacked up at the Citywest Hotel and hit the lovely Asian restaurant, Lemongrass, around 8 p.m. Normally, we were only allowed to have a choice of chicken or beef but that night we landed in and the waitresses and waiters came over with menus giving us a much broader range of options altogether.

We were like kids and we cut loose. Collie Holmes went to town. He ordered prawn crackers, fried rice, spare ribs, and just about anything else that could be fried. Not that the rest of us shied back – an extra portion of chips here, a curry there, spring rolls for the lads. The poor staff were up and down to our tables every two minutes carrying down dishes and plates. Bucketloads of stuff landed out and we ate the absolute shite out of it.

But as we sat soaked in the dressing room after losing to Wexford we wondered if that had been such a good idea. Mickey Coleman certainly didn't think so. Mickey was a real character. He came from Ardboe, a musician and a singer. Over the years he got a couple of games but in 2005 he managed a few League games on the trot and did fine too, kicking a few points against Westmeath. He didn't play very much otherwise in his time with the squad, but he loved being with the Tyrone panel and we loved him being with us too.

After he had played two or three games on the spin, our comedy department got to work on him. It was none of my doing but the other pranksters in the squad looked up a lad from Eglish who I would be friendly with, Brendy Donnelly, and got a pal of Brendy's to prank call Mickey. At that stage the phones with the recording devices had hit the market so when Brendy's pal called Mickey, pretending to be a sales rep from Umbro, the conversation was taped. Our comedians offered Mickey a big endorsement contract – even though he had only played a few games in the League!

There were calls back and forth until your man rang Mickey, explained that he would be in Cookstown the following week, armed with a five-grand-a-year contract.

'Seán Cavanagh gets seven grand with Puma,' Mickey replied defiantly. 'I'll need that too.' The lads, of course, kept recording as they went.

Anyway, when Mickey arrived in Cookstown who was there to meet him but Mugsy and Horse with a big sign saying 'Umbro Deal' raised to the skies. They had completely wound him up.

But when Mickey Coleman stood in the dressing room berating us after that Wexford defeat, there was no light humour to be found.

He gave a big *Braveheart* speech. 'Youse all need to wake up and smell the beans, lads. Youse think you're great with your All-Ireland medals in your pockets but here's the truth – we're at nothing.'

Some lads didn't even look up, but Mickey was right. When we had calmed down the following week at training, Enda

McGinley came out and reinforced what Mickey had said. We were not fit enough. Maybe we hadn't lost the run of ourselves, but we were definitely gone soft.

In fairness we all took a look in the mirror and decided to press the reset button. There was nothing refined or fancy about what we did next – we just trained like absolute lunatics in the six weeks leading up to the Ulster Championship.

Mickey Harte brought us back to basics and that meant a stint at another agricultural college, this time outside Cookstown where we purged ourselves. It had a very basic 'school pitch' feel to it. We went back to our roots and Fergal McCann worked us tirelessly hard for six solid weeks. The ag college was the scene of another stint in hell.

But it turned out that Wexford game was the kick in the ass we needed, and that block of training would provide a crucial base for what turned out to be one of the longest All-Ireland series ever played. It took us ten games to win the All-Ireland that year. Along the way players like Mugsy hit form, McGuigan came back from Australia, Canavan got fitter, and we clicked.

We beat Down well in the first round of the Ulster Championship and drew Cavan then. I came up against one of their players and got a blunt and ruthless education on the mid-June afternoon we played them, one that would stand to me for the rest of my career.

The abuse I suffered at his hands was the worst I have ever endured. I normally stick to the 'what happens on the pitch stays on the pitch' mantra but on this occasion I carried a lot of anger and hurt off the field with me. It was a very warm Sunday and there were almost 20,000 people at the game; typical Ulster Championship stuff. I was due to start my professional exams on the following Tuesday after seven weeks of studying like a professor, rising at 6 a.m. every day to tear into the books. I thought I was on top of things – until I met a certain player.

At the throw-in we shook hands and his was a firm grip that left me in no doubt I was in for a tough afternoon. I had no 'previous' with him and I hadn't marked him before but after a bit of grabbing and pulling me off the ball, and a bit of blocking here and there, he got himself booked. I thought that might soften his cough, but it proved the opposite. As I backpedalled into position, having seen a shot go wide, he tracked me, cleared his throat, drew a hock up and spat in my face. I was shocked. I turned to the referee and said: 'Did you see that? How can you let anyone away with that?'

'I didn't see anything, Seán,' the referee replied.

Your man spat on me five or six times in that first half and each time I looked around to the referee or his linesmen, whoever was closest.

They did nothing.

'We can't do anything about anyone biting or spitting,' one of the officials robotically replied.

'What the fuck? There are 20,000 people watching – how the fuck can you see nothing or do nothing about this?'

Their man stayed at me, pinching and nipping before he actually bit me near the end of the first half as we both fell to the floor trying to ground a breaking ball. Again, I was in total shock. I went back to the official. 'Ref, this is nuts.'

I got no hop off him. In fairness to the referee, this was a typically robust Ulster Championship match and there were serious tackles being made all over the field, so he probably had lots on his plate. But I was sickened.

I went into the dressing room to gather thoughts and in Clones you walk into a changing room where eighty per cent of the space is to the left-hand side – that's normally where Mickey went to give his team talks. But I sat on the right-hand side, where there was space for hardly anyone, and I burst into tears.

I bawled, trying to hide it from my teammates, but you couldn't hide that.

'Jesus, Seán, what the fuck's going on?'

I told them, 'This isn't football, lads.'

Mickey came over to me. 'What's the deal?'

'I'm getting spat on, I've been bitten, I don't want to play this game.'

Mickey and the lads calmed me down. I had already spent most of my Tyrone career getting special attention – shoulders, elbows, knees in the back – but that was nothing. This was my first taste of spitting and biting. A few of the guys came over and put their arms around my shoulder. 'You'll be grand, we'll sort it,' they said.

Gormley came over too.

'What's the craic, boy?'

'Your man is acting the bollox with me,' I replied.

'Don't worry, we'll sort it,' Gormley goes.

And they did.

When the ball came my way at the start of the second half, Conor and I, and two Cavan lads, including my friend, all fell to the ground wrestling for possession. My eyes followed the ball but then I heard it – a big squeal from behind me. My man was howling like a hound.

We had got him back within twenty seconds of the restart

without anyone copping it. To this day I never actually asked what happened. All I know is that the lads had my back.

In the seventy-eighth minute – God only knows why there was so much injury time – Michael Lyng pointed a free after one of our lads was done for shirt pulling. Cavan got a draw. The final whistle sounded, my aggressor came over and shook my hand and instinctively I shook his.

I was still in a dark place when I offered my hand to him, but I was always taught to show respect to opponents. The following Tuesday, my exams started in Belfast, but I was still distracted from the game. I ended up failing the financial accounts exam I sat on the Tuesday. I had never before failed an exam and I never failed one again. I got through on the repeats, but I was completely thrown that weekend.

At the end of the exams one of my lecturers came over and enquired how Cavan had managed to draw with us.

'Don't worry,' I replied. 'It will be a different story this time around.'

For the replay I decided I would run the lad who was on my case ragged. He had gone out with the intention of disrupting my game as much as he possibly could, and he had succeeded.

We met again the following Saturday. A lot of the time Mickey didn't talk very much to us individually, but he came up to me that week and said: 'Get ready. You know what's coming your way.'

Fionnuala's father, Charles, was also on the case. 'Seán, you'd be far better just moving about the field non-stop, so he can't nip you. If you're continually on the move he won't get near you.'

Charles was right. I kept on moving and had one of my best games that year, setting up a goal at the very start of the game for Canavan. With my exams finished I was in a much better place and I just threw everything at my foe.

He tried a bit of crap again, but pretty quickly the game went away from Cavan and that was the end of that. Canavan was taken off to a standing ovation in the sixty-ninth minute, by which time he had chalked up 1-7 to become the highest-scoring Ulster player of all time. After such a tight and tense drawn game, the replay was played out in ceremonial fashion.

I got serious satisfaction from coming back stronger the second day. To be fair to my 'man-marker', as much as I hated him the first day, at the end of the replay he came over with his hand out. 'Seán, you're a special player, you're a serious player.' I shook his hand. Again.

The incident has never left me but anytime I met the chap after that we got on fine. He was a totally different person to the guy I encountered on the field. He was placid, friendly, very caring too, often sending me WhatsApp messages wishing me a happy Christmas and all of that. We never mentioned it again, but we have stayed in touch a bit over the years and, to be honest, I used the experience to great effect. Anytime I got crap on the pitch after that – and I got lots of it over the next twelve years – I drew on what had happened in that game. I had already experienced the worst; what else was there to worry about?

Now we had a date with Armagh in the 2005 Ulster final, a game that would be held at Croke Park due to the huge level of interest in it.

The rivalry between the two teams was still current and it had assumed an iconic status. There were already moments and exchanges between the two tribes that were destined for history, such as Gormley's late intervention which denied Steven McDonnell a potential equalising goal in the 2003 All-Ireland final. Or Oisin McConville and Stevie McDonnell firing them to a win over us in the two 2002 Ulster Championship games we played them in. We didn't know it when we squared up for the 2005 Ulster final, but we would play them twice more in the season and ultimately the legacy of the rivalry would be sorted.

As elders moved on from within the respective tribes, tensions eased. Slowly, the sores from battles of the past have healed. Well, some of them.

But, back then, the drawn and replayed 2005 Ulster finals between Armagh and Tyrone drew a combined 92,140 people to Croke Park.

The Ulster final became a national event. It was said after the season that the three Armagh–Tyrone clashes that year were the best series of games between any two counties in GAA history. I'm not sure about that; I thought they were almost too tense for that to be true and there were a huge number of unforced errors, but only because the stakes were too high, and the two sides were at their peak, fit enough to go at full pelt for seventy-five minutes plus, all over the field.

Here's a backdrop to the hostilities and complexities of that era. By the end of 2005 we had faced each other on five occasions within three years. Armagh had Ulster success in 2002, on the way to winning the All-Ireland title. A year later we faced off in the All-Ireland final and beat them by three points.

When they won, we felt they had robbed us. When we won, they reckoned we had sucker-punched them. Something had to give in 2005.

We just got better as the year went on and, prior to the Ulster final, I was confident. Everything was falling into place – everything except my wild pre-match sleeping patterns. The night before, I shared a room with Conor Gormley in the Castleknock Country Club and, initially, we were given a room just above the smoking area. It was a real warm weekend, there was no air conditioning in the room and when we left the windows open we were basically handed a front-row seat to all the entertainment in the smoking area beneath us. No way could I sleep there, so I asked for a new room. Gormley thought I was nuts but into our new digs we treaded. Eventually Conor nodded off to sleep but of course I couldn't shut the eye at all. I kept thinking about everything and anything, the normal pre-match jitters. At 2 a.m. I grabbed the keycard of the original room and reluctantly made my way down the corridor to it. Gormley got up at six to take a slash and I was nowhere to be seen. He thought I was off out walking around the estate to get fresh air. I met him then at 8 a.m. when I got back to the room after maybe one hour's sleep down the hall.

'Where the fuck were you?' He thought I had been out all night.

None of the lads really knew about my pre-match sleeping habits (or lack of); I never really went into it and always laughed it off – and that's what I did with Conor.

But later that afternoon I suffered a little on the Croke Park pitch and didn't play well. None of us were too hot, except for Stevie O'Neill, who scored 0-10 and roasted Francie Bellew in the process. But it was a low-scoring game in general, we didn't kick on and Armagh got a late goal for a draw, 2-8 to 0-14.

In the replay thirteen days later, we still didn't reach fourth gear. It was a damper day this time in Croker but temperatures were high at half-time when I had a row with Stevie – the only time I had an issue with a teammate during a game, I reckon.

We were frustrated at the break because McGeeney was sweeping up everything in front of Stevie. We wanted to get our man on the ball but each time I looked up McGeeney was there like a bollard in front of him. I tried to run at them and force it that way, but I was turned over a few times.

Stevie lost it.

'Cavanagh, you're not giving me the ball.'

'Well, I'm hardly going to try and thread it through to you with McGeeney standing in front of you, am I?' I asked.

It was pure frustration and we fucked each other out of it. Mickey Harte had never lost a replay as Tyrone manager in any grade but here we were, deep into this rematch, another big game, and we were wondering why we were not doing the business. In the second half another row kicked off – this time between ourselves and them. Within a minute of coming on Canavan was heading back to the bench, with the shirt ripped off his back, having been sent off for his part in a brawl with Ciarán McKeever. He hadn't even got to touch the ball.

With the game in the melting pot we still had a three-point lead. Next thing Stevie was sent off for a second yellow card and we were down to thirteen men. We could no longer keep them at bay and they hit five unanswered points to retain the cup. Both cards were rescinded afterwards – Stevie hadn't even been on a first yellow card, as it turned out.

There was real disappointment that night and yet that loss would prove to be another notable landmark in our lives.

Back at the hotel in Castleknock everyone was quiet and sombre as we reflected on the day. Having lost again to our big rivals, no one knew quite what to do. We congregated for some food and wondered what we would do with ourselves. Everyone had a disco shirt in their gear bags but the mood didn't seem quite high enough for us to hit the town – until Collie Holmes and a few more lads said they were off for a couple of pints.

Mickey was wild annoyed and wasn't about, so the rest of us pulled our shirts on and headed downtown for one of the greatest nights in Tyrone's history. We went mental in Dublin that night, absolutely bananas. I just remember leaving Coppers around 4 a.m. and landing back in taxis with the rest of the lads at the hotel. Inside I could see McGinley mock-wrestling with Gormley; he actually put him through a stud wall in reception at one stage.

Up I went then to the first floor of the hotel where there were people spilling out of rooms here, there and everywhere. There was a wedding party about the place as well and next thing Mugsy jumps out of one of the rooms, armed with a fire extinguisher, and soaks everyone. The craic was good, we partied until 6 a.m. until we called it a day. The Waterford hurlers were staying in the hotel that night and were playing an All-Ireland quarter final the following day and God only knows what they thought of our antics.

A bit like Greenmount Agricultural College, that ended up being the last time the Tyrone panel stayed in the Castleknock Country Club! We were barred. I'd like to say sorry to the staff, the guests and the Waterford boys for what we put them through. Yet, I look back on that evening with massive affection. We had just been beaten by our biggest rivals, but we were still there, still in the championship.

That night, just hours after being knocked off our perch,

after losing to our neighbours, our boys gathered close together and bonded. As we packed our bags and sheepishly made our way past the reception desk and onto the team bus the next day we didn't realise that the spirit and bond we had rekindled the night before would get us back on track and carry us all the way through the rest of the season undefeated.

14

EARTHQUAKE

At the start of August we locked horns with Monaghan in the last round of the qualifiers and beat them handily enough to reach an All-Ireland quarter-final against Dublin the following weekend.

The short interval between games helped us find a rhythm, and the Dublin game proved a cracker. I learned a lot that day. I struggled against Ciarán Whelan, who won five kickouts off me in the air and in doing so went to town on us during that first half. But I found ways to hurt him too, by kicking a couple of scores at the other end. There was a lesson in that. Even if your direct opponent is taking you to the cleaners in one aspect of the game there are ways to redress the balance. He was doing his bit for Dublin but I was weighing in with a shift too, albeit with a different approach.

I didn't have the natural ignorance to block opposing midfielders when contesting aerial balls – and I use the word 'ignorance' as a compliment; it's a skill to be able to fend someone off in mid-flight. So at the break I was taken off Whelan and moved to wing-forward.

We were five points down at half-time and staring into an abyss. But even in the darkest moments you may find a chink of light. I glanced around the dressing room and there was little commotion; never did we feel this game was gone from us. It helped that Mickey didn't do panic, and on such days his demeanour set the tone for the rest of us.

Big Joe McMahon was told he was going on Whelan, and as I went to take a leak in the toilet, I could see he was fit to be tied, almost pawing the floor in his eagerness to get back out there. In the toilet Enda McGinley arrived alongside and said, 'Hey, Seán, we can't go down to these boys! We'll go out now and cut loose. See what they're made of.' That about summed it up. McGinley went out and, along with Big Joe, dominated the middle. Joe snuffed out Whelan, I got going in my changed role, and we clawed our way back into it.

Midway through the half we had upped the tempo, and that's when Mugsy got the ball, took off and sold a succession of dummies as he carved through their middle. I don't know if he suspected he was en route to scoring a goal that would go down in the annals, but as he blazed a trail I sensed something special was on. And sure enough, after sending three flailing Dubs the wrong way he launched a rocket that flew past Cluxton and almost tore the rigging.

The stadium erupted, a wall of sound. It was the spark that ignited our season, and the flame would become a devouring blaze by season's end. Though not without risk of being doused along the way.

After Mugsy staked his claim to immortality we went on a

roll, hoovering up all of the breaking ball, and I assumed we would pull clear and see out the game handy enough. The Dubs even replaced Whelan. But when Bryan Cullen, Conal Keaney and Mossy Quinn hit points they regained momentum. The blue hordes found their voice again, and their players responded. Quinn grabbed the two late points, including a pressure free, and tied it up. It finished 1-14 apiece – our third drawn game in that Championship.

Back then for another replay a fortnight later. By now the games were stacking up, but what harm? Some of our key players were still only getting back to real match fitness – far from being fatigued, they needed the workload.

On the day of the replay, even as we paraded around the field before throw-in, the noise from the crowd of 82,000 took my breath away. I have never experienced an earthquake but as we passed Hill 16 it seemed the ground was trembling – a surreal experience. And when you picked out faces in the crowd, whatever the allegiance, you could read the madness and passion. They were baying for victory.

We had to do it all without Canavan, who was withdrawn shortly before throw-in with a stomach bug. Mugsy stepped up to the mark again and finished with 1-7, all but two points of it from play. I think he won every ball that came his way. He was in the zone.

His goal came midway through the second half and it seemed to deflate the Dubs; you could almost hear the air hiss out of their effort. As the flags went up, Mugsy shot a defiant glare to the Hill, and when the Hill responded with venom he lapped it all up. We cut loose in that game and beat them well in the end.

The games were now coming thick and fast – we had just seven days to rest, rehydrate, and restore aching muscles before an important date with our old friends Armagh. But thanks to the foundations laid from a crazy training regime over the previous three months we were now moving nicely through the gears.

That semi-final, in the first week of September, was in a sense the biggest and most intense game I ever played in. No question – it was bigger than any of the All-Ireland finals. At no time in my career have I gone into a game more focused than I was that day.

I had serious motivation. Myself, Philly and Ryan Mellon were nearest neighbours to the old enemy, and that was a huge factor for us, in particular. There was also the knowledge that I hadn't done myself justice in either of the Ulster finals. I needed a big one this time.

We felt this game would define a Tyrone–Armagh rivalry that had been rumbling for four years. This episode would decide the bragging rights. There was also a widespread view up north that whoever prevailed would not be stopped in their quest for an All-Ireland title. It was all on the line.

Match day. The parade; the anthem. We fanned out and took up our positions, and as the ball was thrown in, Kieran McGeeney invaded my space on the Cusack Stand side and grabbed and grappled with me, a 'friendly' foretaste of what lay ahead. He was there to keep tabs on me for the day. Another easy day at the office, I thought.

Gormley got the ball early and as he shaped to feed it to me I made to free myself from McGeeney. I stepped away, pushing off him as I did. He hit the ground with a serious roar. I paid no heed, but ran on, still looking for the pass as McGeeney tried to hunt me down. When I eventually took the ball from Gormley, I raced at my marker, shimmied him, and stuck it over from forty metres.

Running back out the field I challenged the Armagh captain: 'What's your problem?' Silence.

'What's the deal there?' I persisted, convinced he had tried to get me sent off. Still no answer.

Years later, when we had both retired and were on stage at a GAA event, I recalled the incident and knocked a bit of craic out of it by suggesting he must have been hit by a sniper. Kieran just laughed and said if it ever happened it was too far back to remember!

For me the big moment in that game, and probably the one that made my dad proud – though he would never say it publicly – was when I went full pelt at Francie Bellew, their enforcer and hard man, twenty-odd metres from their goal. Francie saw me coming down the tracks and I swear he was licking his lips – he was about to snap this Tyrone fella in two and it would turn the game.

The collision was brutal, but even though I felt I had been in a car crash I knew I had hurt him too – not that the fecker would show it – because he spilled the ball and it rolled to Enda McGinley, who cut in along the end line, chased by Aidan O'Rourke – until Aidan went down with a ripped hamstring. That left a gap in the heart of their defence, and as Stevie O'Neill was about to exploit it he was fouled in the square by Paddy McKeever. Penalty! Stevie stepped up and blasted the ball past Paul Hearty and we went three points clear.

When the goal was scored and the ball finally left Armagh's full-back line, Francie went down on one knee to get his breath back. I know because I was watching out for it. It took minutes for him to go down. He was some man!

Since we considered ourselves the more mobile unit, we felt we could run the game from there, that they would struggle to contain us, but that was never going to happen. We couldn't get away from them at all; back they came and posted three points in four minutes to draw level.

To and fro it went. We hit three points in two minutes but as we attempted to see the game out, Stevie McDonnell squeezed the ball to our net from an acute angle to put them a point up. My old school pal Ronan Clarke clipped over another and it seemed they were headed for the final. Then they took McGeeney off and the whole dynamic changed.

Once McGeeney left the stage I found space and time. Having been hardly in the game after the restart, I knew I still had ten minutes of good, strong running in me. I would throw everything I had at Armagh.

The ball was kicked out and for the first time I didn't have McGeeney's shadow trailing me. Four of us rose to the skies to contest the restart, I tapped the ball down to myself, ran onto it, raced upfield and kicked a point. Shane Sweeney followed with an equaliser. We went from the cliff edge of defeat, trailing by two points in the dying minutes, to having the freedom of the park. I was able again to gather high ball in midfield. I had eight possessions in those last ten minutes alone, and six times I ran at the heart of the Armagh defence.

At the very end Collie Holmes took off on a solo down the Cusack Stand side. I came looking for it. Confidence soaring, I was going to shimmy, get into open space and hit the winner. Instead, Stevie O'Neill came out from inside and demanded the ball. Collie gave it to him – and Stevie was fouled. Free! Last kick of the game.

Mugsy had been on frees all day and had been doing well. He had three points to his name, two from the spot, but no offence to Mugsy, I didn't even look to him when that free was awarded. I looked around for Canavan and saw him on his knees back in midfield, shattered and breathless after a heavy collision. You might think there was nothing left in him, but this was Peter Canavan. There was never a moment in his life when he ran out of tricks or fuel. He was still the best bet to put that ball over the bar. I ran to midfield, grabbed him by the shirt and yanked him up.

'You're taking this!'

'No, Seán, Mugsy has been hitting them. Give him the ball.'

'Peter, you're hitting that fucking free if I have to march you down there myself.'

He was reluctant, but I laid it on heavy, told him his team needed him. I walked him up the field like a teacher bringing a truant boy to the headmaster's office. I brought him to where Stevie had been fouled, out on the left, facing into the Canal End, and left him there to get his head together.

As Peter gingerly gathered himself, Mugsy walked out from corner-forward with the ball, looked at Canavan, his former schoolteacher, and smiled. 'I don't mind, Peter. I don't mind.'

Canavan hardly engaged with Mugsy; he kept his head down and just took the ball. Paddy Russell, the referee, walked over to him, most likely to say his kick would be the last. I looked up at the scoreboard: 1-12 apiece; seventy-two minutes gone. This was indeed it.

Canavan pulled back a few metres, edging toward the sideline, composed himself and arced toward the spot. On the fifth step he let the ball off his right foot and sent it curling sweetly over the bar. The pressure he must have been under!

Mugsy, the form he was in, might well have pointed that free anyway, but really, in that moment, with so much at stake, Canavan was the obvious man to take it. We trusted him so much, that extraordinary, unwavering strength of character, and it was his moment.

Paul Hearty sent a huge kickout booming upfield, but as he did, Russell blew for full time. We went nuts. Philly jumped into my arms as I started weeping. Typical Peter, he was shaking hands with his marker, Enda McNulty, and Hearty too, before he even celebrated.

We had just seen football at its most intense. The whole country had. Sure, the game was pockmarked with unforced errors but that was down to the ferocity of both sides. There was joy unconfined but more than anything there was the relief of beating them. Our greatest rivals.

We had twenty-one days to get that win out of our system, dissect it all, and get back down to earth. And thank God for that respite! Because it did take time for us to come back to earth. I didn't yelp too loudly with joy because I was seriously sore after my encounter with Francie. To be honest, for the three-week lead-in to the All-Ireland final I could hardly train. I suspect Francie struggled too – I heard he missed a few club games around that time, although few people would have made the link between his injury and our coming together – he was too proud to let anything like that be known.

For the final, against Kerry, we felt that with all the games we had played we would be fitter. Having seen Armagh as the biggest threat back then it was nearly a relief to play Kerry in the final. The final was a good game, but the semi-final was the most intense and satisfying win that I ever had, so the Kerry game didn't completely blow me away. Still, I can see how neutrals might now see it that way.

They got an early goal but it didn't really annoy us too much – we had been behind to Dublin, Armagh and Monaghan in knockout games and won, so we were kind of immune to panic.

We were relaxed and I think we showed everyone our range of skills and passing on All-Ireland day. Mindful of how good their forwards were, we aimed to keep things tight at the back, and thankfully for us, much of the game was played out in the middle third of the field. Kerry kept passing when we thought they might drive direct, long balls into their forwards. They got bogged down around the middle and we tackled like madmen, turned them over, and counter-attacked at speed.

It was a natural, fluid performance and we had seven different scorers. We outfought Kerry to such an extent they managed only two points in the second quarter. We got to land a sucker punch just before the break when Peter took a sublime handpass from Mugsy without having to break stride and placed a low, slide-rule shot past Declan O'Keeffe. Even though there was still a whole half of football to play, that effectively was the game for us, in my opinion.

Mugsy got five points for us that afternoon and Peter hit a goal and a point. By the time that Canavan got that goal in the first half we were starting to feel really confident.

We hadn't scored a goal in the 2003 final and, in fact, Paudge Quinn had been the only Tyrone player to ever score a goal in an

All-Ireland final back in 1986. That made Canavan's goal even more important because it gave us a bigger lift than expected. It was also only Canavan's second start of that season and the fact that we all looked up to him just made it sweeter still. After he goaled I never thought for a second that we would lose. It felt like destiny was calling us home.

He sent us on our way. Stevie and Ryan Mellon were also in flying form and weighed in with great scores. Still, the margin was only three points in the end.

That final was our tenth Championship game of the year but by the end of it we were the ones physically and mentally sharper. Our strength came from the extent and intensity of our preparation. It had to be that way. The game was seen as a clash of cultures between ourselves, the 'puke footballers', and Kerry, with their glorious heritage of thirty-three All-Irelands. Maybe we silenced a few critics with that win and maybe we didn't. It didn't bother us – we were too busy trying to win another title.

Great and all as it was to win a second All-Ireland medal, the sound of the final whistle in that game was bittersweet for me. The team had won and that was the main thing. But did I play my part? I did okay, but I was annoyed that, for the second time, I had failed to score in an All-Ireland final. Growing up, I had looked on every September and imagined what it would be like to score in a final.

I knew in 2005 my chances would be few and slim – I was marking Darragh Ó Sé and that would bring its own pressures. Just as Whelan had done, Darragh beat me in the air, but again I didn't panic, nor did I see any shame in that. I thought I would beat him on the ground, and maybe I did. I certainly got plenty of ball, hit a post and struck a couple of wides. But I also had to look on as Darragh hit two points for Kerry, including a scuffed shot off his left foot that could have gone anywhere. When he hit that one I just wondered, Why is this not happening for me? Am I jinxed not to score in an All-Ireland final?

In my head this was a huge thing. When Philly raced upfield and grabbed a score I said to myself, *Hang on here! Jordan never feckin' scores*.

Philly spent many an evening winding me up over that one. Whenever he spotted the opportunity the question would invariably come out: 'But have you ever scored in an All-Ireland final, Seán?'

'Feck off, Philly!'

It drove me wild. I know it may seem selfish but to me it touched on the essence of the game. You want to play well on the big days, for yourself and for the team. And for me, part of my job description was about grabbing scores. There was validation there. And so there was a bit of disappointment from that 2005 final.

I suppose I had little to be complaining about. I ended up with another All-Ireland medal and a third All Star in a row, but when you're in the middle of it all, this is the madness that flows inside.

Anyway, I got some perspective when we went back up the road the following day and Mickey and Dooher took a detour with Sam Maguire to visit Cormac's grave. It meant a lot to the lads that Cormac got to 'see the cup' before it reached the masses in the big towns like Omagh. It was a lovely touch.

Dooher had kept Cormac very much in mind all the way through that campaign. Not that he spoke much about him or often showed his emotions. But at the final whistle against Kerry it hit him and Dooher cried openly. That's what Cormac meant to him. Nobody overplayed it in 2005, but our fallen hero was a quiet presence at every landmark we reached on that amazing journey.

15

OZ CALLING

When we lost to Armagh in the 2005 Ulster final, Fionnuala was ten thousand miles away in Brisbane, on an undergraduate medical student placement; shortly after the game she sent me a hard luck text. My response was blunt to the point of ignorance: *I'm sure you're not too disappointed.* One line. A full stop at the end. Childish, I know, and something I still regret.

During her three months in Australia we kept in touch via phone calls, text messages, cards – just as you'd expect – but whenever football was mentioned I refused to give her the benefit of the doubt. Fionnuala was from Armagh and that was the end of it. I just couldn't see, in that context, how she would be looking out for me.

Unbelievable in hindsight, but that's the way I was wired and that was what losing to Armagh brought out in me. Because Fionnuala's family were Armagh to the core, I identified her as an easy target and almost took it out on her when we lost. Mind you, whenever we did manage to beat them I gave her a different kind of grief, banging on enthusiastically about the game, driving her mad.

When she came home in mid-August she was full of positive impressions of Australia; she'd loved her time there. Brisbane, she told me, would be a great place to live. And to add to the attractions the Aussies were offering crazy money to get qualified doctors to Brisbane.

That period of our lives was a revolving door because, coincidentally, the Aussie rules agent Gerard Sholly had been sounding me out over a possible move to the AFL.

It was nothing much at the start; he made a few calls and sent me some bits of gear and an Aussies rules football, which Colm and I kicked around on the Moy pitch. I found it easy enough to adapt to the oval ball but I got back to Gerard, told him I was going to focus fully on Tyrone for the year ahead and that I might look again at the lie of the land come the end of the season. At least that was the plan.

News of Sholly's overtures soon made the sports pages and it didn't sit too well with Mickey at a time when we were still trying to get back off the ropes and fight for another All-Ireland. The Australian newspapers reported that the Brisbane Lions had tabled an offer for me to join them later in the year and wanted me to spend a month or two in the city after the international rules tour. All of that was true but the speculation grew legs. A Melbourne newspaper, *The Age*, claimed I had already signed. There were follow-up stories every other day.

Some journalists at home dug a little bit deeper and reported that, four years earlier, between the drawn All-Ireland minor final with Dublin and the replay, five Tyrone players, including myself, had been invited to trials organised by Sholly in Dublin.

I had almost forgotten that episode, but in any case I hadn't turned up – I just wasn't interested at the time.

The hype about Brisbane didn't bother me greatly; I was still genuinely focused on Tyrone. But Mickey, a trenchant opponent of links between the GAA and the AFL, was having to field a succession of calls from journalists when he had better things to do. And that wasn't lost on me – I was aware the Tyrone set-up could have done without the distraction at that stage of the season. I was glad to get back to playing football, and put thoughts of Brisbane aside as we stormed to our second All-Ireland win.

After the dust had settled on our victory, I had a club championship to focus on. I was also under pressure to give Brisbane an answer. The international rules series was coming up and the Aussies said they needed to know where I stood before their pre-season started in November.

Soon after the All-Ireland win, Moy played and lost to Errigal Ciarán in the Tyrone quarter-final. Before the game I got a call from Ger Sholly, and an hour after the game he and Graeme Allen, the Brisbane Lions general manager, were sitting at our kitchen table.

'We really want you in Australia, mate,' said Sholly. 'You can definitely make a great career with us.'

I told them Fionnuala had been in Brisbane and loved it. They had come a long way to see me and that revelation put more fuel in their tank.

'We'll get her a job in Brisbane General Hospital, mate,' they replied as the eyes almost popped out of their heads. 'No worries!'

They handed me a contract form: a two-year deal as an international rookie, worth AUS$120,000. I would have eight designated coaches, free accommodation, a car, medical insurance. They would also pay for my parents to fly over on annual visits. The contract was signed by Michael Bowes, Brisbane's CEO. I wondered was this an offer too good to refuse.

Colm Begley and Brendan Quigley of Laois had both signed two-year rookie contracts with Brisbane around that time, joining a growing Irish contingent Down Under. Tadhg Kennelly had become the first Irishman to win a Premiership title, with the Sydney Swans, while Setanta and Aisake Ó hAilpín were on the rookie roster at the Melbourne-based Carlton Blues.

'We'd love to have you, mate – get back to us soon as you can,' said Allen as he and Sholly hit the road. They said they would look at me during Ireland's two tests against Australia in late October. I just reiterated that I would need time to think it over.

Mickey was one of the first people I rang for advice. He called to the house, sat down with me and helped me draw up a list of pros and cons. Of course, Mickey didn't like Aussie Rules, didn't like the GAA having any involvement with the Aussies at all, so in hindsight – and I say this with great respect – maybe he was the wrong man to help me weigh things up. Over the years I feel that he did influence a few Tyrone lads not to attend the international rules trials but I loved the game too much to really care what he thought. When he would say something derogatory about it, I would always be keen to bounce something back in jest. It didn't make me flavour of the month but, again, I didn't really mind. By the end of our summit meeting we had about five pros and seventy cons. For every pro I mentioned Mickey had at least three cons!

'There's a chance to be a professional here, Mickey.'

'Sure, aren't you at the elite level here and about to become an accountant too? Look how hard you've worked.'

'It would be nice to test myself in a different country, Mickey.'

'But it's not your home country, Seán.'

Fair play to him, he had an answer for everything!

Fionnuala was more diplomatic. She left me to make my own mind up. She loved the Aussie way of life, but she did say that no matter what I decided she was going to finish her training in Ireland and would complete the degree between fourth and fifth year at Queen's University. That took some of the wind from my sails.

Mickey also said something that weighed heavily: I could be a legend in Gaelic Games. It's true that I wanted to leave a legacy. I was a confident young lad with two All-Irelands and three All Stars and I wanted more; to be mentioned in the same breath as others who had achieved great things. I liked the sound of that. I was restless to achieve more. Never content to sit back and reflect on past feats.

I hemmed and hawed over the move, gave it plenty of thought, but I doubt my heart was ever in it. Eventually I made the call to stay put and I don't regret it. Once I made my mind up I can say from the heart that I never again thought about it.

The one thing I would have done differently is how I relayed the decision to Brisbane. They were so nice to me, so unbelievably sound and helpful, and I didn't have the balls to phone them and tell them myself. When it comes to saying 'no', I'm a big coward at the best of times, and I found it especially hard to reject them.

I went to Uncle Seán and told him I wasn't going to do the Oz thing but couldn't bring myself to tell them. I took the easy way out: 'Would you mind making the call for me?'

I'm still embarrassed about it. I should have given them the respect of lifting the phone myself, but I didn't have the balls. I really should have told them straight from the start – there was no way I could ever leave Tyrone.

While a permanent move Down Under was never really on the cards, I got to scratch that itch for a few years when I was invited to play for the international rules series. As I write this, the series stands at ten wins apiece, and while the code and the collisions are not everyone's cup of grog – including among the Tyrone hierarchy – I enjoyed most of the international rules games I played in.

I loved the game ever since I was first called into the 2003 provisional squad by John O'Keeffe. We stayed in the Citywest while we trialled, Hub Hughes and myself sharing a room, and as we lay up watching snooker and chatting about the crazy days and nights of partying since our All-Ireland win against Armagh twelve days earlier, a knock came to the door and Hub answered it. It was Kieran McGeeney.

A bit flustered, I jumped up from the bed, wearing only boxers. Hub too was startled by the arrival of the great man. We were two young messers and he was not only a legend of the game but also the leader of our fiercest rivals and not someone with whom we would take liberties at the best of times.

After a few seconds of awkward silence, Kieran shook our hands and congratulated us on the All-Ireland win. I reckon it took serious character to do what he did. If the boot had been on the other foot and we had lost that game, I probably would have blanked every Armagh rival for six months. Even then I was thinking this must really be killing the fella – but it was the mark of the man.

When Kieran left the room, Hub and I were like giddy kids, hardly able to believe he had actually made the effort to meet us and chat to us as equals and comrades. That's what the international rules did: it brought together deadly rivals and allowed them to get acquainted and even become friends.

I took a bang during the trial the following day, played only twenty minutes of it, and ended up not making the squad, which disappointed me. Hub did make the cut and by all accounts thoroughly enjoyed himself in Oz. I doubt he was overburdened with the pressure of it all.

Fast forward to 2004, with the series at home. There were several standout moments but one I remember in particular. I was sharing a room in the Citywest with Ciaran McManus, lying on the bed eating sandwiches and, for dessert, a huge bag of Starburst sweets. Next thing Ciaran goes into Mr Universe mode, doing press-ups, dips, abdominal isolations, striking poses, and using the furniture as props. He was a beast of a man with muscles on his muscles and I didn't know whether to laugh or cry as he strutted and flexed.

Like Ciaran, I always saw the positive in playing for Ireland, even though there were a couple of episodes that threatened to turn me off the whole concept too.

In 2005 I got on a flight, having finally made the squad under Pete McGrath. But it was a pretty poor set-up. There were seven Tyrone players involved and we were motivated enough, but even we eased back on the throttle when it became clear the series win was beyond us.

The game that year in Melbourne in which Philly Jordan almost got decapitated by Chris Johnson was a disgrace. At the end of that farce I clearly wasn't in my right mind because somehow I swapped jerseys with Johnson instead of telling him where to sling it. Sad to say, we were well beaten both in terms of the match and the fight that year.

That was also slap bang during all the talk that year of me heading to the Brisbane Lions, and in Perth and Melbourne, two AFL heartlands, I was stopped in the street several times by Aussies looking for photos and a chat. I was used to that back home and didn't mind it but getting recognised thousands of miles away was strange.

Another game that rankled was the 2006 meeting at Croke Park where, from the throw-in, the Aussies kicked forty shades out of us and were let away with everything by the alleged umpires.

In 2006 McGeeney and I played together in the Galway test, which we won. There's a great photo of the two of us exchanging a high-five at the end of the game – a collector's item and significant, as we had marked one another in the 2005 All-Ireland semi-final, and let's just say there was no mutual whooping and backslapping that day. But I enjoyed the 'two enemies coming together' theme, and after all was said and done, we were there to win together for Ireland. I never said it to him, but I saw lots of McGeeney's traits in myself, and also in Cormac.

On the Tuesday after the 2008 All-Ireland final, Seán Boylan phoned, inviting me to join the international rules squad again. I told Seán I'd be with him soon.

The Irish squad was training that Friday night at Parnell Park and I happened to be in Dublin at a GPA gig that day, so I waited around for the trial match and arrived in Donnycarney as the caretaker was opening the gates. I was that keen to get going.

Seán and a couple of his kids arrived soon after and he seemed both surprised and happy to see me so soon after the great day. That was my first time to meet him, and we got on from the introductory handshake like a house on fire. In my book this man goes down as one of the most genuine people I have known and I still love meeting him. I like to think my being there so early and eager – and showing up for the trial so soon after the greatest moment in my career – impressed him in turn. Most All-Ireland finalists take time off, whether to drink in the glory or to lick wounds, but I was just honoured to be called up and couldn't wait to start.

Despite my eagerness I wasn't on the plane when the main group took off for Perth; Moy were playing Trillick in the Tyrone intermediate final the following afternoon, a Sunday, and I had to be involved.

That was such a frustrating day for me and the team. Colm got sent off early in the first half, they fouled us for fun, and against a strong breeze I struggled to convert frees. Despite dominating possession and territory, we lost by a point, and the same evening I was in a car headed for Dublin airport and placed on a long-haul flight to Oz in the middle of the night. Happy in a way to be putting that game behind me and turning over a new leaf.

Because I flew to Perth later than the rest of the 2008 squad, Seán Boylan put me up in a penthouse suite of the Duxton Hotel while teammates slummed it below in standard rooms. I got a fair bit of stick about that but the trimmings that came with the room with a view – fresh fruit brought up every day, silk bedsheets turned down and chocolates on the pillow – drowned out the sledging.

The games in Australia that year were special, particularly

the one in Perth – it attracted a full house and Seán made me captain. I stood there, singing 'Amhrán na bhFiann' as leader of my country's team and it still counts as one of my proudest moments. We had a good innings against the Aussies; we won the series by five points, a huge achievement in their front yard. And as the winter of 2008 roared in I returned from Australia with the Cormac McAnallen Cup in hand. That meant the world to me.

I look back on all those series knowing I made genuine friends. In 2008 I shared a room with Graham Canty of Cork and we got on great, despite needing an interpreter to translate each other's accents. We still keep in touch.

For the 2013 series the Tyrone County Board scheduled a relegation match with Eglish in the Moy on the same day we played the first rules game in Cavan. You could hardly make it up. I was assured by Róisín Jordan, head of fixtures – and also from Eglish, by the way – that I should have no bother making Breffni Park for the 7 p.m. throw-in, seeing as the Moy game was at 2 p.m. and, even in the worst case scenario, should be over by 4 p.m.!

It was time for lateral thinking. On the eve of the games I had a few club stalwarts do some essential pitch watering and instructed them not to hold back. The lads were still there at 3 a.m. pumping the contents of the Blackwater River onto the Moy pitch. Not surprisingly, when it was discovered the following morning that the place was more suitable for a swimming gala than a football game, the match was rescheduled for the following Tuesday night above in Garvaghey. Better still, we won.

16

BROKEN TEAM

Leaving home for good would always have been too much for the heartstrings but getting away for a few months from the whole county football bubble was something different. That notion of running off for a while, escaping the goldfish bowl, greatly appealed to me.

That's why I found myself in Chicago in the summer of 2006.

We were dumped out of the Championship by Laois in the middle of July. It was a shocking display, coming at the butt-end of a torturous season.

All year we had talked the talk, about being a 'great' team and how back-to-back titles would guarantee immortality and silence our critics for good. We had resolved we would learn from 2004, when we had been found out by Mayo in the All-Ireland quarter-final. This time we were determined to put things right. Mickey insisted from the start of the year that we were headed for the two-in-a-row, and we had no reason to disbelieve him.

Shortly before we played Derry in the Ulster Championship game, Mickey and his assistant, Tony Donnelly, unveiled their new-fangled attack formation: a four-man diamond. The problem was, the players struggled to buy into it. For one thing, it was too close to the game itself for tactical innovation. And for another thing, we were All-Ireland champions, for fuck's sake, and playing on our home patch – we wanted to take on Derry in a shootout!

Just a few months earlier we had beaten a great Kerry team and we, the players, saw no reason to change our shape for the Derry challenge. But when even our senior lads questioned the new strategy we were assured it was fit for purpose and that was the way we were going to go.

As it transpired, we were a shambles and the season turned out to be an abysmal failure. I doubt the new formation was entirely to blame for our humiliation. For sure we were unhappy with the set-up and I think we played like we were uneasy with it, albeit subconsciously, but we were simply awful in every department and, no matter what tactics were used, we would not have won. From the throw-in Derry rolled up their sleeves and bullied us all over the field, and our response hardly got beyond passive; we seemed to lie down early in that game and never really got up.

Fair play to Mickey for trying something new, but we hadn't enough time to rehearse the system. They beat us out our own gate.

We scraped past Louth at the second attempt in the qualifiers and we were woefully poor in both games. The sky was falling. Before extra time in the drawn game – and with our hopes dangling by the referee's whistle – I saw, for the first time ever, Mickey Harte stuck for words. I still see him standing there that night. He looked to be in shock at how far we had fallen. He was trying to galvanise us but I don't think he knew what to say. There was little he could say, really. We were a broken team and we all knew it.

It didn't help that we lost some of our leaders. That season we lost three key forwards. McGuigan and Stevie O'Neill were injured, and Canavan had retired. Peter was the biggest loss of all. I doubted Tyrone could win an All-Ireland without him. Genuinely.

Chris Lawn had packed it in too. Peter and Chris. Two voices of reason, men that always kept the dressing room honest, men who would talk with Mickey as equals on our behalf.

So, while we went onto the pitch that year as reigning All-Ireland champions, our officer class was depleted. If opponents analysed us forensically they could have seen we were vulnerable without those leaders.

Derry knew that and made a rabble of us. Louth twigged it too and almost beat us. When Laois got us on their home turf in O'Moore Park we finally ran out of road. We scored only six points against them – one measly point more than we had managed against Derry in the Ulster Championship a few months earlier. We were out with a whimper.

Looking back, we were completely dogged by injuries and bad luck around this period and maybe in 2006 we just didn't have the same hunger. We didn't have enough men there to rally the troops either and I ended up giving that extra-time team talk against Louth in Navan just to try and get out of there with a win. We were low on confidence and some of the lads had their heads down and I felt someone had to talk.

On the bus back from Portlaoise after the Laois game, my

phone vibrated, not once but several times. American numbers; expats – already aware that I was now a free agent – looking for me to go out there and play for the summer. I took every call, listened to their pitch, and decided I needed to get away if only for the sake of my sanity. I was twenty-three and had devoted eight years to Tyrone with hardly a breather. Great times, but repetitive enough and often stressful. I was stale and could do with a change of air.

Chicago Wolfe Tones were the first to make contact and I liked what they had to say, but the phone kept ringing and by the time we reached the Red Cow I found myself the object of a bidding war.

Wolfe Tones offered to fix me up in a job that would pay $12,000 for the two months. Then the Ulster club in San Francisco more or less matched that offer. Two New York clubs threw bids into the ring. I gave them all a similar answer – I was too raw at that moment to commit and needed a few days to mull it all over. At the same time, there was a deadline for temporary US transfers and I was right up against it.

If I made the leap I wanted to go with a pal, or at least someone whose company I enjoyed. And so I mentioned the idea to Brendy Donnelly from Eglish and he was all for it. After promising I would try to swing it for him I telephoned Chicago:

'Brendy's a wing-back. He's on the Tyrone panel – a handy player.'

'Aye then, Seán, we'll take him too,' they said.

'Brilliant! Okay, we'll join ye!'

We played Laois on a Saturday night and on the following Monday night I agreed to go to Chicago and play for Wolfe

Tones. Payment for the day job had been ramped up to $15,000. It was a no-brainer.

A few weeks later, I sat back on my deckchair basking in forty degrees heat and sipping a cold beer. The woes of Tyrone football and the Portlaoise debacle that horrible evening were a distant and fading memory. The only taxing question was whether to go for the burger or chicken at Castaways Bar. What flavour ice cream would I have for afters? Did I need a larger sun umbrella?

I loved it there and was totally at peace. I only wish I had gone over earlier, and more often, during my playing career.

North Avenue Beach, on the shore of Lake Michigan, is a real hot spot, a magnet for all sorts of characters and a colourful microcosm of the city's social and cultural life. In that summer of 2006 I popped down there every opportunity I got, blending in with bikers, joggers, chancers, fitness walkers and roller-bladers streaming along the lakefront trail. But I was well out of step with those athletic specimens in pursuit of the body beaut-iful. Instead I would gravitate toward the twenty-somethings partying on the beach, the beers on ice, the jazz band that played throughout the day.

All around there were roller-hockey games, dodgeball tourna-ments, aerobic classes, yoga sessions going on. I thought briefly about getting a pick-up game somewhere – but nah, it was way too much effort!

As soon as Brendy and I landed in Chicago we were put up in the basement of Val McMahon's lovely family home. Val, a Meathman, had married an American, a lovely woman, Heather. They treated us like VIPs and we had a summer to remember.

The day jobs were hardly onerous. Let's just say we didn't

get worked to exhaustion. Occasionally I was asked to take a pick-up truck and make collections or deliveries around the city. That done, it was hit the beach and mingle.

I was out there for eight weeks and we played only three matches in that time. We had training sessions, of course, but it left us with a huge amount of free time – something of which I had really no experience.

One of the lads in the Moy had a bar in New Orleans and we took off there for three days. Four of us hit Las Vegas for a few days as well.

Ger Cavlan and Mugsy were also in Chicago, playing for St Brendan's, but the fierce rivalry between Wolfe Tones and Brendan's dictated that we saw little of them – fraternising with the enemy was discouraged!

Wolfe Tones had some team. About ten county players in total, including Owen Lennon from Monaghan, Brian Mulvihill from Tipperary, Graham Geraghty, Brendy and myself. We won not only the local championship but also the North American Championship. And we had massive fun along the way, cruising around much of the time in the old space wagon lent to us by the club.

As for Val and Heather, their hospitality and kindness knew no limits. They gave us the run of the basement apartment, which had satellite TV with all the bells and whistles and a separate entrance so we could come and go as we pleased.

We would leave sports gear and street clothes in the wash basket and all our stuff would come back spotless and ironed. We had a fully stocked fridge below, and yet Val and Heather – and their kids, Shelby and Fiona – would invite us upstairs to share their table, often for three meals a day.

It was a life of luxury. We would hang at the beach until seven most evenings, then head home for a bit of grub and draw up a plan of action for the night ahead. We spent hardly a dollar.

I would recommend a sabbatical like that to anyone stuck in a rut or a bubble or a revolving door. Just to get away from it all. I didn't once read a paper or watch a match on TV when I was there. Normally I'd be living my life around the club championships and the All-Ireland, but out there I didn't give a tinker's curse who was playing or who won.

Early one morning in Chicago, my phone beeped as my cousin, Oonagh, a Tyrone woman living in Armagh, texted me with the news, and a big 'Yahoo!' at the end of it, that Kerry had beaten Armagh in the All-Ireland final. I just texted 'Happy days' and fell back asleep. I couldn't even get worked up about our biggest rivals getting their comeuppance.

Looking back, I see clearly that the only times during my Tyrone career when I was truly relaxed and at peace were that summer cameo in the USA and two periods of convalescence from long-term injury.

As I packed my bags at the end of that summer and flew out of Chicago on a cool Tuesday morning, I knew I would soon be drawn into that maelstrom again.

When I got back to the Moy and walked into the house, Mummy looked at me and her jaw dropped.

'What in the name of God has happened you?'

'What do you mean, Mummy?'

'You're fading away, Seán!'

I had never even thought about that. Throughout 2005 and 2006 I had felt heavy, sluggish even, and the on-field collisions

The most important people in the world to me, in our garden. Here, nothing else matters.

Fionnuala. She has been a huge inspiration around everything I have achieved.

Baby Seán – I can't wait to watch him grow and fulfil his dreams the way I got to live mine.

Baby Seán with me and Fionnuala.

Clara and Eva. I have some great memories of them in historic football grounds, which I will hold dear for the rest of my days. Perhaps the most exciting day in Croke Park came after we lost to Dublin in 2017. They knew then I would have no more training in Garvaghy and Omagh, and that they would have 'Daddy Time' now. It's long overdue.

My parents' mantelpiece – a small collection of the early years crystal and china; the rest is still in boxes in my attic.

Man of the Match crystal from the All Ireland final of 2008 – the day I reached the top of my sport.

Some of the All Star Player of the Year awards at Mum and Dad's. The team was always first, but I was blessed to gain a lot of individual recognition and awards through my career. These were the cream on top of the cake.

All-Ireland medals are precious. Mine sit in my parents' house.

The stand at Moy football pitch. The club has just grown and grown.

The posts at Moy football pitch –
I spent long hours dissecting those
and kicking points here. I loved
being on my own practising. It
gave me huge peace.

Me overlooking the pitch, where I learned to play
the game. I owe so much to the Moy.

'The Walk' – I walked from the Moy Square down along the riverbanks to clear my head after the May game in 2016.

As you have read, I continued walking for quite some time!

Our basketball net on the front street of my parents' house – where I spent late nights duelling with Colm and Adrian and whoever else was about.

The 'Moy Bridge' and the River Blackwater – separates Tyrone and Armagh. I crossed it to gain an education and met Fionnuala, so it has been good to me!

The next few pictures depict the inclusive, community feel that the Moy has despite its people coming from different backgrounds. Here is the Moy Catholic Church.

The Church of Ireland in Moy Square.

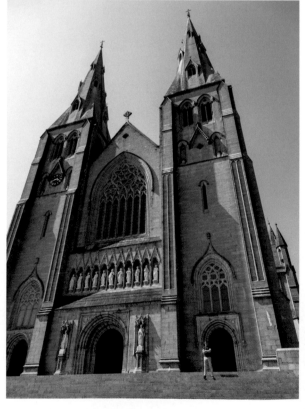

Me in front of Armagh Cathedral, near my school. St Patrick's Grammar Armagh is located on 'Sandy Hill', a few metres from the Cathedral.

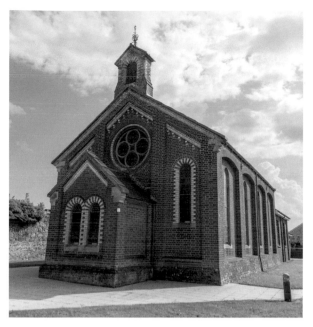

The Methodist Church, yards from Jockey Lane.

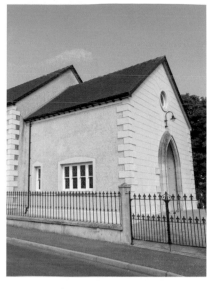

Moy Presbyterian Church, at the end of Jockey Lane, where we lived.

Our proud dad with his three sons on the pitch
after winning the Tyrone Championship.

Bringing home the bacon! The Tyrone, Ulster and All-Ireland trophies at
Moy Parochial Hall, just a few metres from our home.

At work: my office in the Moy.

were taking more and more out of me. Over in the US, in the sweltering heat, I had slimmed dramatically. I hopped on the scales. Eleven stone thirteen pounds. The lightest I had been since the age of fifteen.

Mummy, concerned I might fall down from malnutrition, hurried into the kitchen to rustle up a proper Irish breakfast, and after making short work of it I hit the bed for a few hours' sleep. That evening I was back training with the Moy.

Philly spotted me and let a roar: 'Jesus, Cavanagh! Everyone else goes to the US, cuts loose and puts on a ton of weight. But you come home looking like you've been through a famine!'

And that was it. My brief escape from the bubble was over. Before long, I almost forgot what Chicago was about, the easy way of life I had over there, the absence of all my worries and strife.

I regaled Colm with stories of our adventure. He fell in love with Chicago there and then and has been talking ever since about following in my stud marks for Wolfe Tones. When I retired in 2017 we both flew to Chicago as guests for their end-of-year function. Colm reiterated then how he would love to spend more time there, but he'll be doing well – he has Levina and Chloe, his wife and daughter, to look out for.

Within a few weeks of my return home, the call to arms sounded once more. But again I sensed a kind of emptiness in the Tyrone set-up. I didn't see many young lads coming through. The likes of Raymie Mulgrew had potential, but there weren't too many more.

It felt like déjà vu. We were doing the same things, playing the same way; still minus Chris Lawn and Canavan; Stevie still struggling with the knee; Dooher was injured for spells too. McGuigan had an eye problem in 2006 and broke a leg in 2007.

One day I bumped into Enda McNulty, our Armagh rival from over the road, and we stopped for a chat.

'What sort of gym stuff are youse boys doing these times?' he asked.

I couldn't tell a lie. The truth was we were doing little or no gym training. We told people all along we weren't big into weights and that was the reality.

Philly had managed to cog a weights programme from somewhere and he and I decided we would follow it to the hilt in the modest surrounds of the Moy gym. Philly is one hundred per cent focused on all he does anyway, so there were no shortcuts in the gym with him. But that was about it. As a squad we had no collective or individual schedules or targets. And so we made mistakes.

That's maybe why I bulked up too much in 2006. Lacking expert guidance, I overdid the bench presses, the curls, the squats, and I was carrying the ballast. But after Chicago I was two stone lighter. I had fluctuated wildly and it took a bit out of me. I felt I was drifting.

We did win Ulster in 2007 but it all rang a bit hollow for me. I doubted we could go further. Again Canavan was the missing linchpin – I didn't think we could go the distance without him. We beat Fermanagh, Donegal and Monaghan in Ulster, but we missed him. Chris too.

The great thing about Peter and Chris was, they would get an extra five or ten per cent out of you in training and on match day, but they could have the craic as well. In training they would do all the stuff the younger lads did and more, and then they would head out for pints. They were our leaders and the set-up felt strange without them.

The night before our All-Ireland quarter-final with Meath, Stevie and I watched *Match of the Day* in our room at Carton House. Stevie had been struggling with injury for a long time and he was tearing himself apart.

'All set for tomorrow, Stevie?'

'Nah, Seán, I'm not.'

The expectation for the following day was that he would come on in the hour of need and work his magic by splitting the posts or pinching a goal. That's a nice weight to have on your shoulders, especially when a man isn't fully right.

'I don't want to be here,' he said. 'My knees are not right, Seán.'

Because Stevie was vital to our chances, Mickey had asked him to hang on in, see how the knees might hold up, maybe hope for a miracle. And now Stevie was feeling brutal pressure to perform and he only half fit.

That was something I could relate to. There was always that burden to be fit and ready to get on the pitch and do it for Tyrone. If you were unavailable, not part of that group that was good to go, you need not expect much communication or comfort from anyone. You were either in or out.

Turns out even Stevie couldn't save us the next day. No disrespect to Meath but we saw ourselves as their superiors. As usual, Mickey had us convinced they would be only a speed bump on the road to glory. I still don't know how he does it, but as vulnerable as we were, I was utterly sure we would win.

In fairness we had a few guys showing form: Ryan Mellon, Colm McCullagh, Raymie. But we butchered chances at vital times, and when Graham Geraghty flicked a ball over John Devine's head and into the net the game went from us. We lost by two points.

I trudged into the dressing room and slumped in a corner, wondering if this was how it would be from now. Without our main men we were a flaky bunch. Worse still, emerging talent was thin on the field.

The brother Colm was one of the few showing real potential. His arrival on the scene was about the best thing that happened to me that year; it meant a huge deal to have him in the panel.

Sadly, when he first came in, the narrative around him was negative enough: 'He's not good enough to play for Tyrone. He's only there because he's Seán's brother. Not mobile enough. Can play in only one position. No good to you if there's no ball coming in.'

Colm struggled with all that rubbish. He had fared well as a minor, playing at full-forward before reinventing himself as an out-and-out midfielder.

Mickey employed him at full-forward when he broke onto the Tyrone seniors, but by then we were running the ball into attack and he wasn't getting the service on which he thrived as a minor. Still I couldn't believe the doubters. Yeah, I was his best friend and he is the closest person to me on the planet, but I knew better than anyone how good he was.

Mind you, the first game he played in 2007 was a disaster. After lining out on the edge of the square against Fermanagh he rose for a high ball, fell on his neck, and was stretchered off on a spinal board. I remember walking to where he lay and struggling to deal with it. There was my wee brother with an oxygen mask on him and the stretcher waiting to be slid under him.

Colm recovered well over the next few weeks and having him around made 2007 easier to handle. All through that year I was highly protective of him, and there were training-ground incidents when I was away like a bull looking for retribution if one of the lads took into him.

We would go on to have an amazing time together. I had ten more years playing alongside my brother and best friend: a quiet, hard-working lad who had just as much of an edge and was every bit as competitive as me. It took a while for people to realise how good he was. I have a bit more belief and arrogance, but in the last four years especially he has been at the top of his game.

As kids we hammered lumps out of each other. The two of us ran the parish snooker club across the road from our house, and while we were thick as thieves we also broke snooker cues off each other, off tables, and off anything else within reach. At home we fired PlayStation controllers at each other and at the wall. If we played basketball a fight was inevitable.

We were quite similar when it came to sporting benchmarks and tests – both of us were around level fifteen on the bleep test and close to nineteen on the yo-yo test – and that only heightened the sibling rivalry. Over the years, our Tyrone teammates would be waiting for the two of us to clash. Whenever we were in the same group for bleep tests it was never about beating the others or setting a personal best; it was always about not quitting before the brother. Those runs should have been called 'last brother standing'. We were both wrapped the same way.

Colm is ridiculously stubborn. Even during those years when I knew I had the edge in strength and fitness, he pushed himself through pain barriers to stay with me. Whenever one of us finally cracked, the other would do an extra run just to rub it in.

In more recent years Tyrone have played basketball at St Ciaran's Ballygawley to keep us ticking over through the winter months, and when the teams were being picked, Colm and I, two of the strongest players, were always kept apart.

More often than not both our teams made the final, and that led to many a hot and heavy finish to the winter. Stephen Rice, a PE teacher and one of our masseurs, refereed those games and the abuse he took over disputed calls was crazy.

One night when Colm deliberately fouled me on a fast break – at least that's my version and I'm sticking to it – I totally lost the plot and from point-blank range kicked the ball full force at him. Cue brotherly skin and hair flying. It was comedy gold for the rest of the Tyrone lads and even for the neutrals.

We played squash in Dungannon Leisure Centre in the winter and I don't think we were ever on speaking terms as we left the court. Those games almost led to war, and we wouldn't resume diplomatic relations for a good half hour after them.

The poor lad still has the scars from a quick game of one-on-one as we waited for Philly Jordan to collect us ahead of the 2010 Ulster final. We clashed over a disputed call and I ended up throwing Colm against a pebble-dashed wall and gashing his arm.

To be fair, Colm accepted it all as part of the game. We piled into Philly's car, with Colm's arm streaming blood, and he went out a couple of hours later and scored a goal in the final. Maybe out of pure thickness.

Here's the thing. Colm was, and is, long and gangly and aggressive and the most stubborn person I know. He's also a bloody great player and an even better man. Behind our fierce domestic rivalry we pushed each other to improve. And though younger, he was a huge influence on me. The 2007 season proved another downer but at least my brother was now on board. We didn't know it, but we were about to achieve great things together.

17

THE ENDLESS SEASON

It's late 2007 and I'm sitting in the surgery of the orthopaedic consultant Richard Nicholas as he tells me my Tyrone career is hanging by a thread. He hands me a diagram showing the trauma inside my right knee. The letters BOB jump off the top of the page and I ask what they mean.

'Bone-on-bone, Seán. I'm afraid it's not great. You'll have to manage this carefully. The most you can hope for here is ten games a year. Max.'

I looked up at the wall. Framed parchments, all Latin, copperplate script and strings of letters. Doctorates and diplomas from foreign parts including New York and Brisbane. Just about everything suggested this man knew what he was talking about.

But at twenty-four years of age I thought I knew better. So, while I half listened to him I was already in denial and looking for a way out.

'That's just not going to work for me, Richard,' I said dryly. 'I play around forty games a year. That's who I am.'

I thanked him, shook his hand and went straight to the gym to start on strengthening the knee.

Truth be told it had been bothering me for a year and half at that stage. Always sore after games. So painful in the morning when I woke up. Wear and tear, I was told. But as it got worse, I went for scans and X-rays. I found out both knees were seriously arthritic. 'You have the knees of a seventy-year-old,' Richard told me. It felt like that at times too, but I wasn't contemplating winding down in my mid-twenties. No way. There was more to be won.

Bar Fionnuala, I told no one of the latest prognosis. Not the Tyrone management, not our medical team, not teammates. I feared a life without football. I could not contemplate it for a second. I was obsessed with winning more.

By now I was deep in the bubble, obsessively trying to splice and dice my days between study, work, training, family. Frantically trying to fit every other activity and obligation around my inter-county career. I was just hitting my mid-twenties but already I was institutionalised and knew it. Nowhere else did I feel as at peace or at ease as on a football field, running at opponents, looking for routes to goal, expressing myself. Nothing else could give me that buzz. So getting match fit again was the only option.

Richard's expert diagnosis scared me much more than I ever let on and was the subtext to the most fascinating year of my career. Only now can I really talk about it.

In the weeks and months following, I became fanatical about the knee. I would drop out of training drills I felt might give me bother. Richard's words were always playing in my head, the brain ticking over with the dread of disaster; the notion of missing games through injury.

Being able to play the games was a combination of medical help, recognising the symptoms of my knees being in trouble, and resting when I had to. Add in a dollop of pure ignorance and stubbornness. From then until the end of my career, I had a programme of prehab that helped me cope. This involved physios rubbing me and strapping certain parts of my quads and IT bands in particular to ease the stress on the knee. I also knew that my knee swelled after playing on soft ground, so any time I played on a poor, soft surface I had ice ready and waiting, and then I used compression and anti-inflammatory tablets to cope. During the day I wore an unloading brace on my knee, but it came at a cost – my fashion sense. The brace was a bulky oul' thing, so awkward that it meant I could only wear baggy trousers to work to allow them to fit around the knee. The next ten years involved constant monitoring and reacting depending on how the knee felt. Even a year into retirement, I still have my knee taped with Kinesio tape, which I apply myself every couple of days.

But it took time, and that obsessiveness to play out the rest of my career. And throughout the 2008 League the whole thing weighed on me. I played poorly and the team was nowhere near right either. We were brittle. Lads like Collie McCullagh, after a few years on the panel, were finally starting to break through to the team, and that was a bonus, but some of our key players were only half fit, and some big names who had performed heroics for Tyrone between 2003 and 2005 were out to pasture.

While at work on the Thursday before we played Mayo in the League I was fretting away about the possibility of being dropped

228

when Mickey's number flashed up on my phone screen. Fearing the worst, I headed for the toilet in Uncle Seán's office. That wee cubicle is so tight you have to stand on the lavatory bowl to open and close the door and in the hurry to learn my fate, however grim it might be, I nearly took the door off the hinges.

'Seán, I'm going to change things up this weekend,' Mickey said. That's me fucked, I thought. But Mickey went on: 'I'm putting you on the edge of the square at fourteen.'

Massive sigh of relief. 'God, thanks a million, Mickey! I thought you were going to take me out of the team.'

'No, Seán. Let's see what way you go at fourteen. I've had it in mind for some time and it's worth a shot.'

Mickey isn't a big man for compliments or for communicating on your progress so I was never complacent about my place on the team. I didn't especially want to play at fourteen, but it was better than not featuring at all. So why not?

I went out and played well against Mayo and for a day or two almost forgot about the knee. It wasn't a great League campaign for us but we finished mid-table on seven points and retained our place in the top flight.

Then I was sent over to Oxford to work on a case and spent the month before the 2008 Championship flying to and from England. I had given so much time and effort trying to strengthen the knee that my groin flared up from overwork and I missed a fair stint of training coming into that first game, against Down. I wasn't sharp. Still, we drew with Down and I got a goal and a couple of points. Maybe Mickey was onto something after all! The full-forward experiment suddenly looked like a good idea. Until the following Saturday when they beat us in the replay and left us back on our arses and out of Ulster.

After that loss, management asked if we wanted time off but none of us did. I think we knew the only way back was through hard graft. After the game, Colm and I had pints in the Moy with Tommy McGuigan and some lads from Ardboe, but at eleven the next morning we were both back in the gym at Glenavon House Hotel and we did a rough session there, never holding back.

I still believed we would win the All-Ireland. I don't know if that was just Mickey's positivity weaving its spell, but I was telling people at work the following week we would go all the way. By then we had drifted to 33-1 in the betting, and while I didn't put money on my hunch, I know plenty of people who did.

The hard slog was only beginning. I went down to Louis O'Connor's clinic on the Monday night and he showed me a new contraption. Louis, a great man for the appliance of science, attached resistance bands to my legs and arms and connected them to a VertiMax machine. The aim was to build strength, speed and resistance, and I needed all three.

Apart from mending the knee, I reckoned the VertiMax system would help me gain explosive power, get me jumping higher. So I committed to two half-hour sessions a week with Louis and he worked me into the floor those nights.

The other change I made that summer was to pop down to the club pitch on my own three times a week. I would wait until everyone had cleared off before taking to the field with a bag of balls, whatever the weather. It might be late evening and getting dark, but I found peace there, running and jinking and shooting at pace over the bar. I hit dead balls from everywhere and no matter how well the session went I refused to leave unless I had kicked five 45s in a row out of my hand. It was often midnight by the time I got home, saturated with rain or sweat, but it paid off as I felt the sharpness returning, and confidence in the knee too.

The team hadn't given up either. Poor as we were against Down, we had seven different scorers on the day and hit twenty-one points by the end of extra time. Tommy McGuigan was emerging as a real nuisance for opponents, aggressive, showing for ball everywhere. Joe McMahon was in great form and Dooher was in outrageous shape, doing two-minute runs in Cookstown and finishing the length of a field ahead of players half his age. Losing to Derry and Laois in 2007 had been a complete disaster but this time there was a feeling that the real serious training had only started a few weeks before the Down game. There was plenty more road ahead of us and we still had a lot in the tank.

The fact that Peter and Chris weren't there in 2008 was a real concern early in the year, as we had over-relied on those men in the past, particularly Canavan. The names in the 2008 forward line seemed weak in comparison to previous years, but something clicked as we hit the qualifier trail and I could see players stepping up, guys like Collie McCullagh and Tommy McGuigan, who turned out to be really big players – they were great at picking out passes and quite often I was the beneficiary of them being inside. Peter and Chris remained huge Tyrone supporters, but I'd say they were as happy as anyone to see us move on with new leaders emerging.

We took stock and headed down to Carton House for a training camp as the qualifiers played out. Brian Cody came to give us a talk and we were all ears. His message was simple enough, stuff we had heard before – bully your man, win your own tussles, do the basics well – but, coming from him, it just seemed to make more sense than ever. It galvanised us and maybe that was down to his aura.

We trained like dogs. Despite the fog lingering from that Down defeat we could see a good few stars starting to align. Mickey was a difficult man to approach at times and was happy doing his own thing, rarely asking for input or suggestions from players, so when he brought in the sports psychologist Caroline Currid to work on communication between players and the backroom, it was something of a surprise. The gig was that we had to meet Caroline once a month in Kellys Inn, Ballygawley, and even though I thought better communication was exactly what we needed, my first session with Caroline got off to a rocky start.

'What do you see yourself as?' she asked. 'Are you a starter on the team? You won All Stars in the past, Seán, but are you still at that level?'

I was taken aback and, to be honest, a bit offended. Who was she to be questioning my credentials?

'I believe I'm the best player in Ireland,' I answered, looking her straight in the eye.

Put like that it sounds arrogant, but in the heat of the moment I felt her tone was challenging and a wee bit critical. Fuck it, I thought, I *can* be the best player in Ireland. Why not?

I don't know if herself and Mickey had planned it that way, but she fairly got a reaction from me. And maybe if it was mind games they were playing to get a response, it paid off in spades. Because from then on, whether consciously or subconsciously, I worked like a lunatic in trying to justify my boast.

When we beat Louth by eight points in the first round of the qualifiers and Mickey told me I did well, I barely grunted in reply. I had an attitude, and now I was regaining form and fitness. I began to resent Mickey leaving me inside at fourteen. Convinced that midfield was where I could best help the cause, I spent a lot of training time huffing and bitching, throwing wee sulks and generally letting it be known I was a disgruntled camper. Waiting for supply of the ball frustrated me, whereas at midfield I won my own. I felt I was working hard and was in great shape at training and I wanted to show that.

The way I saw it, we were a running team, and that meant, depending on position, you could spend whole games watching the action from a distance. Opponents tended to target Davy Harte and Brian McGuigan because they were such quality distributors – Brian could put ball on a sixpence and Davy had a sweet touch off the outside of the boot. Obviously if those two boys were shackled, the supply in to full-forward was cut off at source. It meant I could be standing at fourteen with my back to the goal and starved of ball for long spells.

I took no enjoyment out of that, even though we were winning again. How can I explain it? Whenever I was running at teams, I would feel as if a magnet was drawing me in. I thought that running at opposition defences in full flight was where I belonged.

Mickey didn't agree and so now I was making unfamiliar and sometimes futile runs into corners and out onto wings. To compound the frustration, I felt I lacked the blinding acceleration to outpace a jinky, speedy defender. But there was feck all I could do about it and, because as a team we could see the tide turning, I had to suck it up.

By this time the lads were growing beards. Joe McMahon, Mugsy and Ricey were behind the devilment, and the stubble thing caught on. We were like a group of wild men getting off team buses and running onto fields that summer. But we were growing tighter – apart from the face hair – every time we ran out.

The GAA world at large didn't think much of those beards, but that only fed into our belief that everyone was against us anyway.

Before every game Mickey always ensured we had one or more points to prove. In 2003, there was the 'puke football' thing. In 2005, we felt people were against us because Ricey had been spared suspension, with a little help from Feargal Logan, after a clash in the Ulster final. And as we ploughed our furrow through 2008 we managed to convince ourselves that no one was giving us credit, because they just didn't like us.

It was always that way. It was drummed into us that Kerry were the aristocrats, there to be taken down. Down believed they themselves were the aristocrats, and that was plenty of incentive. As for the Dubs, they thought they were Hollywood as well as aristocracy, so motivation was never a stretch when we met them. They were the Fancy Dans from the big city on their own turf, and we played that card of being outsiders, poor relations with massive chips on both shoulders. Even when we played Tipperary in 2015 there was a subplot – the whole 2014 All-Ireland under-21 final episode, where there was so much niggle and bad blood between the counties in that game.

You could go through every county. Mickey made sure there was a compelling and sometimes quite derogatory theme – even if he had to make one up – for each of them. During those years we hung on his every word, but by the end of my career, I have to say, I was weary of all that stuff.

Westmeath were next in the qualifiers, but by the time that game ended I was in Omagh Hospital, concussed. As I back-pedalled in chasing a ball, Justy McMahon came through me, accidentally clipping my ankle and upending me as he contested with his man. I flew into the air, landed on my neck, and lay there in neverland for several minutes before being stretchered out the back of Healy Park.

As they put me into the ambulance I became aware of what was happening. I was strapped down. Fionnuala was there trying to comfort me, the paramedics likewise.

'Ach, you'll be alright, Seán. They're just bringing you to the hospital to get you checked out.'

I was strapped to the bed for the journey, arms and legs, it was like I was wearing a straitjacket and I went nuts, roaring them out of it: 'What do you mean? There's a second half to be played out there! Get these fucking things off me! I'm going back in!'

They had to hold me down. I didn't know what I was saying or doing, and I suppose those experienced paramedics knew that – they just kept telling me to calm down, take it easy.

When I finally settled, they brought me to the hospital and placed me in a bay to await scans and X-rays. Every so often I heard a roar. Then there was an almighty scream. It wasn't the howling of a patient in agony but someone's reaction to a nearby TV, which showed the late goal chance Dessie Dolan missed – one that would likely have won the match for Westmeath.

The scans were reassuring but the doctor wanted to keep me in overnight for further monitoring. Not a hope! I signed myself out. I know it wasn't right, and I would strenuously urge any player reading this not to be as thick and impulsive as I was, but I've done that three times after concussion. And I did it that day even though Fionnuala was with me and begged me to have a bit of sense.

Bizarre as it may seem, there was no one at the hospital to bring us back to Healy Park, so we thumbed a lift from the main road, myself in full Tyrone strip. When we arrived at the ground the team bus had already left, en route to Kelly's Inn for a match debrief, but my dad was waiting to drive me there.

We were only out on the road when I lost my bearings and started shouting: 'Where are you going, Daddy? Hang on! This is not the way!'

Of course it was the way. I was still off with the fairies. Proof that I should have stayed in hospital, but, sure, there was no talking to me.

After beating Mayo by a point, we drew Dublin in an All-Ireland quarter-final. They had hammered Wexford by a hurling score in the Leinster final and had all the look of a team that would prosper on a dry track under a hot summer sun. Fortunately, we got them on a shocking day. It had rained all night and all morning. There was flooding on Jones' Road. We knew in advance there was an ambush to be sprung. The Dubs wouldn't be up for it.

Again, disaster nearly struck for me. We were warming up under the Hogan Stand, doing our tackle drills. Caroline Currid had put Dublin jerseys on the tackle bags and we were bursting them for sport. I was on a base line near the exit to the dressing rooms, ready to knock the stuffing out of anything in blue, when I stepped on a water bottle and rolled an ankle. Down I went in agony.

Louis saw what happened, pulled me into the physio room

and shut the door to keep out prying eyes, before tipping off the boot and sock.

'I'm going to tape this so hard, Seán, that you won't feel anything and you won't have any swelling. It will be highly restrictive, but we'll get you out there.'

After an intensive burst of physio from Louis I ran out and joined the team just before the anthem.

The formalities completed, we took up our positions, and as we did, Ross McConnell loomed alongside me. So, this was the bright new kid in town!

A few days earlier a journalist had arrived from Dublin to Uncle Seán's office to interview me and had raved about Ross. He seemed to be hinting that, given how well Ross was motoring and how indifferent my own form was, I was in for a torrid time in Croker. At least that's what I read between the lines.

Soon the ball came my way up the left wing. I tried to line up a dummy, but McConnell cut me off. Obviously, he had done his homework. For a split second the thought flashed up: maybe that journalist was right! But in blocking off space on my left, Ross left a gaping hole on my right, so I took him on, bounced the ball forward with purpose and just barrelled my way toward goal, holding him off all the time and then smashing the ball past Cluxton from close range. With the ankle mummified I could only guess where the ball would end up – but thankfully it hit the net.

That rattled the Dubs. We hit them hard and dragged them around the place. Then a Conal Keaney goal checked our momentum.

The turning point for me, though, was Joe McMahon's goal. That broke them, the sight of big Joe bursting through and then running back upfield with his huge, dirty beard as we went onto a 3-14 to 1-8 win.

I don't recall what the motivational add-on was when we played and beat Wexford in the All-Ireland semi-final, but I do recall hitting four points from play before being brought off the field after a collision.

I tried a few runs along the side-line but kept breaking down, desperate to get back in and bulling that they wouldn't let me. Again, I was shaken from the blow and wasn't thinking straight.

I pleaded with Michael Harte, our physio: 'Michael, can you get me out there again?'

'Seán, will you stop! You can hardly put one foot in front of the other.'

In fact, as it turned out, that collision left me with two dislocated fingers and my back in traction.

But we were back in an All-Ireland final and that was all that mattered.

As soon as the lower back settled, I resumed my intense training regime. The week before the final, during an in-house match at Ballygawley, with my dislocated fingers taped up, and despite having Ricey on my back doing all the usual Ricey stuff, I scored 2-4 off him. I felt really sharp.

On the Friday night before the All-Ireland final I went back down to the Moy pitch to shoot balls and find some balm. RTÉ were there in the clubhouse filming their *Road to Croker* documentary, but I veered away from all the hubbub, dragged my bag of balls onto the pitch and stayed there till 11 p.m., leaving only when I was happy I had all my kicking boxes ticked and dead balls converted.

If you were to do it now, just two nights before an All-Ireland final, some GPS system would find you out and the manager would shut you down. But that evening I just kicked balls and ran. It was a way of achieving mental and physical harmony. I was at peace on my own patch.

18

THE PEAK

Another place I always found a bit of calm was beside Cormac's grave. Often before big matches I would head over to the graveyard and have a chat with him. I did that on the Saturday morning before the All-Ireland final, just tipped down the road, said a prayer and a quick hello.

Time-wise I was under a bit of pressure. The bus was leaving for Dublin at midday and it was about half-ten when I got to the graveyard, so I didn't plan to stay long. Back then, Cormac's grave stood alone, a good twenty metres from other plots and surrounded by clear-mown lawn. It was quiet there, and as I dwelt in the moment a cat, jet black, appeared beside me from nowhere – or at least I had not seen it approaching.

The cat nestled against my foot. I brushed it off gently, but it leaned into me again and then curled its way around my ankles, pressing against them, for several minutes. At first, trying to concentrate on my moment with Cormac, I thought little of it, but then my mind raced and I felt my neck hairs stiffen: *Is there something going on here?*

Around and around it went, making figures of eight as it rubbed against my shins. That was the number Cormac wore, I thought as I gathered myself, said a parting prayer, blessed myself, looked down – and the black cat had gone; disappeared just as mysteriously as it had emerged. To where, I have no clue. I saw it neither arrive nor leave.

If you think I'm into any kind of hocus-pocus, I can assure you I'm not. I'm not overly superstitious. I have no time for fortune tellers and mediums and those who make a living by letting on to predict events. I don't believe in any of that lark. But I am a practising Catholic. I go to Sunday Mass and I do have faith. When I got out to my car I phoned Fionnuala because I found the whole thing uncanny. Fionnuala would have strong faith too, and since her dad passed away certain things have happened that she might see as signs from Charles.

It didn't end there. After talking to Fionnuala I fastened my seatbelt, switched on the ignition and turned on the radio. And the first thing that came blaring out was 'Gold' by Spandau Ballet. Cormac's song! The one he chose for our 2003 All-Ireland CD compilation. I was spooked and even a little upset. I called Fionnuala again and relayed the latest happening. It was just too mad to take in.

I have no idea if the events of that morning had special meaning or were just coincidence. I do know that, until now, I only ever told four people about it.

One of those was my friend Philly McCann, whose brother, Mark, had died of cancer aged just twenty-four. Mark was Colm's best friend and shortly before he passed away, Colm and I went to Belfast City Hospital Cancer Centre to support Philly in any way we could. Despite what he was going through, Philly was strong, and when we sat down he told me a story. Earlier that evening Mark had leaned over to him and reassured him he was going to be okay: 'I'm alright. Grandad's here.'

Their grandfather had died a few months earlier. Since Philly had told me that, I felt I could confide in him and so I relayed the story of my morning at Cormac's grave.

A few months later I bumped into an aunt of Cormac, and as we chatted away she told me how proud Cormac would have been of us and how much he would have loved seeing us achieve all our goals. Then she mentioned something that had been troubling her. She said that after Cormac died she had taken in his cat, but it had strayed and never returned. I didn't mention my graveside encounter, but again I just told Fionnuala: 'I have no idea what's going on.'

Did Cormac indeed have a cat? Was it a black cat and did it disappear? I'm still not sure. All I know for sure about that graveside encounter and hearing Spandau Ballet on the radio is that, despite the initial shocks, when I headed for the bus that morning I felt strangely settled and at ease with the world.

Still, little was ever straightforward in Tyrone football, and that feeling of calm didn't last long. When we reached our pre-match base at Carton House and were heading out the back of the hotel for light ball drills, word came through that John Devine senior – father of our goalkeeper – had died. It was awful news.

It was only a light kickabout in trainers, but I could see straightaway that lads were distracted. Their heads and hearts weren't in it, and when the first handling drill was all over the shop I drew them into a huddle and told them we would respect John and his family but the best way of doing that was to win the All-Ireland. We needed to stop moping and focus on the job in hand.

It wasn't that I didn't care. The younger John Devine and myself were the same age and had graduated to the senior team in 2002, straight from minor, so we shared more than hotel rooms along the journey. We came from the same batch, and we had plenty of ups and downs together on the field. He was a great lad. And he would have appreciated that, with an All-Ireland final looming, we had to hold our course. So after the kickabout I sought him out and told him we would win the final for him and his family and would join them after the game to pay our respects.

It was desperately sad watching John depart Carton House the night before the All-Ireland, but he had to be with his family. And what could any of us do? There was no time to feel sorry for ourselves. I was just utterly determined that, when next meeting up with John, we would have a medal for him. The way I saw it, we now had another compelling reason to win.

When John left, I headed back to my room. Only hours now to throw-in and I was glad of that; between one thing and another the build-up had been a rollercoaster for the squad.

About three weeks earlier, Stevie O'Neill had returned to our panel, and his comeback was presented by the media as sensational news, almost as dramatic as when, a few months earlier, at the age of twenty-eight, he had announced his retirement from inter-county football.

But to most of us there was nothing outlandish about Stevie's return. He had been struggling for form because of injury and that's why he walked away. Once out of the goldfish bowl of inter-county football and the intense scrutiny that goes with it, he was able to work his way quietly back to full fitness and was in good form with his club, Clann na nGael.

With the final approaching, the question of Stevie's possible return to the panel was raised. Mickey said it was up to us, the players, to decide. We met in Quinn's Corner to discuss it and straight off I could sense there was huge uncertainty. Guys were hedging their bets, not wanting to commit either way. Eventually a couple of lads spoke up and said we should stick with the squad that got us to where we were. I could understand their position – those were fellas that would normally be subbing.

That was fair enough but when they finished I made it clear: this was Stevie O'Neill we were talking about. One of the best forwards to grace the game. He had left the set-up only after being dogged by injuries, and I knew how badly it had cut him up; I had shared the room with him the night before the 2007 All-Ireland quarter-final against Meath and had seen the man in torment.

We all knew too that he was Tyrone through and through and had always put the county first. But here was the clincher for me – I felt he would improve our chances of winning an All-Ireland title. And our history had shown that such chances didn't come around often.

There was another clincher. I was heavily marked back then but I knew that even if Stevie never kicked a ball, his presence on the field would distract attention from me. I was adamant: we needed him. He had to come back. And so we decided to bring him in, even though he himself was slightly uncomfortable with the decision.

All of that had been settled and it seemed every box had been ticked. And on the Saturday night of All-Ireland weekend I slept almost normally, which was pretty much a first for me ahead of a big game. I knew what was expected of me the next afternoon and felt capable of delivering. Going into previous finals with the likes of Canavan and Cormac on the team had always made me feel secure and solid. Now in their absence I knew I had to step up and fill their boots by offering my teammates that same reassurance. I also felt added responsibility because I hadn't scored in the 2003 and 2005 finals. I kept my head down in the build-up to the final. When I was younger I went out and about a bit more, soaked up the atmosphere. But as I got older the consequences of defeat became more apparent and I tended to put the head down, work hard and keep to myself.

Early in the All-Ireland final we were awarded a fifty-metre free straight in front of the posts. I had been clipping them over all summer on my own club pitch, spending hours perfecting the craft, but on All-Ireland final day I addressed the ball, let fly ... and dropped it short. My heart sank. Was I about to have another disappointing All-Ireland? I'm just never going to score in a final, I thought, as I ran back into position.

Thank God, my chance would come only minutes later, when Tommy McGuigan sent the ball in to me and I shimmied around Tom O'Sullivan and clipped it over the bar. The relief! Euphoria! A weight was lifted. And from then on, I couldn't miss. It was just one of those days.

As I ran back to my post I looked at the three letters I had written on my wrist and in black marker: AIM. All Star. Ireland – I wanted to make the international rules team. Man of the Match. I had scribbled stuff on wristbands throughout my career, but this was the first time I put down individual goals. It sounds selfish but there's logic to it. Team-oriented goals like 'work ethic', 'keep my shape', 'support others' – well, I felt I was ticking those boxes automatically. But I was so driven for that game, I reasoned that if I hit my individual goals and at last made my mark on All-Ireland final day, Tyrone would surely win too. I wanted to raise the bar, win an All Star, play for Ireland and get Man of the Match in the final.

Stevie came on early enough and Marc Ó Sé went onto him. I was thrilled and relieved because I was having a good game on Tom O'Sullivan and half-feared that Marc, Kerry's best man marker, would come over onto me. Instead he took Stevie and I ended up having an even better second half than first and managed five points in total. Stevie had them distracted and I led a charmed life.

Tommy McGuigan's goal immediately after the break was a massive statement, but at the other end Pascal McConnell, who had come into goal for John, pulled off some fine saves. The clincher was the flurry of late points from Enda McGinley, Hub Hughes, myself and Colm when he came on. As the game progressed we just kept throwing in fresh legs and experienced heads and Kerry ran out of ideas.

In the lead-up to that final the popular narrative had been the battle between Kerry and ourselves for Team of the Decade. This would be the defining clash, the two big dogs of the noughties lining each other up.

I was so wrapped up in my own performance that the Kerry rivalry thing didn't bother me at all. I actually found the Kerry lads to be sound – unlike some others I could mention, they never gave me grief. There was no running personal feud either, because in our three big duels that decade, I had three different markers – Eoin Brosnan, Darragh Ó Sé and Tom

O'Sullivan. There was no reason to be targeted, no bad blood or bitterness between us.

Just as with Armagh, we actually had huge respect for them. Kerry were the kings of the game, the monarchs of Gaelic football. They were looking for their third All-Ireland title in succession and we knew their forwards could do fatal damage. But we backed ourselves to the hilt. I suppose we were the original breakthrough team, and along our journey we had developed a fiercely independent attitude.

I mean, even when standard-bearers during the noughties, winning All-Irelands, we were always firmly outside the establishment. The put-downs were always the same: *negative; defensive; cynical*. We were the ones who riled the crowd. Nordics with wild, untidy beards. The pantomime villains. The bad guys of the game.

We might have been grudgingly respected but we were seldom loved – though I would like to think that, with the passing of time, we were seen differently, especially after that 2008 final, when we were in control for most of the game. That September day we went to Dublin and seized our third All-Ireland in six seasons. At the end, four points separated the sides.

Were we the team of the decade? Who cares? I can tell you not one of us was agonising over that when the final whistle blew. That debate would rage for a while, but it never kept me awake wondering. Kerry won in 2000, 2004, 2006, 2007 and 2009 while we won three times, so on paper, at least, they had the edge.

But at the same time you have to look at where we came from. Winning All-Irelands is part of the Kerry DNA and they average three a decade. Before 2003 we were All-Ireland virgins. And in all our three big Championship duels that decade, we beat them. Who gets the bragging rights? I don't know.

Anyway, after a year that began with a medical prognosis that I could play only ten games, a season when Down beat us in Ulster and our first-choice goalkeeper lost his father the night before an All-Ireland final, we came out on top. We persisted and got through it. I hit my goals too and then there was the icing on the cake that was the Sam Maguire: they named me Man of the Match in the final. It was a relief to play well and get back home knowing we did the job. It was also a tribute to John Devine and his family, and it was emotional meeting him once we got back home.

After the Australian interlude that year, and back on terra firma, I was swept away by the awards circuit. I managed another All Star and was named Footballer of the Year. I had worked like a lunatic to hit my targets and, apart from the blip of the Tyrone intermediate final, it was very much the perfect year. For a moment or two I reflected on what I had said to Caroline Currid – that I could be the best footballer in Ireland if I put my mind to it. That it happened was simply proof that hard work and ambition pays off.

I didn't know it then but, as a team, Tyrone had peaked. And try as I might, I never reached those heights again.

PART THREE

THE INCLINE

19

MICKEY AND ME

Almost everything was going to plan as we headed into the last week of August 2009. Life was good. We were Ulster champions and about to contest another All-Ireland semi-final against Cork. I was looking forward, when it was all over, to getting married a few months later in December.

Cork were going well too; they had hit Donegal for 1-27 to make the last four and we knew they were a massive threat. But we were in decent fettle ourselves. Stevie O'Neill was having a great year and most of our main guys were back in form, having taken a few months to regain fitness following the injuries and excesses brought on by winning the 2008 Championship. Mickey named me at eleven to play Cork and I knew I would be on my good friend Graham Canty. He would be on my case, but it was a serious challenge that I looked forward to.

For me, there was just one pebble grating under the door. Mummy was laid low the week of the semi-final with a flu, and while doing what little I could to help her I was also pretty concerned about avoiding the bug at such a crucial time.

I got through the week without obvious symptoms and felt in flying form during our kickabout at Carton House the Saturday evening before the big game. I pulled out my luminous yellow boots – courtesy of Puma, who were sponsoring me at the time – and that gave the lads plenty of ammunition to tear strips off me. It was a good bit of diversionary fun on the eve of the showdown.

I looked ahead to the match and felt excited. Playing at eleven would mean flexibility to roam in the way I had mostly operated with my club, dropping back when needed to win ball in the middle of the field or moving in to do likewise at full-forward.

Canty is a good lad and I knew he would be a monster to contain, but I had marked him a few years earlier in a League game at Dungannon and had done well. For good measure I knew he wouldn't kick, spit or nip at me as others had done that season. He was hard but fair, which suited me fine.

That season I felt every game had brought me up a notch. I had set the bar high and had done alright in Ulster against Armagh and Derry. My form had not fully carried through from the year before; I hadn't ignited – but I was chipping in more and more with every game. In the Ulster final, against Antrim, I had got 1-4. And in the All-Ireland quarter-final against Kildare, though Darryl Flynn had been all over me, and I had never quite escaped his clutches – hands, arms, legs, whatever – I had still managed to put in a shift.

Anyway, against Canty I knew it would be all about the football. So I went to bed content and excited. As usual on the eve of a crunch battle I didn't expect to sleep much, but that night is one I will never forget. I had barely hit the sheets when I got the shivers and began to feel weak. Then the hot flushes came. I started to run a fever and it quickly got worse.

I didn't once close my eyes that night. Hot one minute, shivering the next. Soaked in sweat, I got up at about 3 a.m. to change the bed sheets and, while fumbling about, disturbed Ryan Mellon, my room-mate.

'What the hell is wrong, Seán?'

'I'm in trouble here, Ryan. I feel really off.'

'Try to get some sleep. It might help.'

There was no chance. I lay awake, the anxiety now rising, knowing I had to play seventy minutes of an All-Ireland semi-final, not only without sleep but also feeling like my head was in a vice and the legs had turned to rubber.

By 6 a.m. anxiety had become full-blown panic. At 7.30, after struggling to lift my head from the pillow, I phoned Fionnuala.

'I'm in bits here, Fionnuala. I haven't slept a wink. It's a disaster. What'll I do? Do I tell Mickey now or do I just give it a rattle and see how long I can manage on the pitch?'

Fionnuala was her usual rock of calm. 'Don't say anything to anyone yet, Seán. The game is still eight hours away. You might perk up before then. You'll get through this game just like you do every other one. Don't underestimate the power of adrenaline.'

I dragged myself out of bed and headed for the restaurant. Normally I loved my pre-match breakfast but this time I couldn't put a bite in my mouth. The question was now crucial. Do I admit it to Mickey or not? Will I be straight with him or just get on with it and hope for a miracle? You always want to play big games. There's a selfishness there but it's understandable – you've worked toward it and dreamed about it and you want to feel indispensable to the cause.

Tommy McGuigan had been dropped for the Cork game but his form in training had been excellent and I knew he wouldn't let the side down if I dropped out. Still, I agonised and agonised – and in the end the interests of the team trumped selfish considerations. I found Mickey and Tony Donnelly in the hotel's Kildare Suite, took a deep breath and said: 'I'm not in good shape, lads. I don't know if I'm going to be good enough to play. I have no energy, a banging headache and I didn't sleep a wink. I'm just feeling rotten.'

Mickey seemed to take it in his stride. He recognised I was in a confused state and he brought some perspective to it. He said not to panic, as the game was still seven hours away, and to get some sleep. Then we'd see how I was doing later on and make the call.

Back up I went and as I approached my room I heard what sounded like a full-blown disco going in the room next door, which Johnny Curran and my brother, Colm, were sharing. Colm opened the door, and there was Johnny inside doing all his Travolta moves, hip-thrusting and finger-pointing, while 'Rhythm is a Dancer' blasted out from the CD player. *Sunday morning fever, both them and me!* I thought, though I wished for even an ounce of that oomph.

'Hey, lads, do you mind knocking that down a little? I'm wrecked and I have to get some sleep.'

Colm could see I wasn't messing; they killed the backing track, I went to bed and actually managed two-and-a-half hours' sleep. When I woke up around 11.15 I had missed Mass, which was always part of our pre-match routine on big days – breakfast, 10 a.m. Mass, and a round-up meeting at 11.30 a.m.

By now I was feeling slightly more human and thought I might even manage a bit of grub. On the way down to the restaurant I met Tommy McGuigan and I felt a fit Tommy was more valuable to the team than me in my present state.

'God, I heard you're not well, boy?'

'Nah, tough night, Tommy. I got no sleep but I'm heading down to get a bite now and see how I go. I feel much better.'

'Ah, not to worry, I'm in for you anyway.'

My heart sank. So the call had been made. The reality hit: *Fuck it, I'm not going to be playing the All-Ireland semi-final! I should never have said anything!*

It was Mickey's call, and given what he had seen of me earlier, he was entitled to settle on his starting fifteen. I was in a bad way, no doubt, but the couple of hours' sleep had given me a glimmer of hope. A morsel of food would surely help too, and there were still a few hours to throw-in. I thought the way we had left it that morning we would regroup and review the situation. But now I was out, at least, of that starting fifteen.

When I found Mickey in the meeting room he said neither Tommy nor I were to talk to anyone else about it. And it wasn't until some hours later, when the ball was thrown in and there I was on the subs' bench, that people, including teammates, copped that I wasn't starting. Not one word was mentioned of it beforehand.

'What's the story, Seán? What the fuck are you doing here?'

Mickey had his reasons; he had wanted to avoid pre-match distractions. So I played it down, just mentioned I'd had a tough night. I eventually ran on in the second half, got on a few balls, hit the post with five minutes to go, but Cork were better than us and won by five points. Our back-to-back dreams were over and the whole thing wrecked my head, the way everything had unravelled. It was a subdued journey home and a frustrating time for all of us coming back from Dublin after losing a game we felt sure we could win.

Before the game I had agreed with Louis O'Connor that, whenever the season ended for me, I would get surgery on a troublesome right ankle. I had twisted it a number of times that year and the ligaments were shot.

'Whenever you get the chance we'll do it and you'll have to take a few months out after the operation,' Louis advised.

I hoped that time would come after we had won another All-Ireland, but it arrived a lot sooner. Fionnuala and I were getting married in early December, so not long after the Cork game I went under the knife. Colm and Ryan Mellon got the same operation on the same day – all of us struggling with ankles. There we were, the three of us, coming back to our senses together in the recovery wards of the Ulster Clinic and spending the next few months in rehab together. It was freakish.

During all that time and in the run-up to the wedding I didn't hear a word from Mickey. Then in October the extracts from *Harte* were published in a Sunday newspaper. I was in Fionnuala's house when Charles handed me the paper: 'Seán, have you seen this stuff in Mickey's book?'

'ROOF CAVED IN' screamed the headline. Interesting, I thought. What roof could that be? And then, in growing disbelief, I read the text. Turns out I was the one under the falling timber and masonry.

Mickey's take on the morning of that semi-final was very different to mine. He felt that I had buckled under pressure. The 'roof simply caved in' on me. He was 'puzzled' when I told him I was wrecked and hadn't slept all night.

The extracts suggested that Mickey wanted to see things from my perspective but that, 'apart from a few isolated flashes of brilliance', my form 'hadn't been great all season'. I thought I had been doing okay, but fair enough.

'As a player Seán had always delivered,' it continued. 'He was an icon for us and that greatness had been rewarded in 2008. Maybe the pressure was stemming from that recognition.'

Mickey wrote too of how there was a lot going on in my life, from an impending marriage to my role as secretary of the Gaelic Players Association and too many media and commercial commitments. He wondered if the Tyrone management had sufficiently 'addressed all those pressures' during the year. Had the team's 'support structure been strong enough' to share my burden?

'This moment seemed the culmination of a year's worth of pressure and expectation leaning on him. In the end the roof simply caved in.'

God, I was acutely embarrassed sitting there and reading that in Fionnuala's house. I felt betrayed and humiliated. He had made his call not to start me and that was fine – he was doing what he thought best for Tyrone. But I had won so much with this man. Did people now think I had bottled it against Cork? *Pressure. Commercial deals. GPA. Roof caving in.* Those were the words linked with my failure to start the Cork game. I was in utter disbelief.

Take the GPA secretary thing. That role demanded nothing from me. I went to their AGM after we won the All-Ireland and I suppose they saw my profile as a bonus and gave me a job. I was reigning Footballer of the Year, but I was there at that meeting in name only. I doubt I attended one meeting the whole year after that. I did put my name at the end of a sheet but that was about it. Maybe that was the perception, that I was up and down the road all year. But I wasn't.

As with his attitude to international rules, Mickey was vocal against the GPA. I don't know if he disliked the idea of player power, but I do suspect he disliked me being secretary, even in name. In fairness, he never said as much to me – though, again, our lines of communication wouldn't have been humming at the time.

I liked what the GPA was trying to achieve. I felt county players were taken for granted and at the mercy of county boards. I never liked the idea of pay for play but was totally in favour of players getting fairly looked after with mileage, gear and food. For Mickey, GPA concerns were a distraction from the essentials – though to be fair he would eventually mellow on the issue, and the GPA reps are nowadays very much engaged with the Tyrone team and rightly so.

Commercial commitments? I did a few sponsorship gigs throughout 2009. Pictures and interviews. Got a few bob for them. They were all daytime gigs and I had been doing that sort of thing since I was eighteen. Again, no pressure. They never impacted on my training schedules.

The wedding? Fionnuala could testify that I genuinely had nothing to do with the preparation for that. Like most Irishmen about to tie the knot, I was the spare at the planning department – I was just told what to do.

Anyway, reading Mickey's take on things was a shock. And an insult. I had no idea any of that stuff was coming. I was only halfway through my career. I was twenty-five and I thought there was much more success to be had, working with Mickey, the man who had made every player in Tyrone believe we were good enough to dine at the top table.

In the following days, the sense of betrayal turned to shock, then disgust, then hurt again. When the time came to send out our wedding invites I wondered about posting one to Mickey and his wife, Marian, and after giving it some thought I sent the invitation. A few days later I got a voicemail saying he might be caught at something, but it was never confirmed one way or the other. On the day itself he may have popped into the back of the church forMass, but I didn't see him.

I guess I was waiting for an apology, but it never came.

Winter came and went. Our wedding was brilliant and we fully enjoyed it, and once the ankle healed I started to work on my fitness. But I had no great desire to rush back to the Tyrone team either; the whole 'roof caved in' nonsense still didn't sit right with me.

By mid-March, that still hadn't changed; there had been no contact in either direction. We were struggling in the League and had lost two games out of three. Losing to Monaghan in Iniskeen made it three from four, and a couple of days later I got a call from Mickey asking if he could call to the house for a chat.

Five months on from the newspaper bombshell, I was still annoyed and hurt – I had been avoiding going to team training, preferring to work alone on my own rehab – but I agreed to the meeting and Mickey landed over, sat down in the sitting room and attempted to explain what had happened.

His gist seemed to be that the phrasing was down to the ghost-writer and gave a different spin from what was intended, that the context became blurred, but I wasn't buying that. In fact, that explanation annoyed me even more. I felt he should have stood over what appeared in print. It had been a dramatic enough headline and probably sold a few books, so I felt he should have said, 'Seán, that's what I thought at the time.' I wouldn't have been ecstatic with that response, but it would have seemed to me more honest.

There was still a fair bit unresolved, but we moved on. Sort of. It was a frosty meeting. Realistically I never properly forgave him after that. I carried this issue with me for the seven subsequent years I played for him. It broke the respect barrier between us and whilst I never brought it up again, it was never far from my mind. Mickey never really engaged with me all that much anyway, so it wasn't as if I had to visibly snub him or anything.

We just got on with things. We both wanted Tyrone to win more and we were highly driven to ensure that was the case, so we did manage to enjoy some good days together as the years went on. When Brian Dooher retired, I felt I might have got the Tyrone captaincy but it went to Stevie O'Neill, admittedly one of our greatest-ever players. The only problem as I saw it was that Stevie had missed an awful lot of weeks and seasons with injury, whereas I had been playing a long time. And so I suppose I was disappointed at not getting the captaincy and I would say that also delayed the process of putting 'Roofgate' behind me.

For all I won with Mickey, for all the years since we first met – and for all that I admire him – I couldn't say we are close friends. There would still be a distance between us. But there's nothing unusual or sinister in that; I think many of the Tyrone lads would say the same.

Mickey didn't go in much for small talk or banter with us. He seemed content to keep a step back while we the players grew closer to others of his backroom team, the likes of Paddy Tally, Fergal McCann and Tony Donnelly; all of those were on the backroom team over the years and had a good connection with us. Mickey liked it that way and kept to himself. Some lads might go through a full season without Mickey saying a word to them as long as they were doing their jobs. That was grand if you were playing every week. Other fellas, though, didn't always know where they stood.

I never minded too much about any of that stuff. I didn't need to feel wanted and I didn't expect to be coached rigorously. I believed in what I could do and Mickey knew what it took to get us over the line. When he played me at full-forward in 2008 I didn't like it, but I went with it and at the end of the day Mickey was proved right.

Mickey and I differed in our views on several things, the international rules and the GPA among them, but sure everyone is entitled to their opinion, and my only real issue with the man was that book segment. That whole incident is one I have mulled over ever since and even still I can get upset about it.

Mind you, the whole thing did, and still does, generate moments of light relief. When we went to Edinburgh on my stag, the likes of Gormley, Holmes, Mellon, Philly and McGinley made up a song about my roof caving in. I had to go with it then, and I still do. Even at home, if I'm flapping about work or something, Fionnuala will use it: 'Mickey was right, Seán. Your roof is caving in!'

It's something I'll never forget. That one line. In my head. I paid the price for being too honest. Maybe I need to get over it. I look back and I do appreciate what Mickey has done for Tyrone football. He instilled self-belief and a fierce determination to win every single game we played. That's why we won so many McKenna Cups. He brought a group of players through from minor to under-21 to senior and integrated them with the group coming just behind: my group.

Mixing and matching teams is not easy, but Mickey did that brilliantly. He also managed their graduation from underage to senior without missing a beat, and he oversaw the whole thing from there. Under his watch, our self-belief rocketed and we truly feared no one. I would say that the last time we had any palpable fear was going up against Kerry in the 2003 final and that was out of respect for their legend and brilliant track record. Even then, Mickey had us believing we were going to win. Persuading each of us that we were the equal of, or better than, any and every opponent – that is his special genius.

He has a ferocious desire to win, and that has manifested itself in some epic outbursts. One bitterly cold evening in mid-January he and Tony Donnelly were having a kicking duel, hitting over fourteen-metre frees on a frozen pitch in Clogher. Mickey must have missed one free – and sure the ball was frozen I'd imagine – and Tony won. Mickey lost it. For a while afterwards he was in a bull's rage. That's the competitor in him.

Inevitably it rubbed off on us. Of course, it helped that we had the players, but Mickey convinced us no team could live with us at our best, and it was that intense and obsessive drive that got us to the top.

It reminded me of Michael Jordan in basketball. Even if it was a playground dribble, he had to win. You do what you have to do, take down whoever you have to take down, everything to get over that line. Mickey imbued us with that total drive.

It's common knowledge that Mickey is a man of faith. For the last two years before I retired we said the Rosary before every Championship game. And we were happy enough to do it; we were all Catholics and would have been familiar with the tradition. And yet, when you think of it, that took some courage and conviction on Mickey's part. Ireland may still be largely Catholic, but the Church is increasingly on the back foot and many would scoff at such an 'old-fashioned' prayer as the Rosary in the context of elite sport.

But Mickey has huge belief in God; and after what he and his family have gone through, I would say every bit of it was needed to keep him strong.

In early January 2011, we got word that Michaela had died while on her honeymoon in Mauritius. That news was shocking enough, but when details emerged of how she had died, well, that was nearly too much for us to bear. I genuinely don't know how Mickey and his family stayed standing after that, and I can only admire their strength in the face of such devastating news.

I think about Michaela quite a lot. When she was younger she went to most of our training sessions, matches and meetings. She was a constant presence and it was always great to stop and chat with her. After Mickey moved from the minors and under-21s on to the seniors, Michaela was with him all the way. Most of the lads saw her almost as a little sister and she was a big part of our set-up.

She was around the same age as me, so I saw her as a friend more than anything. I first came across her in 2002 when Mickey took on the under-21s and then I really got to know her better from being around Belfast in university the following year.

When we got the news of her passing it was exactly the same as when Cormac died. We were frozen, we were barely able to process what was happening and we certainly couldn't make sense of it. All the lads on the team were rattled and, when we gathered at her funeral, it was the same story – none of us knew what to say to each other, what to say to Mickey, or to his family. We were numb and words felt fairly pointless at that stage. I remember going to the house to pay my respects and hugging Mickey. I would say it was the first time we hugged. I just wanted to show him that we were there for him. We all did.

Soon after Michaela's funeral we had to play a McKenna Cup game in Edendork. And when I saw Mickey appear at the dressing-room door, I felt an overwhelming sense of sadness for the man. I soon understood that he is much stronger than most when it comes to dealing with death and that, while his grieving continues, football probably helped him deal with his huge loss. To be honest, the whole tragic episode was a huge shock then, and it still seems surreal now. Unfortunately in Tyrone football we know only too well of grief and sorrow and we tried to carry on the best we could that year.

Still, it was hard. Michaela had been everywhere with our team. She went on the All Star trips, functions, team holidays and all the other events, so she was very much part of the camp. She was also friendly with quite a few of the players' girlfriends and wives, but then again, from what I saw she was friendly to absolutely anyone she ever met. In the latter years she was on the periphery of our team, but she was never too far away either.

I will always remember her most fondly, though, from the early days. The image of her, as a young girl, watching us from Mickey's car on a wet Wednesday night in some random part of Tyrone as we trained through a winter. And then, as she grew up, she helped us, whether it was teaching us the national anthem or putting together a CD of players' music for the bus journeys. It's hard to think she is gone. I admire the resilience of the whole family for keeping going. And maybe that's why we said the Rosary before games near the end of my career. To get that connection.

Anyway, it was a mark of Mickey's character. It also brought us closer together.

Mickey appears so calm on the line, but we have seen the other side, when he has lost the plot before and after games too. And in the relatively barren years since our last All-Ireland win, in 2008, we've seen that side a little more.

Mickey's team talks on, say, the Tuesday before a game were fascinating, because he always found a new angle. When you're in a bubble you need things to cling to and there were times I came away from team meetings thinking, 'That was brilliant.' Other times I felt certain aspects weren't necessary, such as setting a siege scenario when we played Antrim. No disrespect to Antrim, but they were not going to beat us. But Mickey never left anything to chance and that was why he won so much.

As for tactics, I cannot assess his input because I wasn't privy to it, but he invested huge trust in his assistant coaches. Tony Donnelly would have done much of our tactical work and would be there at meetings with his clipboard: 'Seán, I want you to drive here into the space, retreat there, stick with this formation.'

Mickey would speak largely in motivational terms as distinct from addressing specific tactical plays. But he liked to do that; he likes to step back and let his right-hand man – currently Gavin Devlin – do the tactical talking.

Mickey has earned huge respect. From the Tyrone board, the players and the clubs. I thought he might have gone at the end of 2017 and I was surprised when he took on three more years, but I can see why it happened. He is our most successful manager. People will never forget what he has done.

There are some who want him out and feel that because he has stayed so long the county has missed a generation of good head coaches, the likes of Peter Canavan, Feargal Logan, Paddy Tally and Mattie McGleenan. Guys that might have loved a shot at the job and would probably have brought a different approach and perspective. But would they have done any better? Who knows?

I would love to have played under Canavan but that's all down to who he is. A hero of mine, the teammate I most admired. In fact, I met him lately and remarked that if he was Tyrone manager I would have looked to stay on for one more season. And I would have. How could you not want to play for Peter Canavan? I think a lot of Tyrone players, past and present, would have the same view, and would love to play for Peter. His presence would transform the atmosphere around the team. Peter understands and can relate to lads, he enjoys the craic but, equally, knows when to be serious and work hard.

As it happened the chance to play for him never arose and I ended up featuring for Mickey throughout my entire senior career. We may not be bosom pals, but I still acknowledge that

I achieved plenty under his tenure. I suppose we helped write a fair bit of history together.

One thing both Mickey and I had in common was that we had both climbed great hills for the good of Tyrone. He was the pioneer leading the way, but the rest of us worked hard to follow the trail. I was in my mid-twenties, had three All-Irelands won, a stack of awards in the attic upstairs and yet I never felt much contentment. Instead I yearned for the road again.

I would say with certainty that Mickey was just as hungry for more success. The only thing was that the incline started to get steeper for all of us.

20

BROKEN MAN

Around 2011 Donegal started to get a grip on our game and very soon Dublin got a handle on their game. Slowly, we started to drift down the pecking order. In fairness we never drifted too far and before I ended my career we came back to win Ulster titles and contest All-Ireland quarter- and semi-finals but, after 2009, for the next four or five years, I found the slope harder to hike, the gap between ourselves and those closer to the summit widening.

Late in August 2011, two weeks after Dublin had beaten us in the All-Ireland quarter-final, I got a call from Anthony Tohill to link up with the Irish squad heading to Australia for the international rules tour and I leaped at the chance. Anthony told me to head over to Callanbridge in Armagh, where the team's fitness coach Mike would test us. Mike had a mobile weights room there and when I arrived I saw Darren Hughes from Monaghan, Ciarán McKeever from Armagh and Danny Hughes from Down there too. We warmed up and were put through our paces. We had to do a bench press test, and as Danny was really good at that type of lifting he watched us kick off until we were at his level. I was already broad and strong in the upper body, never really thought bench pressing was for me and rarely got too excited about it, even if some of the lads on the Tyrone team were crazy for it. That night we started off benching a hundred kilos, doing a few sets at that weight and then moving on to 105, 110, 115 and 120 kilos. I was really only going through the motions.

Danny was looking on, half-bored I'd say; he was waiting for us to get up to 125 kilos so he could hop in. On my third lift at 115 I turned to Darren and said that I was starting to feel a wee bit tight, that I might just leave it and go and focus on the runs we had to do outside later in the test.

'Look, we'll give it one go here at a hundred and twenty kilos and we'll leave it then,' Darren replied.

I agreed I'd do one more and that would be it, so I lowered the bar again, Darren on one side and McKeever on the other, ready to hoist it back up if I wasn't able myself. I had it down four inches from my chest and was ready to lift again when I heard this big snap, like a rope hoisted onto the back of a car, towing a trailer, breaking. It was a massive snap and I knew all about it. I let a roar out of me.

'Fuuuuccccckkk!'

Hughes and McKeever grabbed the bar as I lay there. McGurn came running across to me but I didn't know what was going on. I couldn't feel the entire left side of my body where I'd felt the snap and I was in intense pain. I rang Fionnuala's dad straight away.

'Charles, is there any chance of a lift over the road to the hospital? I've done something to my shoulder in the weights room.' Charles said he was on his way. Thank God because the pain was like nothing I had ever come across in my life.

Charles brought me to Craigavon Area Hospital and they had to give me five or six shots of morphine before the pain started to ease. I hadn't a clue what was going on, but the doctors didn't either. Their initial tests showed that the shoulder was in place. No one really knew what to think except that it was a freak of an injury. They kept on going with the morphine until I went to see a shoulder specialist the next day. Again, Louis stepped up to the mark. He phoned Éanna Falvey from the Sports Clinic at Santry and told him what had happened. Éanna got me an appointment with Hannan Mullett, a leading orthopaedic surgeon who specialises in all types of shoulder surgery.

Hannan examined me, and looked at the scans and told me I had ripped my pec major tendon. Everyone has one of these on each side of their body and this clothesline-like link goes from the elbow up to the shoulder and across to the pecs, holding every muscle together as it goes. My clothesline had snapped.

In twenty years of specialist work Hannan said he had only seen one instance of this previously, when he had treated a rugby player after a scrum collapsed on him. His message was stark: 'If you don't get this repaired within four or five days your career is over and you will never play sport again.' He explained how the tendon retracts and pulls away, like a fillet steak shrinking on a hot frying pan, meaning that the line is never properly re-attached to the muscle.

Two days later I had the surgery in Santry. It proved trickier than Hannan had initially thought, as my muscle cord had retracted significantly and had I delayed the operation any longer my playing days might have been over. When I woke up I saw a scar under my arm running all the way up my body and across. When Fionnuala saw me she said I looked like a one-winged chicken! And what use was a one-winged chicken when it came to helping to feed and change our firstborn, Eva?

A few screws had been put in to keep everything in place and off I set about my recovery, working my backside off to make sure I was back within six months. I put myself through three sessions of rehab a day; one in the morning before work, one at lunch and one session in the evening, all forty-minute stints focused on getting me back as quick as I could. I was in a sling for the first month and a half of that process so even getting about and sleeping was a problem, but I got there and made it back ahead of schedule to play Kildare in the first round of the League.

Such was the freak nature of the injury that Hannan asked if he could use it as a case study for an article he was writing for a medical journal. Leaving his clinic after my post-operative consultation I had no idea we would be meeting up again very soon after.

By April I was really starting to come back into myself and see some daylight. The smell of the 2012 Championship was wafting through the air. We had Armagh at home and I felt like I was born to play on days like those. I couldn't wait and honed in on my preparation by playing for the Moy against Derrytresk in the Tyrone league.

It was a mild day, two weeks out from the Armagh game, and with two minutes to go, one of their guys came running out of defence. Instinctively, I put an arm out to break his tackle and I heard a familiar snap – this time on the other side. Straight away,

I knew the pec major tendon on the other side of my body had ripped. Again, the pain was fierce. I hit the deck and roared in agony.

There was no doctor or medic at the game so Karol McQuade summoned Fionnuala down from the stand. Anyone at that match saw how disturbed I was – I was in such pain that I kept kicking my left leg with my right foot just to distract myself from the pain I was feeling in my upper body. I didn't realise it until afterwards, but I had gouged big cuts in my left leg from all the hacking I was doing with my right foot. Fionnuala got some morphine into me, called an ambulance and, after lying on the pitch for twenty-five minutes in the searing heat, I was eventually taken off to hospital.

Before I was taken away, while I was still lying on the pitch, Fionnuala came to me and said: 'Don't panic now, Seán, but your dad has just collapsed and he's on the way to hospital too.' I pleaded with her to look after him. Daddy had been so bothered when he saw me on the ground in agony that he tried to come over to me but, in the heat of the day, he got so wound up that he had collapsed to the ground. They had to call another ambulance for him too.

Daddy smokes sixty cigarettes a day, his diet is ninety per cent salt and ten per cent grease. I thought he was after having a heart attack.

'I don't care about me,' I told Fionnuala. 'I know what I've done to myself – just go and see Daddy and make sure he's okay.' After a while he came around and I could focus on getting myself sorted.

Again, no one at the hospital had a clue what was wrong with me, though I had a fair idea myself. Enda McGinley was a head sports physio at the Craigavon Area Hospital and he advised that there would be a shoulder consultant on site the next day. After a strained few hours' sleep I walked into that woman's clinic and she asked me to put my hands on my hip. I wasn't able to. Without looking any further, she confirmed what I already suspected: the second pec major tendon was ripped. Back to Hannan Mullett for the same craic again. Another operation. Mr Mullett couldn't believe it and said he didn't know whether to laugh or cry. 'This just doesn't happen,' he said.

'Great,' I replied. 'How soon can you operate?'

I got the operation done two days later, missed the entire 2012 Championship but got back playing for the Moy again in August because the second operation had been cleaner and the tendon had been quickly reattached. It was extremely rare to have had this injury twice but Fionnuala is adamant that it was a result of a lifetime of weights sessions shortening the tendons. Still, it is scary to think that a simple gym session could lead to a possible career-ending injury.

That summer was the only one I missed for Tyrone in my entire career.

I look back now and wonder about the madness of it all, reflecting on everything I've had to do in order to play over the years.

For example, I would estimate that I have had between three and five anti-inflammatory injections every year of my life for the last ten years to kill the pain in my body and reduce the inflammation enough to let me play at the weekends.

I know there are bound to be side-effects, but I never asked what they are, and when the medics tried to explain, I just didn't want to know. In latter years especially, when I could see the light fading on my career, I don't know the number of times I went to medics and said: 'I'm in bother here with the foot/ankle/knee. Just make it go away, do what you have to do.'

And they would. And the pain would go away. Time and again the medics asked me to reconsider what I was doing, for the good of my long-term health, but I wouldn't listen. I batted them away. Nothing I ever did was illegal or prohibited but it was reckless, downright stupid and smacked of desperation just to play the next game.

I got to know the medics personally and some of them became good friends. In 2016 we beat Cavan in the Division Two NFL final – my first time captaining Tyrone in a final. I went into a clinic in Belfast on the Wednesday before the game. I could barely walk; I hobbled in. But after an injection into the joint, I walked back out, free as a bird. 'Just get me back out there.' That's all I ever told them.

Every time I got injured and sought anti-inflammatory medicine, Louis said to me that I should think long-term and be more patient about my recovery, but he was talking to a brick wall. My attitude was, if he didn't help me I would find someone who would.

When I was in the zone, I just didn't care. There was a total disregard for my safety. It's always about the next match. I have to play. Tyrone need me. Mickey Harte needs me.

As a result, I have played more times for Tyrone than anyone else. But will that help me in my old age? I just got used to pain, learned how to deal with it, became an expert in anti-inflammatories. I got to know what medicine worked and what didn't. Ibuprofen, Dilatrend, they did nothing for me. In the end, Naproxen was the only one that was any good to me. I would go to a doctor, ask for a box, ten strips with ten tablets in each strip, and I would use them before and after games. Over the last few seasons, just to be able to play a game at the weekend, I knew I had to start taking anti-inflammatories on Wednesday. I would take two Naproxen on Wednesday, Thursday, Friday and Saturday, and by the time Sunday came around I would know I had enough inside me to play freely. Otherwise I would have taken the field with soreness in my hips, ankles, knees, groins, ankles. With Naproxen, I was free again.

I mentioned very little of this to Fionnuala because I knew it would scare the life out of her. She knew of my obsession, that striving-to-win-at-all-costs mentality. But she sees the other side too – I have had pain every day for the last ten years. There is not a part of my body that has been unaffected. When it gets cold, one of my fingers starts swelling in pain because I broke it so many times. Anytime I go outside the house just to play a bit of basketball, I have to strap the ankles because there is no support there.

Both knees are goosed. I did my right one a decade ago and my left three years back.

My two shoulders have been pinned, my right ankle has been pinned too and one reconstructed.

That's part of the payback for playing football the way I did. It was not like I ever stood back and waited for the ball to come.

I still don't consider myself as bad as other lads I soldiered with. Poor Dooher was way worse than I ever was. I actually felt sorry for him one evening near the end of his career when I saw him hobbling into training. He was so bad that people wondered if there was something seriously wrong with him. And yet he was the one leading the way in training and matches. An absolute warrior.

I was never as sore as that but it wasn't pretty at times either. Everything I did fell within the permitted drug test medical guidelines – our doctors and medics would have told me what was fine and would always have advised me on the dangers of depending on anti-inflammatories. We were made aware of everything we could and could not take. The Irish Sports Council test GAA players regularly, and I averaged two tests per season during my career, which helped keep me fully informed too. Same with the rest of the panel. I was never a big one for taking creatine or protein powders and thought they were a fad, but when it came to getting back on the field, my outlook was way too short term.

Perhaps the biggest regret I have, medical-wise, is that I have been concussed between four and six times every year and played through games in many of those instances.

Concussion protocols are thankfully in place now but more than once I was able to convince the medics that I was good to go when I was actually all over the shop. Against Monaghan in the first round of the 2015 NFL I was playing full-forward when I went into a tackle with Drew Wilie and hit the ground. A few Monaghan lads came steaming in and I got a knee to the side of the head from one of them. I can honestly say that I had no clue where I was during that first half.

At the break Michael Harte, our physio, came over and said, 'Seán, there is no way you can go back out there.'

'Michael, will you go away? I'm fine,' I replied, and I went off, puked all over the place, convinced the rest of the medics I was fine too, and went back out onto the field. I can't remember one bit of that second half.

There were times I was hardly able to walk straight, feeling disoriented, yet I managed to convince the medical team that I was okay. Stupid.

Only now that I have children do I see how unfair I was. On the medics. On others. And on myself. Would I let my own son play through a concussion? No way. In 2003 Vinny Corey and myself clashed in the under-21 Ulster final at Enniskillen and I was as bad that night as I ever was, vomiting for hours after the game, struggling with a migraine. At 11 p.m. the guys in Craigavon told me I had to stay overnight but I had exams a few days later and said I couldn't. I made a few enquiries, looked into it, and found out that I could legally sign myself out. So, I did. Many's the time.

I am worried about my long-term health as a result of what I did. I would like to think if I was to do it again I might this time look after my body better and not take so many painkillers, but I'm not sure if I would follow through on that. I was addicted to playing in the biggest games and I was willing to do whatever it took to get me ready for battle, ignoring detrimental health risks. Most mornings now I struggle to walk downstairs because of those ankle and knee injuries. Who knows what sort of shape some of my internal organs are in after twenty years of tablets and injections?

It's not a good idea to go down that road. It's a risky business and it showed a total disregard for myself and others. But that's what happens with an obsession. You become selfish. You are fuelled by a demonic desperation to win.

To win at all costs.

21

TELL ME LIES

Fionnuala and I had our first baby, Eva, on 26 April 2011. It was a magical time for us, and Eva has continued to bring incredible love and joy to our lives. But the warm glow we enjoyed in the days and weeks after her arrival was mixed with unpleasant background noise from anonymous quarters.

All through my career I've had to endure an awful pile of horse shite being spoken about me. Right from when I first played underage for Tyrone, stories started to emerge and grow legs. Thanks be to God, Fionnuala has been there with me through thick and thin for most of it. She knows how quickly rumour spreads and, more worryingly, how easily it sticks.

I'm not the only victim of fake news; many of the Tyrone boys have suffered their unfair share. But I'd say few have been such frequent targets. The odd time it can get to me because I feel sad and angry that my family are affected. Mostly, though, I have just brushed it off.

Did you hear Seán has dropped out of university? Cavanagh fell out with his dad and has moved out of the house. Seán is leaving the Moy and going back to play with Coalisland. Or he's joining Armagh Harps. Some sort of row with the lads in the Moy. Just heard, Cavanagh is going to Armagh. He's ticked off with Mickey and the whole Tyrone set-up.

It's not much fun when some lad tells you the juicy story he has heard on the grapevine and looks for your reaction. In his mind his nugget of information is gospel. Worst of all, though, were the rumours about my marriage.

They started with random snippets. One day I was in a local shop and bumped into a clubmate who said he was sorry to hear Fionnuala and myself had split up. Soon after Cathal McCarron told me he heard I had gone off with the winner of the Tyrone Rose competition and was moving to Omagh with her. Those were outrageous suggestions for a man who spent the majority of time at work, training or strapped up with ice.

At work one Tuesday morning, soon after Eva was born, I got a phone call from Philly McQuade, taximan and Moy club stalwart: 'Are you about, Seán? Look, take a run out of the office, will you? It'll only take a minute.'

He probably wants me to sell tickets, I thought.

I popped out and sat into his taxi, and Philly gave it to me straight: 'You need to do something about these rumours, Seán. I'm going around in the taxi and people are saying you ran off with a woman and Fionnuala showed you the door. I heard it in Armagh, in Blackwatertown, and I heard it in the Moy a couple of times this week.'

'Huh? I know this has been going around, Philly, but can you find out where it's coming from?'

'Seán, it's coming from everywhere. You have to nip it in the bud.'

Fionnuala was on maternity leave and whenever she was around Dungannon we would meet for lunch, which we did the following Friday in Linen Green, a shopping village outside the town. As I pulled into the car park the phone buzzed. The lad at the other end gave his name and said he was writing a story for a popular Sunday newspaper.

Feck's sake, I thought, another interview! And this late in the week, two days before our Championship opener with Monaghan!

'Alright there, how's it going?' I said.

'Seán, I'm just following up on a story that you've taken up with a woman and got kicked out of the house.'

'Huh? Sorry?'

'It's on Wikipedia.'

I was gobsmacked. I didn't know much about Wikipedia.

'Huh? Who put that in?'

'I don't know, Seán. I'm only following up the story.'

'Well, I can tell you this. I'm actually meeting my wife, Fionnuala, right now. I'm on my way into the coffee shop.'

'Seán, we're running the story on Sunday.'

'You're what? I'm sorry, you'll have to give me a minute here!'

I hung up and went inside, and Fionnuala knew straight away something was up.

'I have no idea what's going on here,' I told her, 'but a newspaper is running a story about us this weekend – that our marriage is gone and that you kicked me out.'

Fionnuala is much more bullish than I am at taking people on. Where I'd be diplomatic or tactful she takes the direct route. If someone is hedging or waffling, she cuts to the chase. She took the phone off me, dialled the number and got your man from the newspaper. I sat there in disbelief. Why the interest in us? I wasn't bloody famous. I was a boring accountant from the Moy who played football for a hobby!

'I'm Seán Cavanagh's wife,' she said. 'What's going on here?'

He told her they had information from several sources that I had been given the door and was away with another woman. Fionnuala told him he was following a false lead. We had a two-week-old baby, for God's sake. Fionnuala also referred to the defamation of character of two professional people and told him that if such an unfounded story were to be published it would be highly detrimental. She thanked him for the opportunity to explain what he had heard and ended the call.

Sensing she was getting nowhere, she told me to phone Seán Potts, head of Communications in the GPA. Seán said he sympathised but there was little the GPA could do. 'These guys do this stuff. They can work it a certain way, saying "it is believed" or "it is reported" or "allegedly". They've done it to so many people over the years.'

It got worse. 'If you do manage to prove it's untrue, it will likely mean a trip through the courts and having the money to pursue them and get an apology. Then, at best, you'll have to wait six months to see that apology buried in small print at the bottom of a page.' He added that, if the story was going ahead, the newspaper could potentially get more out of it in sales than they would stand to pay out in compensation.

Disbelief again. I had dealt with journalists all my life and found them all grand. I never believed someone would willingly make headlines and column inches out of someone based on an untruth that might ruin their family and their life. Of course, in this instance I was dealing with newshounds, not sportswriters, but it was still a horrible shock to the system. My head was everywhere. But Fionnuala and I were the happiest we could have been with our beautiful baby daughter at home, needing all our love and attention. And we agreed that this was a case worth fighting for.

Back home that evening, I said to Fionnuala, 'Here, I need to get out for a while. I'll go for a bit of a walk and clear the head.'

Fionnuala followed me out to the hall and told me not to sweat it. 'What will be will be, Seán. We can't do much to stop them at this point.'

All very well, but I spent forty-eight hours before the Monaghan game stressing and beating myself up over something that wasn't true and was out of my control. Still, Fionnuala was rock solid and uber-determined that we present a united front and face down the detractors. First thing Saturday morning, she suggested we get out and show people that what they were hearing was all lies.

We surrounded ourselves with good people, sought advice from those we trusted and were grateful for my cousin Oonagh, a Tyrone woman living in Armagh, for her constant support, and Uncle Seán, who called in a few favours from a barrister he knew, a big Tyrone supporter, Kieran McGarrigle, who gave us advice once it seemed that the papers were going to print a story.

'We'll drive to Lowe's butchers [a GAA hotspot] in Stewartstown and we'll take Eva with us,' Fionnuala said. 'And then we'll go to Cookstown and the two of us will walk up and down Main Street with Eva in the buggy. Then Dungannon. And then Armagh.'

She had a full-blown campaign strategy. At first, I thought she was crazy but she insisted on going out and about and so we did it. We went off, mingled with friends and acquaintances as we normally would. Showed Eva off to anyone who stopped to chat. Acted like a normal young family, which we were. And do you know what? I believe it worked, though it was a few weeks before I realised to what extent.

A couple of lads from the Moy, friends of mine, later came to me and said that because of the rumours they had been walking on eggshells around me. They were delighted and relieved to have seen us out together with the baby and to be able to tell themselves, 'Aye, we should have known, it was just more of the usual bullshit about Cavanagh.'

As it turned out, nothing was ever run in print. I had a couple of restless nights before the Monaghan game – Eva had been crying in the wee hours and I had been sweating over what might appear in the papers – and I wasn't exactly full of the joys that Sunday morning. But none of the papers ran with the story either then or later.

Oonagh is an amazing girl, someone who has been there my entire life. She was one of the few people to whom I had mentioned the newspaper shenanigans, and she had been out bright and early in the morning to buy all the papers and let me know everything was okay. Her text on the Sunday was heaven-sent – I could finally focus on the game.

Maybe Fionnuala's idea to go walkabout had worked! It's a small community we live in. We made a point of being seen by so many people. Good news can sometimes travel fast. Maybe it had nothing to do with the story being scrapped. But it's sad we had to do something like that to stop a scurrilous lie from appearing as news in a national paper. And it hurt us deeply that so many people 'enjoyed' the rumour and didn't bring it to our attention.

We went out and beat Monaghan by two points. And as the days passed and people saw Fionnuala and myself going about together as usual, the whispers mostly petered out. But that whole saga was awful. I was a professional in a job that demanded people's trust. I was a married man with a new-born baby.

What freaked me out most was meeting Fionnuala's family while wondering what they might think they had let their daughter in for. True to form, I would have chosen not to mention the elephant in the room. I wasn't inclined to bring it up with them. Fionnuala did. Her attitude was, 'No, let's fight this, Seán. Let's bring it out in the open and make people aware it's not true.'

We reckon we know who was behind the rumour and finding that out in itself proved a sickener. It was an individual with whom I had been friendly for a while before we had lost touch. All the evidence suggested that this fella, if not the original source of the rumour, was uniquely placed to shoot it down at source but didn't. And when it wasn't rebuffed by him, someone who knew me pretty well, people assumed there was some substance to it.

Angry, I phoned the individual in question. Not surprisingly, he pleaded total innocence. But to this day, any mention of the name of that lad is banned in our house.

It's just as well Fionnuala never doubted me. Fortunately, in such matters a woman's instincts are usually sound. She had been there from the very start of my Tyrone career and knew me better than I knew myself. She still does.

In any case, if there had been doubts, she wouldn't have needed a GPS to track my movements. I was training four nights a week with Tyrone and another night with the Moy and the other days in the gym. Not much time for playing away from home!

By the way, that rumour also followed me onto the field of play, long after it had fizzled out closer to home. Armagh, of course, let me have it. When we played them in the third round of the qualifiers in Omagh late in July, and beat them well, it was dredged up: 'Cavanagh! Doing the dirt on your wife, you sneaky bastard!'

It wouldn't have bothered me, only I was marking Fionnuala's brother at the time. If I had lashed back, Charlie, an entirely innocent party, might have been dragged into the middle of it. That would make some picture – Charlie and me in opposing jerseys but fighting on 'the same side'.

It was thrown at me over the years in club scenarios too. With twists and variations. But, sure, what could I do? There's a whole lot of verbals go on in the modern game and some of them are harmless and even a bit of fun. Others are vicious, but I couldn't be going to war over all of them – I'd be getting red cards and early showers every weekend.

I would be more concerned at how easily something false and malicious can spread – or 'go viral'. Wikipedia as a news vehicle for a story that wasn't true? What's the world coming to? Who controls that site? Everyone and anyone does, so I've been told. Including nut jobs.

22

THE FOUL AND THE FURY

It's one thing to have stuff said about you behind your back, but another to have your name dragged through the mud on live TV in front of hundreds of thousands of viewers.

At the start of my career with Tyrone, playing for the minors, I got an insight into Joe Brolly when, on RTÉ, he ran that pretty critical rule over our team. Fair enough; he was entitled to his opinion.

When Tyrone started winning senior All-Irelands, Joe thought well of me – or so I was told. People in the media had a job to do and most of the time they were sound. And if analysis was negative that was grand too, as long as it wasn't personal. In any case it could never be as hard on me as I was on myself.

People would point out things written or said about me and Brolly was sometimes part of the conversation. For ten years or so it was all good: *unstoppable force; out of this world.* That's just what I heard. I thought some of it was over the top. Sensationalist. But positive at least. According to Joe, I was the best thing since sliced bread.

In August 2013, we beat Monaghan by two points, 0-14 to 0-12, having played the entire second half with fourteen men after Martin Penrose was red-carded.

Near the end of that game, Conor McManus broke through on goal and there was no doubt in my mind where the ball would end up, so I dived on him and pulled him down, conceding the free instead of a goal. It was both calculated and cynical. As Dessie Mone ran to David Coldrick, calling for the red card, I made sure to get my spoke in, insisting we all knew the rule – it was yellow and nothing more.

We hung on for an edgy win and at the finish I half-apologised to Conor for the rough injustice. Fair dues to him, he admitted he would have done the same thing had the roles been reversed – that was the jungle we lived in. We shook hands and went our separate ways.

In the tunnel Colm Parkinson stopped me for an interview and told me Brolly had gone on a rant about me in the RTÉ studio and would I care to defend myself. I admitted that while it didn't look good I had taken one for the team. I told Parkinson that the laws of the game dictated I would get a yellow card so after weighing everything up I took Conor down knowing I wouldn't get sent off but I would stop him from scoring a goal. I also told Parkinson I would be the first person to advocate bringing in the black card, because I had probably been pulled down more than any player in my career.

But I conceded at the end that while most players would do the same thing in my position, the whole incident didn't look good.

I thought no more of it until we got home and the whole village seemed to be talking about the criticism. I wondered what he could have said, so I looked it up, watched it just the once and part of his analysis was: 'Seán Cavanagh, who is a brilliant footballer, but I tell you what, you can forget about Seán Cavanagh as far as he's a man. What he did there tonight was a total and absolute obsenity.' And there was a fair bit more in a similar style.

He looked set to explode. At first, I kind of laughed it off; I didn't really see a massive deal in it myself. I just felt that, whatever way the wind was blowing, that lad would have his own say. And he would most likely be over the top. Sure enough, he was, and this time he got personal too.

Did it annoy me when it was my turn to get a rap? Not really. I actually felt he was dead right in calling out the tackle – it was totally cynical. But I don't make the rules of the GAA. Most teams operate with the unwritten principle that, if a man is through on an open goal you stop him any which way you can. What I did was unsporting and not how I ever wanted to play football, but the punishment was set in stone: a yellow card, which is what I took. Had it been a red card offence, I may have thought twice about pulling Conor down.

I had no complaints about accusations of cynicism. But as the days passed after the game I began to see how rubbishing my character hurt Fionnuala and my parents; they were more sensitive than me to such talk.

To be honest, after I took Conor down, my main fear was of facing Fionnuala, because she had read me the riot act over previous incidents. Just a couple of weeks earlier, as we scraped past Meath in the final round of the qualifiers, I had been booked for dragging down one of their lads as he raced out of defence. Fionnuala was annoyed and asked me later why I had done it.

As far as I was concerned, there was no case to answer. I had played well and scored eight points – my highest ever haul for Tyrone in a Championship match – and yet she was asking me why I had pulled a bit of a professional foul. I told her I had to break up play and was happy to take a card for it. It wasn't pretty, but nobody died and we won the game. 'Don't be getting yourself booked, Seán!' she replied. And she meant it.

We played Monaghan on a Saturday, but the scrutiny only intensified on the Monday when Joe went on *Ireland AM* to talk about his charity work with the Irish Kidney Association and again mentioned the incident. The whole thing blew up online and clips were all over Facebook and Twitter that evening. I guess if it had happened a few years earlier, it would have been seen once on live TV and that would have been about it. Now, though, the whole country had a chance to see the incident if they had missed it live, watch Brolly's outburst and then click on it multiple times. To this day, you can download it if you so choose. It soon became clear that the fallout from my tackle was going to rumble on.

I was in work that morning when a client phoned on a business matter. Being from a Protestant background, he admitted to having no interest in Gaelic football, but he was curious about something he had seen or heard. 'What have you done, Seán?'

'Do you mean the football?' I replied. 'Yeah, we scraped the win. Happy days! We're in the semi-final.'

'But were you caught taking drugs or something?'

'Huh?'

'I'm seeing headlines with your picture. "Cavanagh cheat" and stuff like that.'

'Oh right,' I laughed, half nervously. 'God, no, it's not as bad as it sounds. I pulled a lad down. That's just sensational headlines.'

I played it down, but my client needed a bit of convincing and I was mortified. Right there and then I knew the backlash had consequences bigger than I had imagined. People were less laid back about it than I was. I was living in that bubble. I had enjoyed a few weeks of fine form; Tyrone were back in an All-Ireland semi-final, somewhat unexpectedly; and I was aiming for another All-Ireland. But this 'cheat' stuff was becoming a nuisance.

I would have hoped I had a decent reputation, that whatever faults I had, people saw me as a solid lad. But now, when my name was mentioned, the words 'cheat' and 'cynical' and 'dark arts' often followed. That was strong.

On the Wednesday, Brolly phoned me in work, somewhat apologetic; it seemed the whole thing had come out more forcefully than he had intended. He was mumbling away and seemed to be backtracking. I'd nearly rather he had stuck to his guns because his words seemed futile to me.

'Ach, look, whatever,' I said. 'It didn't bother me.'

And it mostly didn't. But the fallout hurt my family and that's different. Being called out for a bad tackle is fine. Being dismissed as a decent human being is not. That's over the top completely.

It was strange. Most people who understood the game weren't bothered in the slightest. By then Gaelic football had gone down what you might call a pragmatic, clinical route and people accepted that, within certain parameters, players did what it took to get over the line. But the fallout definitely intrigued and maybe influenced people who didn't know the game; they wondered if this Cavanagh fella really was a thug and a cheat.

Coincidentally, the black card, where a player is sent off and replaced by a substitute for cynical behaviour, was officially introduced not long after my textbook rugby tackle on Conor, and I remember chatting to David Moran soon after, during the international rules tour in Oz. David was talking about the perception that my actions had inspired the tweaking of the rules. The idea was funny, but the reality was that the black card had been voted through Congress in 2013 – long before I went rogue against Monaghan.

Two years earlier, in the 2011 All-Ireland final, Kevin McManamon had run untouched through the Kerry defence and rifled a goal that ultimately won the Sam Maguire, and David reminded me how, after that final, the Kerry defenders were slated by teammates as well as management for their failure to stop McManamon. David agreed that my Tyrone teammates would have been even more furious had I waved Conor through.

Still, I wish I had an All-Ireland medal for every time a club player has blamed me for bringing in the black card! The irony is that I would have benefited more than most from the black card in my early career. In fact, I wish it had been brought in ten years earlier.

Later, at an event in Croke Park, I met another Kerry player, Darran O'Sullivan, who like myself had spent years getting blocked and dragged by defenders, and again we spoke of how Kerry had given McManamon freedom to roam, whereas I had done what was needed. I took comfort from the fact that both David and Darran, lads from a purist football county, knew the score.

So too did Conor McManus, in fairness to him. The two of us were chatting at the 2013 Irish Daily Star GAA Awards, standing at the bar, when Brolly approached. He walked over, hiding under his coat in mock embarrassment and contrition. Pantomime stuff for the benefit of all those looking on.

'Get out of here,' Conor said to me, and I did. I walked off – I couldn't be listening to the other lad.

I suspect that as much as Joe likes to have a rant he also wants to be popular with the players, one of the lads. Me being me, I didn't engage with him over the years, even when he was bigging me up. That's just because I didn't like the sensational stuff he came out with, the way he ran people down.

I would say I have only ever spoken to him twice, and one of those occasions was at a Q&A in Edendork in 2008. As I went up on stage he started genuflecting, making a silly show of hero worship. I just didn't respond; I have no interest in that kind of comedy routine.

Look, I was cynical on the football field at times – I haven't always been an angel. And fouling McManus was not the worst thing I've done either. Were there times when I took a dive to win frees? Yeah. Did I deliberately pull a man down or block his run? Yeah. Am I entitled to criticism for that? Absolutely right I am.

But I never went out to hurt anyone. Despite all the grief I had to take – body checks, high elbows, high knees, spitting, gouging – I never stooped to any of that. And in my book, all those things are ten times worse than what I did to Conor.

The labels 'cynic' and 'cheat' stuck with me for a long while. They were even thrown at me in club games, and, fair enough, I have to live with that.

Thanks mainly to Joe's rant, which I feel showed he was completely out of touch with modern-day Gaelic football, a tackle that might have been soon forgotten took on a life and ramifications of its own.

And because the words 'cynical' and 'Tyrone' already seemed to sit handily together, it didn't help the team's image. It was bad PR all round.

I watched the clip only once. To this day, though, I still wonder why some others in that studio didn't stand up for me, or try to balance the debate, if only by pointing out that, given the rules, such last-ditch tackles were inevitable.

In retrospect, I guess some of the tackles I made that year illustrated my willingness to do whatever it took to win. Fionnuala would ask why it was so often me instead of a team-mate standing in the breach. I suppose the answer is that I was willing to do what was needed and take the rap, even if it was my own reputation on the line.

In basketball, if you commit a flagrant professional foul, you're gone. Should it be likewise in GAA? Yes. Or maybe a penalty for the team on the end of the cynical tackle? Yeah, I would go along with either of those.

I'm now working in the media myself but I'm still in touch with the modern game and I know how players flout the rules. I'd be astonished if a pundit such as Tomás Ó Sé – someone only recently retired from playing – reacted as Brolly did to a bit of professional fouling. Analysts like Joe are a long time away from the game as players and a lot of things have moved on or regressed – depending on your way of thinking.

My views on the issue have never changed. As far as I can see Joe is on a different planet. I know he's an emotional fella and I'm aware the TV programmers are fond of juicy soundbites and even controversy. But I would never in a hundred years come out with that personal stuff.

Every season Joe seems to manage three or four outbursts.

Maybe it was just my turn. Did it bother me? Only when it hurt my family. Is he my friend? No. Will I be courteous if and when I meet him? No problem. I hold no grudge.

And you know what? If Conor was bearing down on our goal tomorrow and I was the last line of defence, I would do it all again if the team was in trouble. Most people who know how the game is played these days would understand. For all the shrapnel that flew, I wouldn't change a thing.

23

CAPTAIN ALL AT SEA

Not long after the 2013 season ended, Mickey Harte called me and invited me to take the Tyrone captaincy. It was a massive honour. I had wanted it for a while, but when Stevie O'Neill got the nod before me, I had just assumed it would never happen for me.

The gig itself proved a rollercoaster. A captain needs to do everything his teammates are doing. And more. If he takes shortcuts and fails to lead by example he cannot expect to talk and be taken seriously. When Mickey gave me the armband, I had to wear it on a damaged body – weak knees, dodgy ankles, creaking joints and muscles – but the adrenaline helped me cope. I was already obsessed but I found another level. I wanted to be a great leader. I gave all I had to Tyrone. I would devote every waking second to the winning of another All-Ireland.

I saw some good times. Lifting the Anglo-Celt Cup in Clones in 2016 and 2017, and doing it with Colm there, was brilliant. Actually, just to say I was captain of Tyrone was enough. I had already captained the Moy, Ireland in the international rules and Ulster in the 2015 Interprovincial series, but leading Tyrone had a lovely, special ring to it.

First, though, there were dark days. Losing to Armagh in the 2014 qualifiers, despite the fact that I got five points, was one of the lowest moments of my career. It was embarrassing.

One thing the captaincy did was to encourage me to engage with Mickey. I had to buy into his methods. There were times over the years when I might disagree with what was going on in the camp and I would always have spoken up – if I felt there was any point. As captain, however, there were times when I had to suck it up too, as I felt I was Mickey's ambassador within the squad. It might be tough at times to toe the line, but that was my place. On certain issues I was probably more measured as a captain than player as I had to be an advocate to both the manager and the team, but I still said my piece when I felt it was right to do so.

Sometimes we were given tactical instructions that made little sense to me, like conceding kickouts to teams such as Armagh in 2014 and Meath in 2013 – teams I considered way below us at the time. In the past I might have spoken out, but regarding matters as sensitive and crucial as team tactics I decided that raising my concerns might have been divisive within the camp. So I said nothing. Was that good leadership on my part? All I can say is I took that stance for the right reasons.

When I retired, not long after Monaghan beat Tyrone in the 2018 Ulster Championship, I was down in Dublin at a GAA launch and was asked by journalists what I thought of the defeat, and how Tyrone had no marquee forwards. I gave an honest answer, as I always do, saying that our defensive style had stopped several brilliant young forwards in the county from progressing and that we lacked a structure in the forwards. I told the reporters I felt that was a reason why some of our forwards who came through the system over the past six years hadn't really kicked on, lads like Darren McCurry and Kyle Coney, especially.

It didn't go down well at all. Soon after, Horse Devlin, my former teammate and current selector, took issue with those views in a newspaper piece. Horse is an incredibly emotional person and obviously took my comments personally, despite the fact that they were quite general in nature. I've known him down through the years and so his words didn't really surprise me all that much either. Horse openly wondered if I had done my job as captain well enough. He said that I should have raised any issues I had when I was in the panel, rather than airing my views in the media. And he seemed to suggest that, if I had been a stronger captain, we might have got further along the line.

But I'm confident that if you asked the players who I captained from 2014 to 2017, you would get a much more positive outlook. I set out to be very much a players' captain and although there were loads of side issues I loved the buzz and challenges we embraced as a team. I was incredibly proud to lead that group and Mickey spoke quite often about how I deserved to lift Sam because I was that type of captain.

I took that as a compliment because, contrary to what Horse thinks, I did often raise issues as captain with Mickey, making suggestions right from the start. That's the type of person I am; I'm not one to sit back and accept whatever is already in place. The reality, though, is that even though I tried to pick my battles carefully, my views were seldom taken on board.

In my first year as captain, the lads pleaded with me to get better training gear. Along with Dermot Carlin, another long-serving player, I contacted O'Neills, the company that designs GAA gear. After taking counsel from the squad, we had items specially designed, backchecked the samples with the lads, and after they agreed what they wanted, we put the order in. The whole process took a couple of weeks to get right. Ultimately, though, Mickey went a different route and decided to proceed with a new set of gear he felt was right.

That is just one example, but it was a sign of things to come.

During video analysis sessions I would be very vocal on certain points, as would some other players, but ultimately we were talked over if it didn't suit the script prepared. Guys began to seriously fear the analysis sessions, as they were normally negative. In terms of tactics, the management team never asked me to contribute privately either, but that's fair enough. Mickey is the manager and, no matter what Horse thinks, the reality was that I understood Mickey better than most. I knew that, no matter what I or anyone else said, it would be his way. That's autocratic leadership, and I can talk about it all day – but the facts are that some of the best leaders in the world share similar traits and characteristics and the approach has paid huge dividends for Mickey and Tyrone over the years. Calling it autocratic leadership is not a criticism, per se. I have seen similar styles in business, too. It's just not my style.

Around the same time that Horse came out with his comments, my clubmate Philly Jordan wrote a column saying that I had made life difficult for Mickey and that I must have been thinking about my media career, learning from Joe Brolly and Pat Spillane about making the headlines. I'll admit, that surprised me. Philly lives just a hundred metres from me and I thought if he had any issues with me he would do it face to face or even send me a message.

But the key point of my argument is this. Philly left the Tyrone panel in 2011 and the points I was making regarded the style in which we played from 2013 onwards. After Monaghan beat us in Omagh in the 2013 League, we adopted a more defensive, counter-attacking approach. It served us well in many games because we had great players who could carry the ball through the transition, and we also had Colm as a sweeper.

But I still feel that system took away our ability to beat the very best.

The quality to win was still there but some of our greatest scoring forwards became transition players and the confidence drained from them every time they were withdrawn in games – sometimes with the ball never coming near them. I mean the likes of Darren McCurry and Kyle Coney, great lads who should be household names in the game but whose game never really got the chance to develop as a result of our style.

We copied Donegal's success, and it took us to Ulster titles in 2016 and 2017, but I genuinely feel that, if we had been more adaptable, maybe we could have taken down one of the bigger teams. Every time we faced a Mayo, Dublin or Kerry, they had the tools to stop our transition game and we knew nothing else. It means that players sacrificed their own attacking flair and instincts in favour of keeping formation, following instructions and focusing on set plays. None of that came all that naturally to me. In fact, it went against all my instincts but I was captain. I had to toe the line. When I was inside the group I totally believed it was down to bad luck and that we would eventually win back Sam, but on reflection it feels like opportunities were lost because we were tied so tightly to a system. Back then I didn't watch, read or listen to any media coverage but now that I am involved in analysis myself I can pause and rewind, see things in different light. That's why I spoke up about our attacking flair being curbed.

Maybe Horse feels I should have spoken up more while I was in there, and Philly might not agree with me either, but Mickey is incredibly good at convincing players that the system he chooses is right and, as captain, I very much felt I had to buy into it all. We had some of the most skilful and best players in Ireland in the team I captained. I just hope that the current generation, with the likes of Mattie Donnelly, Peter Harte and Tiernan McCann, can eventually win Sam. These guys deserve to and they have the talent to back it up.

But back when I was in the role there was a lot going on behind the scenes. When it came to having a training weekend away, for instance, Mickey would look for my input and I was happy to contribute. Then there were other issues that kept cropping up and seemed to defy consultation and resolution. Brushfires that were never put out.

There would be complaining over the budget that was available for food after training. Lads were always on about that, and efforts to help drained my time and energy. Getting more variety in our post-training meals was an issue and, to try to help, I even wrote up recipes, but things would stay as they were.

Some lads gave up. There was a pizza shop five minutes from our training centre and they would order and pay for a pizza and collect it on their way home while their meal was going cold back in the centre. Meanwhile, we knew what the Dublin lads had on their menus and that only fuelled resentment.

Word of our difficulties reached the media. In February 2017 someone calling himself a 'disgusted Tyrone senior footballer' sent an email to Newstalk's *Off the Ball*, stating that each player had been asked by the county board to contribute £15 for sports equipment.

The email claimed we were operating on a shoestring and players were waging an 'ongoing battle' with the county board over mileage allowances and other expenses. I got a call from Newstalk's Adrian Barry asking me to comment. Another tricky situation to be put in.

I still don't know where that email came from. I suspect it was generated by someone in the camp and sent from a fictitious address. But there was truth to the sports equipment claim. Those rehab bands and foam rollers were ordered, and every player was given one of each. They cost £30 per man but the board would only cover half and looked for the rest from the players.

I guess we resented that. But it was only one of a number of issues, like having no gym that could accommodate full squad training at the Centre of Excellence in Garvaghey and having our trainer, Peter Donnelly, constantly struggling to find one for us.

Lads didn't always get their expenses on time and I would have to plead their cause. There were issues with match-day tickets; we were due four per player ahead of Championship games – and they'd be in big demand among family and friends – but I, for one, never got the quota.

After Colm had a scan on his knee, he got letters from the medical centre threatening legal proceedings if he didn't come up with £2,000. The bill obviously hadn't been paid at that point. It wasn't ideal to be dealing with that sort of stuff. Our sponsors and Club Tyrone were extremely generous. It was the distribution of funds that was our issue. We wanted money to be directed at the team's preparations and I say that knowing my first cousin, Raymond McKeown, was county board treasurer at the time.

Bitching over food, ticket rationing, moveable gyms, battles over petrol money – it seemed everyone had a gripe and as captain I got to hear all about it. Early in 2017 it was revealed that Tyrone had spent €484,127 on their inter-county teams compared to the €1,632,448 spent by Mayo, the team that knocked them out of the All-Ireland at the quarter-final stage, so I guess that illustrated the gulf that was emerging despite everyone in Tyrone trying to do their best.

Soon after I did a media event with Bernard Brogan and he landed in with wee Tupperware containers full of granola, yogurt, and a rice-and-chicken dish. He told me he had picked up those goodies at training the previous night. There was I with a sandwich and a protein bar I had bought in a nearby shop, and knowing we were way off the pace compared to Dublin.

I guess when the Dubs started dominating under Jim Gavin we looked at their template to find out where we could improve. It was an accumulation of small things that maybe frustrated us. We always felt our players were good enough to beat them, but they were able to bring into the fold people like Jason Sherlock, who worked specifically with their forwards, and Bernard Dunne, who looked after mental preparation. That brought new ideas and different approaches and helped keep things fresh. They didn't have to worry about food; it was all cordon bleu.

We were way behind Dublin in terms of planning and support. But at the end of 2017 Mickey brought Stephen O'Neill in as forwards coach and you can tell Stevie is making serious inroads.

Still, this was five years after Dublin recruited Sherlock. We have lots of ground to make up.

Perhaps the biggest issue as captain was dealing with the RTÉ boycott. In June 2011, *The John Murray Show* had aired a sketch that was woefully insensitive toward the Harte family after the death of Michaela. It prompted Mickey to withdraw cooperation with RTÉ, and you could perfectly understand where he was coming from. The problem was that Mickey wanted us, the players, to support the boycott.

Hand on heart – and it was obviously nothing to the pain endured by the Harte family – but that stand-off with RTÉ was an extremely sensitive issue during my time as captain.

Before the start of the 2016 season we felt a truce was about to break out. A county board meeting announced that the new Tyrone sponsor McAleer & Rushe wanted the players to work with the broadcaster and conduct interviews with the company logo in view – normal practice with major GAA sponsors.

During a meeting with Mickey present, the chairwoman Róisín Jordan asked if everyone was happy to resume business as usual. There was unanimous assent – or so it seemed. But a while later, when we played Armagh in the McKenna Cup, Mickey pulled me out of a team huddle and instructed me to tell the lads not to engage with RTÉ after the game. I suppose I should have told Mickey to convey the message himself. Our players had just been told they could decide for themselves whether to talk to RTÉ, but we all sensed it wouldn't happen. I was willing to chat to them, but not at the risk of falling out with Mickey or jeopardising the team.

Later that year, when one of the lads was named Man of the

Match in the qualifiers, there was a crystal ball to be collected. The player looked at me, wondering what to do, and I said that, while he obviously wouldn't be talking on air, he should at least go out and collect the award. He decided not to and so never got the piece of crystal, prompting his parents to write to RTÉ wondering why. RTÉ replied that, since he didn't turn up to accept the award, he wouldn't receive it, although I think RTÉ did eventually give Mattie the trophy.

Another night Róisín asked me to do an interview with Darragh Maloney after a League game.

'No problem, but you'll have to clear it with Mickey,' I replied.

We won the match and as I came back into the tunnel Darragh was standing there. I popped into the physio room to get strapping ripped off and was in there when Róisín arrived to tell me that Mickey wouldn't clear it. Mickey had made it quite clear to all in that area that 'we aren't speaking to RTÉ'. Point made!

From 2015 through 2017 the issue was never far away and players didn't know where they stood. Whenever one of them asked my advice I replied that, if in doubt, it was safer to just keep the head down.

I feared I was letting the lads down. The RTÉ thing wasn't our battle to fight. And then I could absolutely sympathise with Mickey. I have two daughters myself and the thought of them coming to harm is beyond comprehension. The whole debacle, years later, it is still there for everyone to deal with.

Those other matters of budgets and expenses are insignificant when you consider what people close to Tyrone football have gone through. We ploughed on and still got down to Carton House for training modules, but things had changed dramatically with the recession. Understandably. During the good years, when we were winning, we got so much gear – maybe half a dozen T-shirts and jackets in a season – you'd wonder where to put it all. But in latter years, we barely got a T-shirt and a tracksuit. It was a huge contrast to the boom years.

I remember when Art McRory called me in back at the start, we would have a barbecue in Augher after training. We'd be doing laps of the pitch with the mouth-watering aroma of steak and onions wafting in our nostrils. Afterwards, we'd sit down with the steak and all the trimmings – baby spuds, veg, pepper sauce – and chat with teammates. It was like a boys' night out.

Fifteen years later, I found myself sitting after training with three lads, eating something that resembled a school dinner, with half the team missing. The restaurant where we ate is well known for good food but the quality was restricted by our budget. As the years went on, the game became more professional, more time was demanded of us and the training load went through the roof, some of our standards away from the pitch slipped.

Oddly enough, all that hassle and strife only fed my obsession; I was intent on quenching all those fires so we could perform to the max on match days. By now the body was creaking, but I felt I had to be there and take a full part in every session. And that entailed some unorthodox preparation.

After the 2016 Ulster final I got hamstring tendonitis and, as things had been going well, I didn't want to miss a game. The physio gave me a programme with a twenty-minute workout to be done four times a day – an isometric hold whereby you lie face up and arch the back for thirty seconds at a time while putting pressure on the hammers.

Working at Cavanagh Kelly, I got a brainwave. I would fit in a couple of those exercise sessions during office hours. I would seize a meeting room, put a brush across the door – there were no locks – take off the trousers and lie down under a table to stretch the hammers.

It's only fair to admit that those private physio sessions affected not only me but also colleagues. There were ten other managers in that busy practice and, depending on the take-up of meeting rooms, they might find themselves locked out because there was a brush across a door and a lad inside lying under a table doing hammer holds in his jocks.

I would hear people approaching, a rattle and a banging at the door, and agitated voices wondering why they couldn't get in. There were panicky moments when I feared the brush might slip and some innocent client would get an eyeful of me in nothing but shirt and tie and skin-tight pants. No one deserved that.

24

TUNNEL VISION

'Daddy, will you bring us up to the park?'

It was a Saturday morning in February 2017 and Eva hadn't seen her daddy all week long. She wanted to hit the playground for a go on the swings, a shot on the see-saw, a run around. A bit of craic.

But I wasn't zoned in to her, what she needed from me, or what Fionnuala needed from me. I was only tuned in to one frequency – Tyrone football.

'Nah, girls, I can't. We're playing in the League tomorrow and I've to keep myself right.'

Fionnuala looked at me. Almost with disdain. The girls were most likely disappointed but if they were I didn't even see it. I probably had stretching or something to be at. I was a robot. Computerised. There could be no deviation, nothing to upset my pre-match routine.

I look back now and cringe. What the hell was I playing at?

The obsession only intensified as I ended the home run phase of my career. A fourth All-Ireland medal had become the biggest fixation, the heaviest drain on my days, and I absolutely tortured myself in the pursuit of it. As captain I found myself preoccupied with everything around me – except my work and family. Shame on me. Whether it was a McKenna Cup final or a meaningless League game in freezing February, I was fretting.

I tortured Fionnuala too. I broke off connections with close friends that had taken a lifetime to build up. I was Tyrone captain; I had to lead. Nothing else mattered but football.

Everyone depended on me. Or so I thought. In my head there could be no straying from the script I had laid out for myself. I was meticulous in the chase.

It was not a sane approach. It was not real life.

'Seán, can you collect the kids on Tuesday and Thursday?' Fionnuala might enquire. They would be in her mother's house in Armagh and would need to be picked up at 5.45 p.m. But that was the time I was due to eat before I went training, and sure you can't eat properly in the car.

'Nah, I can't collect them,' I'd reply, and I'd leave it to Fionnuala, who would have to finish a busy day in the GP practice, collect the kids herself, and only get home after 7 p.m. At the time, I never saw any of this as being unreasonable.

'Look, Fionnuala, you married me warts and all,' I would reply. 'I was a county footballer and you knew what was involved. I have not changed over the years.'

But I had. Back when we met first I was motivated and determined, but I wasn't ridiculously gripped by the game like I was in my last few seasons with Tyrone. I hang my head when I reflect on those final two campaigns.

Every hour of the day meant something but all of it is meaningless to me now.

I got scorpy too. I was thirty-three years old, had done it all, but I still never missed a session as captain, even if the body really wasn't fit to take part in half of them. For some of the winter gym sessions with Peter Donnelly, half of the boys didn't show up, maybe because there was no urgency at that time of year. That enraged me. I was in ribbons most of the time with pain, but I never wanted to let Peter down and I felt that the captain should be there anyway, so off I would trot to the gym, squatting weights that I wasn't able to squat. I used to wear long skins underneath my shorts to hide the heavy knee bandage I was wearing. I didn't want to show pain; I didn't want people to throw their eyes up to heaven when their captain began to miss sessions.

There was one evening I literally had to pull myself out of the car, an hour before the other players arrived, just to get warmed up so I could squat 150 kilos with me knee in shite. I would get through these sort of sessions, shower and meet Mickey Moynagh, our veteran kit-man who's been with the Tyrone seniors over twenty-five years, who would hand me two massive bags of ice.

Whenever I suffered I would think aloud: 'You only have a short time left in your career, Seán. Go manic for the final six months.'

I did. I sacrificed it all. At times it took from my performances in games because I was over-thinking everything, putting my body through things I shouldn't have.

But you could hear the talk around the place.

'Cavanagh's not the same player of old. His legs are gone.'

I totally believed that I was the same player. I fully believed that I would front up if the team needed me. The beauty of it was that I had scientific data to back that up. After training and matches we were handed GPS readings as feedback and that data showed I was still competing at the top end within the Tyrone panel. I was covering nine kilometres per training session and maybe hitting ten in games. Most players in the middle sector of the pitch cover between seven and nine kilometres.

Speed tests showed that I could still compete too. I was still hitting top gear. In 2017 I was reaching 9.2 metres per second in runs; 9.3 metres had been my personal best in 2013, so I was still doing okay. That's pretty fast, about thirty-six kilometres an hour. I was seeing all that data and ignoring the public perception that I was fading. I had skills and experience, and despite my pain and injuries I had the times I needed to do my job.

What I lost, however, was a once effortless ability to recover and go again. I had always been able to run and hit top speed and then do the same moments later. In training I noticed that even a run at eighty per cent pace with a twenty-second turnaround would leave me struggling. The likes of Petey Harte, Tiernan McCann and Niall Sludden were upping the ante in that regard, and I was aware that I was slipping in terms of recovery; but that was the only tangible evidence I had to hand. Otherwise I was putting in as much – if not much more – than others and I was holding my own.

This led me to get narky with guys who did not show up for training.

I would go to Mickey or Peter Donnelly. 'Where the hell is so-and-so?'

When I would eventually meet them, I wouldn't go for outright confrontation, but I'd enquire where they'd been the previous night.

It all did my head in, though. I saw Peter making a huge effort and there were times – although not too many – when half the squad would be missing. I would see him deflated and I would share that flatness. But I would be raging too. An hour earlier I had walked out of a house with two kids crying for their daddy, a wife busy at work, to go training on a dodgy knee. And then later that night I might see a picture of some lad who had missed training posting a picture of himself in some nightclub on WhatsApp.

'What is this about?' I would ask no one in particular.

Now, that stuff didn't happen all that often. Most of the time, lads were tuned in and disciplined, but whenever it did happen I would lose it. It didn't take much to set me off, in any case. It's gas. I met Peter recently and he told me that the biggest problem Tyrone have now is they can't stop fellas from training. In fact, some of them are doing way too much on their own.

I became more verbal on the field too; I was narkier and nastier. I never went out thinking that I would be too personal, but there were times when I let myself down badly near the end of my time with Tyrone. In 2017, I was black-carded against Donegal for tangling with Paddy McGrath. A few years earlier I would have totally avoided a situation like that.

In my head I decided I would do whatever I had to do to win the next ball, to win that game. If that meant taking a man down, grand. The McManus tackle was the start of all that in some ways, but as the final curtain began to fall I felt an increasing onus to harden the team's resolve and exterior. My personality was changing on the field. Two years after that McManus tackle, we had played host to Kerry in the League. They were All-Ireland champions from the year before and we gave them a guard of honour when they came to Omagh. Mickey was sick at the time and not on the line. But he had come to meet us in Kelly's of Ballygawley before the game and in the dressing room I felt I needed to take on more responsibility in his absence. I told the boys to form the guard of honour so tightly that Kerry could barely squeeze through it. I tried to intimidate them, to turn the gesture into an uncomfortable experience for them. We closed the line tight as they ran through and tried to make a point in the process. *Ye won't get it easy today, lads.* Early in the game I lined David Moran up and hit him with all I had. I was booked. Again, it was a tackle that I wouldn't have made five years earlier. I could see a trend forming – I was happier to sacrifice myself if it meant we won games. It was just about winning.

I would stand on the field and encourage teammates to pull opponents down if they breached our rear-guard at a crucial stage in the game. I openly shouted for lads to do that during Championship games, like the Ulster finals of 2016 and 2017. In 2016 we managed to get two points ahead of Donegal and I screamed at the lads to pull them down anytime they got near our half.

'Do not let them pass, knock them back,' I roared.

And then play would go on, I'd run after the ball and I'd think to myself: That's not you, Seán. That's not how you were brought up and it's not what you stand for.

I had resented people who did that sort of nonsense to me; I had spent much of my career not getting involved in that silliness, but now I was in the thick of it. I regret that big time. People will say that the game in general has slipped to that level, but I was responsible for my own actions. I was willing to do whatever it took to win.

Another regret I have is my tangles with Michael Murphy. We were close enough during the international rules series of 2013 but when we met he was Donegal captain and I was leading Tyrone. We squared off every time we met each other.

In one game, he missed a free and I was straight in his face.

'Murphy, you fat bollox.'

I squirm with embarrassment and remorse even thinking back on that. As soon as I had it said I was mortified. *Jesus Christ Seán, what are you at? You're not that sort of lad*, I thought to myself.

I had read that article where Michael said he had looked up to me as a kid. Did I need to go on with that sort of shit? No, I didn't.

Was it worth it? No.

There were times in games when I would just go into a ruck and grab him, feeling almost obliged to start a row.

Did I need to do that?

I didn't.

I regret it. I should have steered clear of all of that.

Guys had targeted me for years and disrupted me. There was a perception that I was easy to throw off my game if you got in my face. But that was no reason to start playing the hard man with others.

Gerard O'Kane was in my face one day – before a McKenna Cup final – and it led to one of my teammates losing patience with me and coming over for a word in the dressing room.

'Jesus, Cavanagh, see the next time a lad puts his hand on you? Grip their thumb and bend it back. They'll not do it to you again.'

He was sick of seeing me man-handled and doing nothing

about it. But by the end of my career I was following his instructions to the letter of the law. Lee Keegan came over to me in the 2016 All-Ireland quarter-final and started pulling and dragging out of me. I grabbed his thumb, jerked it back and told him that, next time, I would break it. By the final innings I was doing whatever it took. For years I used the discipline and tools that were given to me through basketball to ignore and overcome the thuggery and dark arts, mostly. In my latter years I had succumbed to it. I'm not proud of that.

But what hurts me most about that time was never being around at home. I would waltz in at night from training, maybe after 10 p.m. Fionnuala would have put down a long day in work, collected the girls, fed them and put them to bed around 8 p.m. They'd keep half an eye open in the hope their daddy would come up the stairs for a late cuddle. And I'd tear back the road from training with the same aim. I'd come in the door and rip straight up the stairs to them. I'd have them wired and roaring laughing within minutes.

'Ah, Fun Time Frankie is home,' Fionnuala would shout up the stairs.

She would have worked hard to ease them into a routine, but I would come home then, take them out of their slumber, play a bit of Lego with them, lie in bed beside them, read them stories. They were supposed to be asleep, but I was having the craic with them.

Clara would usually chance her arm: 'Daddy, I'm hungry – will you get me some cheese on toast?' Then Eva would look for those wee Percy Pig jellies that you get in Marks & Spencer; treats not normally permitted on weekdays, never mind at 9.30 p.m. when they were supposed to be asleep. I'd ramble down the stairs and rustle them up a snack, sneak back up and tell them not to tell their mother. The girls loved me for it. I loved it too. It was like, *Here I am girls. I'm the good craic one here.* Fionnuala was right – Fun Time Frankie.

It was all an act of compensation because I knew I hadn't been there all day. Maybe I hadn't been there all week. Yeah, we tacked on Ulster titles in 2016 and 2017 and, yeah, I did well in those games. But, really and truly, what was it all about in those latter seasons? I went completely overboard and cut people off.

Regrets? I've had a few alright.

25

GHOSTS OF DRESSING ROOMS PAST

As the light dimmed on my time with Tyrone I became not only more desperate and narky, but also lonelier. There were times I pined for the lads I had started out with, the vintage of 2003 and beyond.

On match days in 2016 and 2017, I'd peek down the bus and see boys who were blessed with magnificent skills. To be honest, they had more skills than many of the lads on the team of my early days. Technically gifted, they could do things with the ball some of us could only dream of. But, as of yet, they didn't have the character of the lads I began with.

When a match was there for the taking, the question was: 'Could these young bucks conjure up something to pull a game from the fire?' That part of their character hadn't fully formed by the time I got off the stage. Please God it will come; I think it will. Back when I set out on the road I was blessed to take the journey with fellas who would make things happen. Whenever we went behind on the scoreboard, lads would be salivating for the ball, bulling to make something happen. And they nearly always did pull a rabbit from the hat.

Those lads were sorely missed. On match days in recent years, I perched myself at the top of the bus, three rows down on the right, beside Mickey Moynagh. I trusted Mickey first and foremost. He was a link to the golden days. I pined for the ghosts of Tyrone dressing rooms past.

Truth is I had more in common with Mickey than with my younger teammates. But at thirty-four, how much could I have in common with, say, D.D. Mulgrew, nineteen and just out of school? We were from different generations.

I'm the oul' lad now. Times were simpler when I started out. We didn't have our heads wired up to iPhones or iPods. We went and played games, played hard, won medals and went out together to celebrate our achievements and even examine our failures. If lads were hobbling on the night of a game, you still knew they would be in training midweek. Sore hamstrings? See you Tuesday. That was the character and the ethos of those involved. They were tough boys.

I am not being selective with my memory either. Even back then I didn't click with everyone on the team. Outside of football, I wouldn't have hung around with most of them. But on the pitch, those fellas had few equals.

It rubbed off on me. I remember the reassurance and resolve I felt when, for example, we went nine points down in that 2003 Ulster final. As soon as we got level, they launched a long ball in and Dan Gordon got a jammy fisted goal. We had to claw that three-point lead back as well, which we did. I remember winning a kickout late on and about eight of the lads came to me screaming for a ball I had won from that possession. They demanded responsibility. That's what I want to see from the current lads. It's about the only area they need to develop to make the breakthrough.

They must look out for each other on the field too. If someone was beating lumps out of me way back, I knew Gormley and Canavan had my back. In later years, I tried to be that minder for the new lads. I'd see guys roughing up Tiernan McCann in his early days and I'd go in to add my weight.

But, off the field, I struggled to keep up with them. They are gas to listen to chatting about YouTube or using the Snapchat lingo. When in full flow, I would sit back and remember just how out of tune I was.

They're all great fellas and I think the mental toughness and resilience will come as they develop. That confidence might come with maturity and success, or even flourish more with a new management in time. I believe in the ability of the lads and think they can achieve great things. I did miss my old gang, but I was proud to captain the younger lads too.

Late in 2017, when I finally retired, I spoke to the lads in Kelly's Inn and told them how I felt. They would need to step up, man up and become leaders in their own right.

It probably hit me hardest in late 2016 when, after being sent off, I sat on the line for the closing stages of the All-Ireland quarter-final with Mayo. I'm in no position to have a pop at the lads – after all, I had let them down by getting the line – but I was praying one of them might buy me a chance to make restitution. A chance to make it up to them.

I sat in the Hogan Stand knowing that if McGuigan or Dooher were out there they would have got on the ball and won a free or conjured up a score to draw in those last few minutes. They would have been cute enough to manufacture something and I have no doubt we would have salvaged that game. Guys like those don't come around often but hopefully the current panel can continue to build their resilience, just like the way Cathal McShane and Harry Loughran snatched late scores against Meath in the qualifiers this year.

These guys maybe have more pressures than we ever did too. They have social media and antisocial media to contend with and it's become clear that those things bring their own pressures.

The day I knew I was truly past it came in late winter 2016 when one of the lads came in as brown as teak. I tried to get the banter going: 'Jeez, lad, there's a nice gloss off ya.' And he looked me straight in the eye, not missing a beat – 'Ah yeah, I got the tan done today' – and off he went and unpacked his bag. Like, what's the issue?

I sat down feeling like I was one hundred years old. Seriously. Seán Teague used to beat lumps out of me when I first started marking him in training back in 2002 – and the only reason he beat me up was because I was young and fast. Imagine if I'd swanned in all tanned. He'd have killed me stone dead!

But society has moved on. And I haven't.

It's the same in all counties. Even before games, lads checking that the ankle socks match up, the boots are sparkling, the shorts are just right.

In 2003, the idea was to get the baggiest shorts in the kit-bag because nobody wanted to be showing off a big fat arse or drawing attention to his other bits. You'd shout to Moynagh, 'Throw us a thirty-six there, Mickey!' Now they're down to size twenty-eight because the lads want to look sexy. The shorts are like compression pants.

One day I went to Mickey looking for a size thirty-four. He had fifteen of them left in the bag.

'Is no one taking size thirty-four any more?' I asked.

'No. All the boys want is twenty-eight or twenty-six.'

The boys are in such good shape now that jerseys have gone from a duffle-coat-sized XL to slimline in fifteen years. When I started out, the Tyrone shirt hung like a flour sack on me. Then they went to large and then medium, which was a wee bit tight for my liking. Then Moynagh started getting orders for small sizes until so many were looking for the small size that the whole team had to wear them. I had to get help taking the feckin' thing off. I was like the Incredible Hulk bursting out of the shirt, trying to get it over my head, drenched in sweat. Over the last few years we got Championship casual wear from a local shop, Cuba. Guys were constantly bursting buttons and having to roll up sleeves. I was consistent; I just went for the bigger sizes!

I recount all this and I'm smiling, but there's a cult of the body beautiful in present-day life. That's a societal issue and it's largely down to the world of social media, the world all the boys inhabit. Back in the day, no one cared about appearance – except Mugsy. He was a unique character anyway. We used to rip him apart for looking so sharp, but sure he'd be laughing back at us.

As my career wound down I was the odd one out in a panel of thirty-five or so. There were times I'd look at a lad and think: *Will you show me a bit of personality! You have all the footballing talent in the land – will you just come out of your shell and use it!*

I wonder too how Mickey keeps open the lines of communication. He always took players as he found them and through the generations he generally kept his distance anyway, so maybe that's part of his plan. Still, players have confided in me that they struggle with that approach.

It's a fickle sport at the best of times but, leaving aside the fact that I'm a cultural fossil in comparison, I would love if the Tyrone lads came out of themselves more over the coming years, because they are certainly good enough. Across the board, some lads seem to play in fear of making a mistake. Modern-day GAA tends to home in on meticulous video analysis, where every dropped ball and bad pass is put under the microscope. If this is not followed up with something constructive it can make for an insecure player and team.

The 2003 boys used to drool at the prospect of two-on-two shooting drills. It was a chance to show what you could do, to force the manager to pick you. In latter years, however, I would see heads go down, lads letting on they needed to tie a bootlace, and maybe ducking their go in the drill for fear of being exposed because they were low on confidence.

It brings me back to Ryan Mellon. Ryan himself would tell you there were days when, like us all at times, he might have had a below-par game. It may have been during the McKenna Cup or the League, but throw Ryan into Croke Park on the likes of Tomás Ó Sé and he came alive. The bigger the day, the better he played. You could bank on that. The balls and grit and self-belief of that lad!

The current group need that. When they get to Clones or Croker they just have to emerge from their shell. I think that will happen. They have the raw materials. They are a great bunch. I guess that time just caught up with me – not only on the field but also in the changing room and on the team coach.

26

HOME COMFORTS

There was an evening, not long after I was sent off against Mayo in 2016, when I was down with the club team, trying to get ready for the upcoming Championship. I was there in body, not mind. I was struggling to get going. Our manager at the time, Paul Doyle, twigged as much. He came over and told me to head off for a holiday somewhere with Fionnuala and the kids. We hadn't a game for three weeks and I wasn't much good to him the way I was. What was there to lose?

Paul was right; my body language was rubbish and the club deserved better; they had always stood by me. Fionnuala and I made a last-minute booking and took the girls off to Puerto del Carmen in Lanzarote, thanks to a friend and huge Tyrone supporter, Jimmy O'Donnell, who gave us the use of his apartment, just to get away from everything. I tried to tune out, to stop thinking of football and focus on family.

My head wasn't there for the first few days; it was still back in Croke Park. Fionnuala would try to snap me out of it: 'Ach,

Seán, come on! Will you go and see to that child, make sure she's alright.'

Eventually I stopped moping and got back in the moment. I would look across the ocean and lose myself in the noise of the waves crashing on the shore, be thankful for what I had. I found a way to get past that mental torture of having been sent off. I began enjoying my family again.

It wasn't an easy process. We were only ever a hundred metres from an O'Neill's jersey or an Irish accent. People approached for a chat and meant well, but I had gone on holiday to hide from people and put the red card behind me.

'Tough one last week, Seán.'

'Aye, not great now.'

'God, ye could have won it. Should have.'

'Aye, maybe so.'

'Will you be back?'

There wasn't much getting away from it, but Fionnuala had a theory that if we followed the tanned legs we would be okay, as they couldn't be Irish legs! Sure enough, down the road we found some respite: a wee beach where local divers went for snorkelling. That spot was crowded with Germans, Spaniards and French, and that's where we spent much of the week – just to buy a little time to ourselves. Football was the last thing I wanted to talk about. That was the effect of just one incident in one match.

A year later, after losing to Dublin, and this time knowing it was curtains, I genuinely feared I would never be the same again. I wondered how I'd replace the buzz of seventeen seasons of intensity, triumph and adversity with Tyrone. Like, how do you replace something like that?

The first step was to do what I've done my whole life. A few days after losing to Dublin, I ambled down the road to the Moy pitch. Tyrone was over; it was time to go back with the club and fully embrace it. Straight away I knew the atmosphere was good; we had two great managers and a good set of lads on the panel. I knew I was back with people who loved me for who I was. They were people I loved in return.

Being with the Moy was refreshing. I wasn't a slave to the GPS or the heart monitor. It wasn't about leaving the house and the three girls at 6 p.m. in a mad rush to get to Garvaghey ahead of everyone else. It was about leaving the house at 7.15 p.m., putting in a shift with lads from your home place, having a laugh, and being back up home at nine.

Soon after I went back, baby Seán was born. It was early November 2017, and his arrival gave me added perspective. My family would need me now more than ever and I would need them just as much. Yes, there was despair and bewilderment for a while after the Dublin game, but it soon passed, and it had to. I really started to enjoy being with the Moy full-time again and I loved training with them. It was like getting back to my childhood and adolescence.

We went on a bit of a run too. After Tyrone's season ended, the club played a few League matches and, for the first time in about twenty years, that competition actually wound up before the local championship started. That in itself gave us some structure. We weren't pulling up trees – we were eighth in Division Two – but we could see the road ahead and we started to regain a bit of form as the championship loomed. Free from the pressures of being Tyrone captain, I was playing the game I love with a smile again.

I owed these lads. Through my time with Tyrone they had been there for me. Many's the night over the last few years I would pop down to the clubhouse around ten and use the gym. They had given me keys and fobs to the place and that meant access all areas. Not every club gives its players that sort of freedom and support.

That was down to people like Mooner. Karol McQuade, if you recall, is the lad who I pledged to, at the end of the 2002 All-Ireland final, that we would be crowned champions the following year. Mooner is also my next-door neighbour and I'd say he could have been voted clubman of the year in any of the past thirty years and there would have been no quibble. He's one of those lads who lines the pitch, cleans up, constantly extends the helping hand, and still togs out to play. At thirty-eight, he took the field in the 2018 All-Ireland intermediate final at Croke Park with six minutes to go. He deserved every minute he got out there – and more.

Every club has a few families that are the heart and soul and driving force, and in the Moy the McQuades are a classic example. I reckon that in any given season over thirty-odd years, there's been at least one of the brothers playing for the club. Francie, Karol's elder brother, is current chairman. The sisters have helped with fundraising and of course the essential sandwich-making, as well as playing and being involved in administration. Their father was chairman, their grandfather honorary president.

We live in Clover Hill. Mooner is beside us, Colm is beside him, and Philly Jordan is literally a kick of the ball up the road. A gang of us will often be out on the front green with our kids. They could be playing away while we'd talk football or basketball. There would always be some analysis to be undertaken.

It could so easily have been different. Our clubhouse was torched in an arson attack in late 2015. The pity was that the hours prior to the fire had been filled with hope and promise. About fifty teams had converged from all over Ireland, from Dublin to Donegal, for an underage tournament. Colm and I had been down presenting medals for Martin Conroy, a referee and the Moy's youth co-ordinator. Martin organises that competition and he and his family are GAA to the core. A few short hours after that lovely tournament had run its course, the place lay there, burnt downstairs and all charred upstairs.

A couple of hoodlums, who were not GAA followers, went to a petrol station, filled containers, broke a window of the clubhouse, poured fuel in and struck a match. In terms of infra-structure, it devastated the club, but it did not break our spirit. In fact, the outright condemnation across the entire village was overwhelming. Neighbours and locals, who would likely once have opposed the GAA, contributed large sums to help rebuild it. It was this goodwill which formed the momentum for the success that was to come. That arson attack actually led to the gelling of a previously disconnected society.

Those lads were caught for the crime, but a year or so later, following repairs and restoration, there was another arson attack and this time we never found the culprits. Again, there were suspicions it was sectarian. This time around, two people were picked up by the CCTV cameras of the nearby Jordan International, a haulage company owned by Philly Jordan's brother, Gary, but their faces were not clearly recognisable.

Seeing the place burn a second time was tough, but at least the damage wasn't as bad as before. After that we had CCTV installed in our own premises. We also put in shutters that must be rolled up and down when people want to get in and out at night. It's sad that it has come to that. The Moy had its share of troubles way back, but there had been no real issues for most of a decade.

That whole thing upset me no end. It hurt everyone in the club. You'd feel especially for people like Martin who put so much in. But it was a case of sticking together, shoulders to the wheel, and we rose again.

A few months later my office in the Moy went on fire after an electrical fault and Mooner was there with me beyond midnight trying to salvage what we could and helping me cope with the aftermath. When I moved offices to Armagh he was there again helping, unloading furniture, and he was there again when I eventually got to move the office back to the Moy.

It's thanks to people like Mooner that our club is so welcoming. In the past two years we have had a couple of lads from a non-GAA background playing with us. A couple of fellas who play rugby came to us lately and it's great to see.

We hoped the arson incidents would not deter anyone from different backgrounds wanting to join the club, and thankfully it seems they haven't. In fact, the whole thing has made us appreciate those lads even more.

About a year ago Ryan O'Neill said that a lad called Rob McCleary (aka Rab) would like to try out with us. By all accounts Rab was a seventeen-stone rugby player standing six-foot-three and could kick a ball seventy metres. Good enough for us, we thought, bring him down.

When Rab arrived for training we discovered he could indeed put the ball into orbit. The problem was, most of his missiles headed for the River Blackwater instead of the goalposts. But he embraced us, and we welcomed him. He's around my age, so I made it my business to sit near him in training and get to know him. He's a good lad, with a nice manner about him, and though he didn't get onto the field in the All-Ireland intermediate final at Croke Park, he was on the bench and very much part of our journey.

Would anyone have even considered that possible just two years ago – that a club like the Moy would have players with no GAA pedigree? Not a chance. But things are changing all the time around our community. For the better. A shared-campus school, the first of its kind in Northern Ireland, is under construction and I hope it works. I think it will. It's essentially the amalgamation of two primary schools: the regional (Protestant) and the Catholic one, which was outdated and unchanged since I was there in a former millennium.

Anthony Tohill heads the governing body in charge of that project and he explained to me how it will work. There will be a number of separate classrooms, some for the Catholic students and the same number for the Protestant students. I fervently hope they will eventually all come together, and it will be brilliant when it does.

Even within our club you see the Moy lads now heading off to play rugby with Dungannon or Armagh, and that is another sign of better times. There is far more harmony around. Sport can obliterate cultural and sectarian differences. Kids are making friends in school and saying, 'Hey, why don't you come to play Gaelic with me?' And the same with rugby. It's all happening spontaneously and organically – and that's the best way. Wouldn't it be fantastic for the Moy to have an even wider net to embrace the talented children in our village, irrespective of which of the four churches in the village they attend on Sundays?

When the Moy went on our great run in 2017 and 2018, we could see the mood around the village lift. Shortly before we played our All-Ireland intermediate final I met a neighbour, a prominent Orangeman who once upon a time might have been marching down roads. He pulled me aside and wished us luck for the All-Ireland final.

'All the best Saturday, Seán!'

'Sorry?'

'We wish ye the best. It's great.'

'Uh, thanks a million!'

That was when the extent of what we were achieving hit home. In former times that lad – and people like him – wouldn't have had the slightest interest in GAA, or the inclination to acknowledge what we were doing. To hear a staunch member of that community wish us well was unreal. They were proud of us. It knocked me for six. Such experiences touch me far more than success on a field ever could.

Episodes like that stood to us in 2017 when we started off on a run of wins I could never have envisaged. I'll put that journey into perspective. Aged fifteen, I took the field against Killyclogher for my first senior Championship game with the club. Over the next twenty years I think I won just eight Championship matches, and most of those were at intermediate. In those two decades we were either on a brief flirtation with senior or back down to intermediate. Whenever we reached senior we would suffer the ignominy of being knocked out in the first round. Sometimes we suffered the same humiliation at intermediate.

I always had it in my head that at some stage we could give it a good rattle at intermediate, but as the years flew by our hopes faded. We had great players over the years: Philly, Ryan Mellon, Colm, Harry Loughran. Between those lads and myself we amassed eleven All Stars for the club. We grew up watching Plunkett Donaghy and idolising him, and so role models were not a problem. But for whatever reason we couldn't get our collective act together in the Championship. We were an easy touch.

Throughout the lean years, I had to listen to my dad get crankier about the trophy drought. He had been part of the 1979 and 1982 juniors – the last Moy sides to win silverware – and he kept telling us that thirty-five years was too long a time to wait for another cup.

We started the 2017/18 Championship with all three of our county players – Colm and Harry and myself – fully fit. And the League was out of the way. Those were two positives. We were up against Augher in the first round and, having finished six places above us in the League, they were hot favourites. That night I was due to make my debut as an RTÉ analyst and I was worried that if we lost there might be a backlash. Lads might say my mind wasn't on the game. Thankfully, we scraped through by a point on a dirty wet day and off we set on a magnificent journey that would bring the good people of the Moy all the way to Croke Park.

Along the way we beat Cookstown in the Tyrone semi-final and faced Derrylaughan in the final. Not long down from senior, they had walloped Eglish, another fancied side, in the other semi-final. Derrylaughan had four or five county minors and under-21s and a few lads with senior experience. They were unbackable. But we backed ourselves and beat them too, by a point.

Huge credit to the two boys in charge: Gavin McGilly and Austin Kelly. Gavin will surely go on to have a fine inter-county career in management. I played alongside him at schools in St Pat's Academy and we won a few Ulster colleges titles together. He had helped Paddy Tally land a Sigerson Cup for St Mary's and he was one of the lads we looked for to take on the team.

Austin Kelly, or Audy, had been with us in 2013 when we managed to make the Tyrone senior semi-final, and he went to train Dromore for a few years after that. But we got him back and he and Gavin provided us with the perfect blend. Audy would stand back, a traditional, old-style manager, while Gavin was upfront and personal. A happy combination.

As a coach, Gavin also developed several of our fringe lads and that was to prove crucial. He kept ramming home the importance of 'just one point' – how one point was enough to win a game. How right he was! Of all the games we played en route to the All-Ireland intermediate title, all bar two were decided by a mere point.

Having won the Tyrone final, we faced Carrickmacross in the Ulster Club Championship. I asked Conor McManus for a lowdown and he deemed them virtually unstoppable. Conor reckoned they should have been challenging for the Monaghan senior title, since they had won most of their games at intermediate level by ten points or more. But we beat them 0-9 to 1-5. Again, we fought like Furies.

The likes of our full-back Tommy McNicholl and centre-back

Niall Conlan had been there nearly twenty years and had retired more than once. I still have the WhatsApp messages from 2017 begging Tommy and Niall to give it one more season.

Give us a year, lads.

Nah, Seán. Family commitments.

But they came back, and they gave everything, and it was so worthwhile. Those guys are real warriors; they would eat the grass for you. Each day we played, they came good. We were strong down the spine with Colm, myself and Harry. Elsewhere, lads who might have been peripheral in previous years started to hit new heights.

Colm, at midfield, won a lot of possession, but crucially he marshalled the defence too, and that gave the platform for our All-Ireland win. We established a tough, solid defence and took it from there. Our defensive stats show that we held Derrylaughan, who had scored 3-16 against Eglish, to nine points. Carrickmacross were averaging maybe 2-17 in games but we kept them to eight points. In every game a trend was evident: ferocious defence, McGilly's coaching, and the emergence of youngsters.

Mark Gribbin was one of those lads who emerged at high speed. The ultimate testament is that he was deployed to mark Caolan Mooney when we played Rostrevor in the Ulster final. Mark, a lad who a few years earlier looked like he might not even be good enough for senior club football, did a serious job on a guy who had played professional AFL just a season or two before. We beat Rostrevor by a point too.

We got An Ghaeltacht in the All-Ireland semi-final. They were down to play Dr Crokes in the Kerry Division One league final and we couldn't figure out for starters what the hell they were doing in the intermediate grade. Genuinely, we thought our run would end there. So too did our supporters.

'Lads, ye've done us proud but the day out against those Kerry lads is your final. Enjoy yourselves!'

I'm an eternal optimist but that stuff seeped into my head and I sensed a good few things would have to go well for us to win. After all, they had seven or eight lads on Kerry panels, underage, junior and senior, and while we had a strong core I wasn't sure we could match the quality of the players in their squad down to number twenty.

We were to play them in Portlaoise soon after Christmas but after it lashed rain for three days, the game was postponed. That was a sickener for us because, not only had Fionnuala, the kids and most of the Moy stayed in Portlaoise the night before the game only to be told to come back next week, but when we looked out at the biblical floods, we were also thinking 'Ambush!' The game was switched to a week later and the wide-open prairies of Semple Stadium. Those Kerry aristocrats must have been licking their chops.

We were almost brainwashed into thinking we couldn't win this one. Sure, weren't we going to the home of the GAA? The best pitch in Ireland outside of Croke Park? Match day arrived, and we were almost going down to make up the numbers and enjoy the experience. But let's not get humiliated, lads!

But we dug in, got a foothold in the game. They led by a point at the break and as I spoke in the dressing room I could feel the belief building, and with it our dander. 'They're only fucking human, lads! Are they even that good?'

It was like one of those Rocky Balboa moments, when he hits Ivan Drago and finally the punch lands. Despite the myths, Drago was human after all. Our punches started to connect.

Tom Loughran stepped up. He was given a man-marking role on Éanna Ó Conchúir and after forty-two minutes Éanna, frustrated by the close attention, lost it and hit Tom a haymaker to the midriff. It really was getting like *Rocky IV*.

I complained to the linesman, Éanna got sent off, and the whole Ghaeltacht team turned on me. Marc Ó Se, who was marking me, went ballistic. I was having none of it: 'Hey, Marc, if I punched you, would you be happy about it?'

The whole thing kicked off and they were clearly raging with me for the remainder of the game. And with normal time up, they still led by a point. Desperate, I ran out the field to Colm, who hadn't won a ball all day: 'Colm, you've got to win one fucking ball! And when you do, just get it in to me!'

I took off back to full-forward and spoke to Harry: 'Colm's going to win a ball, Harry, and you and I have to find a way of scoring a goal.'

Within twenty seconds, Colm had fetched the ball and pumped it in, and Harry had it dancing in the back of the net. I still scratch my head at that one.

There may have been just seven hundred and fifty Moy supporters present, but until the day I die I will never forget the howl that greeted Harry's goal. It was like a deep yelp of relief, as if a knife was suddenly being withdrawn after inflicting decades of hurt. It was one of the most special moments in my career. Our supporters were like a sixteenth man. They believed in us, diehard club men and their families. The Laverys, the Farmers, McKearneys and a load more like them.

With two minutes of injury time played and still a few minutes left, we pulled down the shutters and won 1-5 to 0-6. Mad as he might have been, Marc was a perfect gentleman as we shook hands at the final whistle. Thoroughly gracious in defeat, as you would expect of a great sportsman.

We had to adjust our settings as we prepared for the final showdown with Michael Glaveys of Roscommon, the club of the late Dermot Earley and his brother Paul. No one around the place had given us a chance in the semi-final but now the mood swung diametrically. This, after all, was a Roscommon team – how could they possibly live with a team from Tyrone?

The traps were set for us if we wanted to fall in.

EPILOGUE

Saturday, 3 February 2018
All-Ireland Intermediate Final, Croke Park
Moy Tír na nÓg 1-10, Michael Glaveys 0-7

This is the proudest day of my sporting life.

I know Paul Earley well from his time in charge of the Ireland international rules team, and from early the previous summer he had been telling me what a fine young team was emerging at Michael Glaveys. I was forewarned well in advance and we put everything we had into preparing for that final.

We beat them by six points, but do you know what is so special about it? The pictures I have with Fionnuala and the family. Wee Seán and the girls. Colm and Mummy and Daddy. My neighbours. Friends. They form a circle and hug me tightly. My eyes are wild red and I struggle to deal with it all. I'm choked up, much as I was when I walked off the field after being humiliated by Dublin a few months earlier. But this is emotion of a vastly different kind. This time I am finishing a season with All-Ireland glory, surrounded by my friends in the mecca that is Croke Park.

You may know from reading my story that I have no GAA

photographs in the house, but as the bulbs flash I just know these pictures, of us, the girls and the wee man, will have to go on the walls. Same as the ones from Semple Stadium after we won the semi-final.

There may have been only five thousand at that final but it might as well have been a hundred thousand, it meant so much to us. Those are the pictures that will adorn the walls of our house.

There is something fiercely tribal about what we have just achieved. Going to hug Tommy McNicholl and Niall Conlan afterwards, guys I've campaigned with for twenty-five years – well, that genuinely means more to me than any other embrace.

I meet Daddy and he even makes an awkward attempt at some sort of a man hug, though he keeps a lid on the emotions. *Come on, Daddy, let it out!* He is struggling too. He manages only a few words: 'Isn't it hard to credit what happened, all the same?' He's been saying the same thing every day since. And I suspect he'll talk about this every chance he gets for the rest of his life.

My legs, arms and lungs are burning again, but this time only with pride. All around me are people from my own patch. We arrive home mid-evening and go straight into PBs, the local bar for our club. B. J. Mullen's hardware store have given us a big truck on which to parade up through Moy Square. Coming up the hill, I feel every bit as excited as when we arrived back to Omagh to a crowd of thousands with Sam Maguire in 2003. It feels better, to be honest. There may be only a few hundred this time, but as I look around I know most of the faces: family, friends, neighbours.

I see Uncle Malachy, who has travelled from London for every match. I spot two friends, one who flew from Australia, the other from the USA. It's hugely emotional.

For twenty-five years these people have stood full square behind me in all I have done. Protected me when rumours flew. Grounded me when my career became media fodder. Lifted me from the heavy ground when I was in danger of sinking.

I look at Mooner – he's like a kid on Christmas morning – and think of all he has done. The likes of Mooner would always level with you. There were mornings after a big day when I would bound out to the garden, having maybe played well and posted a few points the previous afternoon. My chest would be out. I might even be fishing for affirmation of how well I played.

'Good oul' game yesterday, Mooner,' I'd venture.

'Hey, I wouldn't get carried away, Seán. You missed three or four. You were a bit selfish going for that goal too.'

On the other hand, if I'd played rubbish, he'd spot that my head was down. I'd sneak out to the shed to get firewood, trying to keep a low profile. But sure, he'd be out feeding the dog, waiting for me to surface: 'Hey, don't be worried about that county stuff, Seán. The only game in town now is next Sunday with the Moy.'

On top of that trailer now I see guys that have improved as players, made comebacks from retirement, fellas who have kept me steady through the craziness of the county scene, the massive highs and devastating lows. They told me how proud they were of me, and they never put me under pressure when I was struggling with Tyrone. And to be able to give something back to them – well, even thinking about it, I'm close to tears again.

A night or two later I sit down with Fionnuala and survey the madness of the previous twelve months. A lifetime with Tyrone gone, All-Ireland champions with the Moy, wee Seán arriving on the scene, a new accountancy practice up and thriving. I tell her I wish I could freeze this moment in amber.

The girls are sound asleep upstairs, and the wee man is having his bedtime feed and winding down for the night. I love my girls more than anything. Every so often when Tyrone play and they see the number 14 shirt on Mattie Donnelly or Cathal McShane, they ask, 'Daddy, why is he wearing your jersey?'

'Ach, girls, it's not my jersey–I only had it for a while,' I reply.

It will be nice to say to the three of them in years to come that their daddy was out there for so long. That will mean more to me than anything. Having the wee man in our lives is a massive blessing. One of the reasons we called him Seán is that I want to leave him with a legacy. I want to pass on anything I've ever learned. I want to offer him every best chance in life.

I'm counting down the days until I get to watch my son play, be it down in the Moy field or in Croke Park. The girls will always have memories of sunny days in Clones, but wee Seán will see the pictures of Semple Stadium and Croke Park and will know he was there and his daddy played for the Moy and Tyrone and did his best for the cause. And he'll know that, all the time, behind the scenes, his mummy kept the show on the road and tolerated twenty years of manic obsession to make it possible. We have the pictures from Semple Stadium of him in Mícheál Ó Muircheartaigh's arms and what a special moment that was. I am looking forward to filling him in on the legend of that man in years to come.

We have a lovely home and I'm so proud of my family. My business is up and running over a year and the only difficulty is in head-hunting enough staff to keep up with a growing list of clients. Essentially, much of the energy and commitment I formerly gave to Tyrone now goes into my business, but the work has recharged me too.

Meanwhile, the Moy have renewed my love of football and I'm enjoying the bit of media analysis too. I hope life will always be this good.

As Fionnuala puts wee Seán to bed, I get back on the WhatsApp and start harassing Tommy and Niall again, trying to get one more year out of them. After sixteen months on the go, the lads need a break. Still, we are unique. Get everyone together again over the summer and we could take off on another run.

I'd like to think I'm no longer obsessed, but I'm as motivated as ever. Some people see the Moy's success as the end of a journey but I'm thinking we can give the senior Championship a shot now. I still think deeply about the game. I always try to plan things and of course I will forever lie in bed at night, fretting or fearing that I missed something.

Each morning I get up and challenge myself to make sure today will be better than yesterday. And just as Cormac did, when it comes to the day's end, I reflect on how I fared. The last twenty years have seen heartache, with the loss of Cormac, Michaela, Mark McCann, and those tragedies are seldom far from my mind.

I would say they made me more resilient. I take every day as it comes. I'm thankful for a wonderful family, a nice job and a fine home. But there are new paths to be explored. The girls and the wee man will have their own journeys and we want to be there with them along the way.

I'm not proud of some of my actions toward the latter end of my Tyrone career, mouthing to referees and opponents, sledging decent lads like Michael Murphy. I let myself down believing it was for the greater good of helping Tyrone win. At the start of my career certain players abused me and I detested them for it. Yet, when I got older, I became one of them.

I will apologise to those lads whenever I see them, and I hope they accept. Fionnuala hated the cynicism of my later career but I was desperate to win one last time and I couldn't see what she was getting at. Now I see things more clearly. She was right.

I'm only nit-picking, though. In the end I got that one final victory – an All-Ireland with the club in the most unlikely circumstances. That just crowned everything. I could never have expected such a happy experience so late in my playing days.

This crazy obsession of mine has brought both joy and torment over the past twenty years. The fixation with winning came from within, it roused me and veered on the dangerous at times.

But if you were to hand me back time and ask what I might change, I would say ninety-nine per cent of what I did, I would do all over again.

PLAYER PROFILE

Seán Cavanagh

NFL debut: versus Dublin 2002 – as sub, replaced Jarleth Quinn at midfield

First full NFL appearance: versus Roscommon 2003

Senior championship debut: versus Armagh 2002 at full forward

Senior Football Championship appearances: 89

National Football League appearances: 104

Dr McKenna Cup appearances: 46

Total competitive appearances: 239

Senior Football Championship Scored: 9-185

National Football League Scored: 9-167

Total: 18-352

3 All-Ireland Senior Football Championships

6 Ulster Senior Football Championships

1 All-Ireland Minor Football Championships

Courtesy of Paddy Hunter, Tyrone-based journalist

ACKNOWLEDGEMENTS

Seán Cavanagh

I would like to thank Campbell, Ali and the Black & White Publishing team for affording me the unique opportunity to bring my autobiography to print, illustrating my life experiences and the highs and lows of my sporting career.

Mummy and Daddy, thank you for the enormous sacrifices that you made in providing Adrian, Colm and me with the very best of everything life has to offer. The example you have set of being hard-working, committed and loving parents has influenced my life both on and off the football field. I love you both.

Colm and Adrian. For being exactly what brothers should be – loyal, supportive and competitive. It has been your ambition and will to win that has driven me to success and that sibling rivalry that has us so close.

My cousin Oonagh. You are the sister I never had. Your unwavering support in sport and in our accountancy work together make us a formidable force. A true Gael, even if you do live in Armagh!

My uncle Seán for inspiring my academic career and for your

unrivalled support in all things GAA. I will be for ever grateful.

I would like to thank, most sincerely, the GAA community. From its headquarters in Croke Park to the volunteers, players, coaches, kit men and sandwich makers. We have an organisation which rivals and surpasses any sport and I am immensely proud to be a small part of it. I thank you for the opportunity to have played Gaelic Games since I was a young boy and for the opportunities to play our native games – from small parochial pitches to world-famous venues. It's a privilege to be a guest in your clubs, the length and breadth of Ireland, USA, Asia. Thank you for your generosity and hospitality.

I wish to thank the Tyrone GAA family for their support and encouragement, from my first game in the Red Hands jersey at the tender age of seventeen until I handed the jersey on to the next generation in 2017.

Moy Tír na n-Óg. I hope to be able to repay you all in some small way and give back to the club what I have received ten-fold from you all. The opportunities afforded to me, the unwavering support, the generosity of spirit shown to me from you all is humbling. My love of GAA and my success throughout my career can be attributed to the skills and characteristics I learned on the banks of the Blackwater – football on the Tyrone side, antics on the Armagh side!

Long-time friend and brilliant writer, Damian, for being as honest and genuine as the day I met you fifteen years ago. You were the first sports journalist who Fionnuala and I met on this exciting sixteen-year adventure and you made such an impression on both of us that night, that we've followed your success and been friends ever since. Thanks to Ruth and the kids, Jamie, Chloe and baby Aaron, for giving your daddy the time to listen to me ramble for nine months about the life and times of Seán Cavanagh. Tedious work! Thank you, Damian.

Most importantly, my beautiful wife Fionnuala and our three amazing children, Eva, Clara and Seán, for sacrificing so much to allow me to achieve my dreams and ambitions. Always encouraging and supporting me, following my career all over Ireland. I hope to be able to repay you for your faith and love.

Damian Lawlor

My wife Ruth and I first met Seán and Fionnuala at a GAA function fifteen years ago and we have been friends ever since.

Seán is just a brilliant guy, the most obliging lad you could meet, and Fionnuala is class personified. I was absolutely honoured to help write *The Obsession*, the story of one of the greatest Gaelic footballers of all time.

I took the book on in late 2017. It was a busy time for us both. Seán was expanding his newly established accountancy practice and I had just started back in full-time education at DCU, pursuing a master's degree, and had also agreed to join the Tipperary under-20 football backroom team for the 2018 season. It was almost overwhelming trying to combine everything, but it was of great comfort that Seán is so easy to work with. Nothing was ever a problem and he is an open book himself in many ways.

A lot of other people helped me along the way.

Campbell Brown, Ali McBride and Emma Hargrave of Black & White Publishing were most encouraging and professional from start to finish. So too was the book's copy-editor, Brian Langan.

Richard Gallagher and Pat Nolan were a massive help, looking over chapters for me, putting me back on course when I had veered elsewhere. Two most loyal and great friends who tell it as it is.

Simon Hess and Declan Heeney at Gill Hess were most enthusiastic in their promotion of Seán's story.

My course administrators at DCU, Padraig McKeown and Martin Molony, went out of their way to assist me in fitting everything in around my course work and I am most grateful to them.

Finally, to my family. My parents back in Kilruane, John and Mary, have always encouraged me and offered solid advice. My wife, Ruth, has achieved great things in her own career and is fully supportive of mine. She was right there with me every day as I put Seán's thoughts down on paper. It was such a busy time for her too, as we awaited the arrival of our third child in the midst of all that was going on around us. To Ruth, Jamie, Chloe and Aaron, I hope I make you proud. It's safe to come into the office again.